▶▶ Choosing & Using BOOKS
WITH ADULT NEW READERS

MARGUERITE CROWLEY WEIBEL

Neal-Schuman Publishers, Inc.
New York   London

Published by Neal-Schuman Publishers, Inc.
100 Varick Street
New York, NY 10013

Printed and bound in the United States of America.

Library of Congress Cataloging-in-Publication Data

Weibel, Marguerite Crowley.
    Choosing and using books with adult new readers / by Marguerite Crowley Weibel.
        p.   cm.
    Includes bibliographical references and index.
    ISBN 1-55570-211-2
    1. Readers for new literates—Bibliography.   I. Title.
Z1039.N47W45   1996
028.5'35—dc20   95-46252

For Mathias and Brendan and all new readers

Table of Contents

Acknowledgments

I could not have completed this project without the help of several colleagues in the library and literacy communities, and I am grateful for their help and support.

At Ohio State University Medical Center, I have worked with the Advance One project, a workplace literacy program for hospital employees, as a tutor and consultant to the project. I am grateful to Rachael Turner, Director of Advance One, for her support and insight into the work of teaching adults to improve their reading and writing, and to all the students in Advance One who have participated in classes in which I have used some of the readings recommended in this book.

At the Ohio State University Health Sciences Library, I thank my director, Susan Kroll, for supporting and encouraging my research and writing in the area of libraries and literacy, and all the librarians and staff of the library for their help in tracking down books, making copies, and encouraging me to keep going.

At Columbus Metropolitan Library, I thank Barbara Fellows, Assistant Director of the Main Library, for her support over several years of my efforts to link public libraries and literacy students. I am also grateful to Louanne Conner, Macrina Kershner, Jeri Kladder, Beth Riemenschneider, and Kerry Wolf for suggesting titles for the bibliography, and to the staff at CML, especially those at the Whetstone branch, who processed over 1,000 books for me over eighteen months.

Barbara Shapiro, Coordinator of Adult Services for the New York Public Library, invited me to participate in a New York Public Library Staff Development Institute for libraries and literacy teachers working in NYPL's extensive literacy program. At that institute, I met several wonderful librarians who inspired me with their enthusiasm for books and reading and suggested several titles as well. I am particularly grateful to Karlan Sick for her help in suggesting titles from the young adult collection, and, of course, to Barbara for her invitation.

Susan O'Connell, middle school reading teacher for the Boston Public Schools, also suggested fiction titles appropriate for adults, and I thank her.

Last, but never least, I thank my husband Stuart for his support, perceptive comments, and occasional prodding, and my sons, Mathias and Brendan, who, over the past twelve years, have taken me on a journey through the wonderful world of children's literature and who make every journey a joyous one.

Introduction

If the Statue of Liberty is the city's gate and welcome sign, the Library is its horizon, its sense of possibility: gain hope (and power and pleasure), all you who enter here.
—David Remnick

All of us who are readers have stories about the books which started us reading: stories about books in which we discovered characters that were so much like ourselves, books which transported us to times and places vastly different from our own and opened up possibilities of other ways of living, and books which answered the questions that no one around us seemed willing or able to answer. For me, one of those books was *Little Women*. I vividly recall sitting on my parents' bed, totally absorbed in the nineteenth-century New England world of the March girls, then looking up for a moment and being startled at the sight of the iron fire escape outside the bedroom window and the sounds of traffic, kids, and summer in the city five stories below.

But what stories do our adult literacy students have? For them, there were no books to convince them of the power and magic of reading. Or worse, books and frustrating experiences with reading convinced them that they were incapable of entering this world of books where other, more successful, students seemed so comfortable. But we who are readers know that it is not just the ability to read that makes us readers; it is the *power* of the books themselves that makes us *want* —and love—to read. It was this power of and love for books that, in many cases, led us to become librarians, teachers, or volunteer tutors. We firmly believe that books and reading can change lives. We need to have an equally strong conviction that it is never too late for someone, no matter what their earlier experiences might have been, to experience the transforming power of the written word.

There is no better place than the public library to find books that have the power to make our adult students readers. Libraries serve everyone who walks in the door, without regard to educational background, income, social standing, or interest. Whatever you may want or need to know or read, you are welcome in the library. Writing in the *New Yorker* about the 100th anniversary of the New York Public Library, David Remnick described Room 315, the Main Reading Room of the Library, as "the most democratic room in New York," a room that is "an inclusive—*wildly* inclusive—house of knowledge and art and information."[1] Room 315 is a room where great writers have researched their books, where immigrants have found books in their native languages to offer comfort while they also read books to improve their English, where the unemployed have read job ads and researched companies for which they might work, where sons and daughters have gone to find information about their ancestors, and where the city's workers find an hour's respite from the toil of the day browsing through a collection of art or photography or found inspiration in the poetry of others who have faced the trials and tedium of everyday life. While Room 315 in the New York Public Library might be the most famous and exalted of public library reading rooms, it is only one of thousands of such rooms in virtually every city and town across the country, where people of all ages and stages of life and from every economic and social class can freely go to find whatever it is they need from the treasure trove that is the library.

How to Use This Book

Choosing and Using Books With Adult New Readers is different than most literacy bibliographies because it goes beyond merely recommending and annotating titles that are appropriate for adults learning to read or trying to improve their reading skills—it discusses a multitude of ways to *use* those books with adult new readers. The books I have chosen are all found in the general collection of the public library. While many public libraries have special collections for adult new readers, and those collections offer books that will be interesting and useful to literacy students, they are but a meager sampling of the wealth of materials any library has to offer.

A Look Inside

The book's chapters outline the diversity of resources available to tutors and students who seek them out in the library.

Chapter 1, "Reading Pictures," suggests art and photography books that offer new readers interesting, informative, amusing, beautiful, and challenging pictures to discuss and write about. "Reading" these pictures also provides students an opportunity to describe what they see, infer relationships within the picture, react to a mood or an idea, connect the picture to events or people in their own lives, and imagine themselves in the circumstances of the picture. These are all skills that successful students must eventually apply to the written word.

I recommend selected poetry collections in Chapter 2, "Wisdom and Delight." Many wonderful poems can communicate ideas, insights, and experiences in simple, but certainly not simplistic language. Most of these poems were actually written for adults, yet just happen to be very easy to read. Even students who have difficulty reading some harder poems can still understand the ideas and images contained within them if the poems are read aloud.

"Stories from the Human Family," Chapter 3, recommends stories that, whether real or imagined, tell us something about ourselves, and our fellow human beings. These books span many different genres, including collections of letters, newspaper columns, essays, memoirs, and other true stories. I've also included fictional stories here that are accessible to new readers, especially those who have mastered basic skills and reached the stage where they need "real books" to read if they are going to maintain their skills and—even more importantly—become hooked on reading.

Chapter 4 delves into "A World of Information." Most adult literacy students' poor reading skills inevitably led to poor performance in most subject areas when they were in school, so they missed learning much of what society considers "general knowledge." Similarly, they continue to miss current information that better readers gain everyday from newspapers, magazines, and books. This information is essential background for an understanding of the way the world works. The titles suggested in this chapter cover a wide range of topics from health to crafts and many will be found in the children's collection of the library. Children's books cover just about every conceivable topic, are written at levels accessible to adult new readers, present information in a straight-forward narrative, and are accompanied by clear, often compelling photographs and drawings. Although any adult will find the choices listed here appealing as well as informative, some adults may be sensitive about using children's books. The books listed here, though, are not condescending and never identify children as their target audience.

Chapter 5, "You Could Look It Up," continues an examination of a particular kind of informational material—reference books. New readers need to learn basic information skills in order to thrive in the Information Age. This chapter will suggest some exercises to help new readers use the variety of print and electronic reference materials available at the library.

Picture books are "Not for Children Only" as Chapter 6 reveals. Many picture books are truly visually stunning works of art; it is a shame if only children get to enjoy them. Some of the books recommended here are truly picture books for all ages that will appeal to many adults. Others are suitable for family literacy programs in which adults learn to read to the children in their lives.

Finally, Chapter 7, "Finding Books Suitable for Adult New Readers," reviews the methods I have used to find the books I recommended in earlier chapters and suggests other resources to help librarians and teachers identify additional books for new readers.

Selection Criteria

As is the case with most bibliographies, and certainly one like this based on the vast resources of a public library, this list of books represents only a sampling of what is available. While most of the books listed have been published since 1990, several titles are older than that. I deliberately chose to include some older books, not only because the individuals titles were good ones, but also because they remind us that the library has books we no longer hear about through book reviews or publishers' flyers, or in books like this one. Out-of-print books still have something to say about who we are as a people and how we live our lives. This is particularly true of poetry, fiction, collections of letters, essays, and memoirs, and other literature that doesn't rely on factual information but on the understanding of the human heart.

Not all of the titles listed here will be available in all libraries, although they can usually be obtained through interlibrary loan. If a particular title is not readily available, however, a similar one might be. Recognizing this, I have tried, especially in the annotations of older books, to explain why the book may appeal to new readers and thus help tutors and librarians identify similar books in their local collections. This list of books is as important for the *types* of books it suggests as it is for the actual titles it recommends.

The books and methods mentioned here are for students in Adult Basic Education (ABE) classes and literacy tutoring programs which serve students who speak English as their native language but are unable to read it very well. However, many of the books and methods, and certainly the principle of finding numerous resources within the general collection of the public library, apply to programs and classes that teach English to Speakers of Other Languages (ESOL) as well. Adaptability to ESOL classes is mentioned in annotations for some titles, but experienced teachers will recognize other possibilities.

Finally, I have attempted to identify books that represent, by their authors and by their subject matter, the range of cultural diversity which exists both within literacy classes and America in general. While my primary concern has always been the quality and potential usefulness of particular books, I hope that all literacy students will find themselves represented in the pages of the books listed here. I also hope they will find much in common with characters who come from times, places, and cultures different from their own. That, after all, is one of the real glories of reading.

Reading Levels

For all the books listed (with the exception of those in the art and photography section), I have assigned a reading level of beginning, intermediate, or advanced new reader. These categories are intentionally vague, because each student's own ability and interests should determine the choice of reading material, and because I wanted to expand the possibilities of books available to all new readers, not restrict them by arbitrary measures meant to apply to a group of hypothetical students. Using broad standards such as these three categories allows tutors to consider more of the qualitative aspects of a particular book, such as whether the writing flows with a rhythm and a semblance to real speech that makes it easy to read, whether words are repeated in ways that assist an inexperienced reader, whether the illustrations, photographs, drawings, or diagrams enhance both the look of the book and the accessibility of the information, and, perhaps most importantly, whether the subject of the book will appeal to a particular student or is about a topic he already knows something about (and can thus apply his prior knowledge to help him understand the book's meaning).

Beginning New Reader

In general, the beginning new reader level corresponds roughly with grade levels 1-3 and indicates books that contain familiar vocabulary, generally simple sentence structure, relatively large print, and a spacious layout that includes a lot of white space.

Intermediate New Reader

Intermediate new reader level corresponds approximately with grades 4-6. These books introduce more complex sentences. Fiction books at this level require the reader to make some inferences and apply other critical thinking skills, while the nonfiction books expect an understanding of some background material or historical references.

Advanced New Reader

The advanced new reader level, roughly grades 7-8 and beyond, includes longer stories, more complex sentence structure, greater use of imagery, metaphor, and inferential thinking, and, in factual texts, greater detail of explanation.

Books and Libraries Change Lives

In her keynote address to the 1995 annual meeting of the American Library Association, former Poet Laureate Rita Dove called libraries "a house of the spirit where the past comes to life and the future is cajoled to sit and chat." "They support the interior life of our society," she said, and "bridge the past, present, and future as well as the relationship of thought to heart."[2] Those of us who are librarians and literacy teachers eagerly nod our heads in agreement, but her words become even more poignant when we learn from her poems and stories that Dove's own family's past includes ancestors who were slaves and therefore forbidden to read or own books. Dove has a visceral as well as intellectual understanding of the power of books to shape and change lives which she has passed on to us through the gift of her words.

It is my sincere hope that *Choosing and Using Books With Adult New Readers* will help librarians and literacy teachers convince their students that books indeed have the power to help them change their lives, and that those books are waiting for them at the library. Read on to find those books which will envelop your adult new readers the way *Little Women* enveloped me on a summer day so long ago.

Notes

1. David Remnick, "Room 315 at 100," *New Yorker.* (May 22, 1995): 5.
2. Rita Dove, Keynote Address, American Library Association Annual Meeting, Chicago, June 1995. Author's notes.

Chapter 1

Reading Pictures: Art and Photography Books to Inspire New Readers and Writers

Looking at the pictures discovered on the walls of the Caves of Lascaux and in the tombs of the ancient kings of Egypt, we find evidence that pictures—the making of them and the looking at them—matter to human beings. We can look at the artwork on the ancient caves and tombs and feel a connection to people who lived so long ago we can hardly measure the time. We see in their pictures that these ancient peoples had the same need we do to understand their world, to communicate the ideas and pictures in their minds, to express their feelings of joy, sadness, and wonder. We sense their attachment to the physical world and their quest to find meaning in its mystery. These distant human cousins left little or no written record, but from their pictures, we can "read" some part of their life story.

Pictures tell us stories, not only about times and people of the distant past or in distant places but also about ourselves and those with whom we share our time and place on earth. Pictures strike deep emotional chords, sometimes eliciting feelings we could not articulate in words. Pictures connect us across borders of time, geography, and culture and give a human face to historical facts and figures. Pictures help us find common threads in different circumstances; they also help us see the familiar from a new perspective. In other words, looking at pictures involves the same intellectual activities that reading does: learning new facts, considering ideas, incorporating the ideas or information into the body of knowledge we already have, seeing something of ourselves in the circumstances of others, and responding to the humor, sadness, or beauty of a story or an idea.

Looking at pictures with new readers, tutors and teachers can help literacy students exercise these intellectual skills using the stories and ideas presented in paintings and photographs. Students can describe what they see, connect the picture with their own experience or memories, compare the content or the effect of various pictures, express an emotional reaction, consider differing interpretations or suggest several levels of meaning, imagine what the painter or photographer might have had in mind when creating the picture, and form an opinion about the effectiveness, power, or beauty of the image. These are the same critical thinking skills that students will eventually apply to stories and ideas presented through words.

Even the smallest public library has numerous art and photography books containing pictures that will appeal to new readers and offer them opportunities to "read" the content and discern the feelings and ideas expressed. For beginning new readers, "reading" the pictures found in art and photography books can be incorporated into the language experience method of teaching reading which is frequently used with students at early stages of reading. Language experience is a method that teaches adults to read using their own language and experiences as the reading material. With this method, tutors engage students in a conversation, write the students' words, then teach them to read their own speech. Tutors then use the words and sentences of that language experience story to teach the students some basic skills such as vowel and consonant sounds, contractions, or whatever other elements of language present themselves in the experience story and are appropriate for the students' abilities. Initially, students create language experience stories based on their own family, work, or everyday lives. While it is always a good idea to root initial reading experiences in the students' own circumstances, it is also important to move students beyond the familiar to a consideration of the experiences and ideas of others. Generating language experience stories from the pictures presented in art and photography books will help students make that transition from thinking about their own experiences to considering the experiences and ideas of others. This is an important step toward helping students develop the skills necessary to read from a wide range of sources.

In a similar way, art and photography provide a good starting point for writing exercises because they provide information and ideas that students can describe, compare, react to, or connect to their own experiences and ideas. Since writing is an integral part of learning to read, asking students to write in response to pictures, even if only a sentence or two, helps them to begin writing at the very early stages of their literacy program.

This chapter suggests ways to use art and photography books with students at various levels and in both classroom settings and individual tutoring situations. The bibliography that ends the chapter lists suggested titles. The books chosen combine appealing format with content that covers a wide range of potential interests. In all the books, there is a mix of pictures with written text. Sometimes the text is limited to captions describing the pictures; sometimes it is a more extensive explanation of the events pictured or the artist whose work is featured. But in all the books, it is the pictures that carry the story or convey the message. Teachers may choose to read some of the written background to students or ask them to read if they are able to do so. Knowing the background of the artist or the historical context of a photograph may help students see connections and layers of meaning beyond the literal. Teachers can make those decisions based on the interest and ability of the students.

All of the books listed in this bibliography were found in the public library of a medium-sized city. The majority were published in the last ten years, but some are older than that. One of the great and sometimes overlooked contributions the public library makes to its community is that it keeps books on the shelf long after their popularity, but not their potential usefulness, has faded. Collections of historical photographs still have much to say to our contemporary society, and many books remain appealing and relevant over long periods of time. Most of the titles listed here will be available in public libraries across the country, but even if specific titles are not, others which serve similar purposes will be. This list is, of course, but a sampling of the many possible titles that will inspire new readers to consider the ideas and images presented by pictures.

Using Art Books with New Readers

There is a wide range of style and content among the art books found in any public library. Some books feature paintings that are almost photographic in their representation of the physical world, while others present a perplexing view unique to the particular artist. Some concentrate on paintings or drawings, while others feature various artifacts from particular cultures. When choosing art to share with an individual student or with a class, teachers should look for books they find interesting and attractive, or books they believe will have a particular appeal to their students, then share their reasons for choosing the book with the students. Prior knowledge about the artist or the work is not necessary. Format is also an important consideration. Many of the books mentioned in this bibliography open with a discussion of the artist, his or her life, influences, and work. Sometimes this is a scholarly discussion; sometimes it is intended for the general reader. What makes these books particularly appealing for new readers is that the color plates showing the work are printed all together in the second section, which is often more than half of the book. The plates are usually presented just one or two to a page with little, if any, intervening text. This format allows the students to browse through the pictures, picking one or more to talk about, without encountering lengthy explanations. Teachers can then choose to read from or mention any part of the text they consider of interest to the students.

Some collections of art incorporate a comprehensive range of style and period within one book. *Masterpieces of the Metropolitan Museum of Art,* intended to introduce the general reader to the treasures held in one of America's major museums, is one example. New readers browsing through this book will find Turkish carpets, Asian pottery, African statuary, and American colonial furniture, as well as paintings from cultures around the globe (but particularly from the masters of Europe and the United States). With a book as comprehensive as this one, teachers may ask students to describe objects or pictures they particularly like and explain their choices, tell whether any pictures remind them of a time, place, or experience from their own lives, or imagine the life, interests, ideas, or feelings of the artist.

Other art collections take a narrower view, focusing on the work of individual artists. For example, several titles in the bibliography present the work of "folk artists," that is, artists who are essentially self-taught and whose work sometimes lacks correct perspective or other indications of mastery of technique. Nevertheless, they convey stories, ideas, and feelings with great power and originality. Margot Cleary's book, *Grandma Moses,* presents the work of this celebrated artist who only began to paint seriously when she was in her sixties, but who has inscribed images of rural America on the nation's collective memory. Grandma Moses's work is a vivid evocation of a particular time and place. Students looking at her paintings could describe the many details that make her pictures so appealing then try to describe a scene from their own memories, using as many telling details as possible. Another folk artist whose work appears in two titles listed in the bibliography is Horace Pippin, a black artist who is now enjoying renewed recognition. Though his arm was damaged in World War I, Pippin managed to paint powerful pictures of his experiences in the war and as a black man in America during the first half of this century. The book *Horace Pippin,* published by The Phillips Collection in Washington, D.C., presents a simple but beautiful introduction to his work, while Judith Stein's *I Tell My Heart: The Art of Horace Pippin* offers readers a more comprehensive look at his life and his work. In addition to these collections of his paintings, Mary Lyon's biography *Starting Home: The Art of Horace Pippin,* written for children and listed in Chapter 4, examines his life in the context of his paintings. Teachers might read sections of the biography and ask students to consider how the artist's life informs his art.

Artists inevitably reflect their own lives and circumstances in their paintings, and they, in turn, influence the views of those with whom they live and work. George Bellows was a painter whose work explored subjects not commonly considered "art" at the time he worked in the early twentieth century. Considered a member of the group known by some of their critics as the "Ashcan School," Bellows and his colleagues found beauty in the ordinary—in hard labor, in sporting events, and in the sometimes gritty environment of the urban centers of that time. Their paintings focused attention on the harsh conditions of life that others might rather ignore. Students looking at the work of George Bellows might consider the conditions which Bellows depicted and compare them to conditions in American cities today, or they might consider where they find beauty in their own world.

Another painter whose work will be accessible and appealing to many adult literacy students is Jacob Lawrence, an African American painter who combines words and images in series of paintings that tell stories from the history of blacks in America. His Migration Series, reproduced in *Jacob Lawrence: The Migration Series,* is a stunning collection of sixty panels, each depicting a particular aspect of the migration of black people from the agrarian South to the industrial North in the days between the world wars. Each of these panels could stand on its own artistic merit, but as a group they tell an extraordinary and vivid tale of hardship and determination. To "read" these panels is to learn a lesson in the power of art to convey not only the facts of history but the impact that history had on the lives of the people caught in particular circumstances. Students might choose one panel and describe the picture as well as the content, then consider how the manner in which Lawrence chose to present his subject affects the viewer's ability to understand the picture.

Several publishing houses produce series of books focusing on particular artists, and two in particular would be attractive to new readers. The Rizzoli Art Series, published by Rizzoli Publications, Inc., offers paperback books with artwork reproduced on large pages that give viewers a sense of the scale of the original, but the books themselves are thin enough to carry and browse through easily. Each title contains a fairly small sampling of the work of the artist featured, but it is enough to introduce the reader to that artist's style and subject matter. Among the artists included in this series are Michelangelo, European masters Vincent Van Gogh, Claude Monet, and Edgar Degas, and twentieth-century American painters Edward Hopper and Roy Lichtenstein. The *Edward Hopper* volume is specifically discussed in the bibliography. The Watson-Guptill Publications Company also produces a series of attractive and accessible paperback books which highlight the works of many famous painters, including Americans, as in *Winslow Homer Watercolors*, and *Whistler: Landscapes and Seascapes*, both listed in the bibliography.

After students have had experience looking at and reacting to art from various artists who paint in a representational style, consider introducing them to works of abstract art. Abstract art presents viewers with a different kind of challenge than does art that more or less resembles the familiar. Looking at abstract art, viewers must allow their minds to wander in response to an image that the conscious mind does not recognize, to make associations, to let feelings determine a reaction, to try to imagine what an artist might have had in mind when creating the work. Asking students to write all their reactions in response to a work of abstract art would be one way of encouraging them to write creatively, to write whatever comes into their minds rather than what they think a teacher might expect of them.

Georgia O'Keeffe is an American artist whose work might serve as a bridge between representational forms of art and abstract art. In a collection of her work titled *One Hundred Flowers*, for example, she has painted flowers in such minute detail and vibrant colors that they become almost magical. Describing these pictures will challenge students' vocabulary as well as their powers of observation. Georges Boudaille's book, *Jasper Johns*, and Enric Jardi's *Paul Klee* both present abstract artists whose work includes objects that are recognizable but distorted, truncated, or combined in ways not consistent with real life. These distortions lead to questions about why the artist did what he did and what affect it has on the viewer. These questions require abstract thinking, a skill good readers must develop if they are to progress in educational goals beyond basic literacy.

There are hundreds of books published expressly to introduce children to the world of art, and many of these books will also be appropriate for adult new readers. Two particularly good collections of art and literature have been edited by Charles Sullivan and published by Harry N. Abrams, Inc., another publisher specializing in beautiful art books. *Children of Promise: African-American Literature and Art for Young People* is a collection of art and literature from African American artists, while *Here is My Kingdom: Hispanic-American Literature and Art for Young People* presents Latino art and literature. In both books, students will find beautiful and intriguing images matched with excerpts from prose and poetry, sometimes directly, sometimes only indirectly related to each other. Imagining why particular words have been paired with particular images will help students look more deeply at both and perhaps see layers of meaning not apparent at first glance.

Using Photography Books with Adult New Readers

Collections of photographs offer new readers and their teachers the same kind of opportunities to use words and discuss ideas that collections of art do, but they have the added advantage, at least in most cases, of being a more familiar medium. Teachers can choose from a wide range of photography books to engage students in intellectual exercises that will help them develop the comprehension and critical thinking skills they will eventually apply to print. Some collections of photography document our time and culture. For example, *A Day in the Life of America,* edited by Rick Smolan and David Cohen, presents a montage of American life through photographs taken by more than 100 photographers on one particular day, May 2, 1986. These pictures show Americans in small towns and big cities, on farms, at work and at play, in family groups, among friends, or enjoying solitary moments. Browsing through such a book, literacy students can find pictures that remind them of their own lives and interests, pictures that suggest other lifestyles and pursuits, and pictures that raise questions of personal values. Viewing the book as a whole, students will find a perspective that inspires reflection on the extraordinary diversity of land and people that is America.

Other collections narrow their focus to a particular place. Bruce Davidson's *Subway* is a good example. Here we find, in the relatively small universe of the New York City subway system, a picture of urban life in microcosm: workers and students travelling to and from the routine activities of their lives, citizens alert to the ever-present threat of violence, families en route to graduations or a day at the seashore. In these photos, we see the ugliness and grit that people commonly associate with subways, but we also see the buildings, bridges, and waterways that define New York take on an unexpected beauty when framed by the window of a subway car. Looking at these photographs, students familiar with urban life may find resonance in the faces of the riders pictured, while those whose lives are spent in smaller places may be fascinated or perplexed by the cauldron of people and activity to be found within an urban subway system.

Still other collections reflect changing social structures. Although published in 1975, Betty Medsger's collection, *Women at Work: A Photodocumentary,* presents a view of the changing face of the American workplace that remains timely. This book shows women at work in jobs ranging from traditional nurse or teacher to precedent-setting roles as telephone line workers, miners, firefighters, and surgeons. As with all photography collections, students can choose particular pictures to describe in detail or react to. Teachers can also take students beyond that first reaction by asking questions that encourage them to probe the deeper issues a book such as this one raises. Are there any clues in the picture that help you know how the woman pictured feels about her job? Imagine yourself a woman in a precedent-setting job such as miner or a man working as a nurse. How would you feel? How would you respond when people ask you why you have this "different" job? Are certain jobs only appropriate for men or for women? Which jobs and why? What happens when women take jobs traditionally held by men? How does this affect women and their view of themselves? How does it affect men? What happens in a community when women work more frequently? Who takes care of the children? What economic forces are causing this shift in the workplace? How is the economy of the community changed when more women work? A book such as this offers new readers a chance to consider and discuss social issues which are important to an understanding of our culture but possibly intimidating to those who are unable to read about them in newspapers and books. Such books also have an important place in any ESOL classroom because they offer students from other countries a glimpse into American culture and an opportunity to talk about differences they see between this new culture they find themselves immersed in and the different one they left behind.

Another book which focuses on the contributions of women, in this case black women, is Brian Lanker's collection, *I Dream a World: Portraits of Black Women Who Changed America.* This book highlights particular women, some famous but others not, who have influenced our culture through their work in the arts, politics, and entertainment. Each of the women also gives a brief statement about her life and work. Teachers can read the statements to students, then ask them to make connections between the woman's life, her work, and its effect on American society. The portraits in this collection also send their own message. They are formal and stately, conveying a sense of nobility that befits the courage and dedication all these women have applied to their work. Teachers may wish to discuss this with students, asking them to examine the pictures closely and consider how the manner in which the women were photographed affects the viewer's impression of them.

On the lighter side, some photography collections document the many activities that Americans participate in or observe in moments of leisure. Walter Iooss's *Sports People,* for example, is a stunning collection of photographs which capture that combination of beauty and fierce determination that makes professional sports appealing to so many people. Looking through a book such as this one, students can describe the particular skills of individuals pictured or consider the similarities and differences between the basketball player working in concert with his teammates and the solitary ice skater practicing jump after jump.

Photographs also teach us about history. The rare nineteenth-century photographs found in Russell Freedman's *Children of the Wild West* present a picture of the grim reality experienced by the families who made their way west across America in the last century. These photographs show the details: the broken wagon wheels, the harsh weather, the meager possessions, the treasured mementoes that had to be chosen so carefully, the uncertainty etched on faces, and it is these details that tell the pioneer's story with an immediacy and power that words alone could not match. This particular book was published for children, but its format, subject matter, and style make it very appropriate for adult new readers. Looking at photographs such as these, literacy students might compose a letter to be sent to friends and family left behind, describing the rigors of life on the trail, or they might imagine themselves in the pictures, trying to explain to the children why they believe this difficult journey will be worth its price.

For the many years of its publication, *Life* magazine recorded the twentieth century in pictures. In his book *Life Classic Photographs: A Personal Interpretation* John Loengard presents a collection of photographs that, as he says in his introduction, "retain their power to surprise. Their depiction of a subject is telling and concise. They are rich in detail. They are apt, dramatic, and simple."[1] Looking at these photographs, students can recall memories of events that occurred within their lifetimes or react to pictures of events they never experienced. They can connect the events pictured to similar circumstances from today's world or imagine how such an event might look were it to happen today. They can discuss whether the photographer was trying to convey any message by his choice of subjects, angles, or details, or they can write in words what the photographer presents in images.

Sometimes history can be told through the life of one person whose particular talents match or conflict with his time and place in a way that makes a powerful story. Such a person was Paul Robeson, grandson of a slave, scholar and champion athlete, acclaimed actor and singer, and tireless crusader for civil rights at a time in this country when such talents in a black man were all too easily overlooked or scorned. In *The Whole World in His Hands: A Pictorial Biography of Paul Robeson*, Susan Robeson documents her grandfather's life through numerous photographs, recollections from those who knew him, and brief sections of text describing the events of his life. New readers can "read" the life of this extraordinary man by paging through all the pictures and captions or by listening to the tutor read the more extended text. Robeson's life raises numerous opportunities for discussion about racial discrimination, black history, contributions of black artists, and opportunities artists have to use their talents to contribute to the common good, even in the face of danger and discrimination.

Photography is obviously a potent tool for recording history, but it is equally useful as a means of recording personal moments and aesthetic interpretations of the world we live in. Renowned photographer and poet Gordon Parks uses his camera for both purposes. On various assignments for *Life* magazine, Parks travelled widely to record the events and people of the twentieth century, but at the same time he also recorded a very personal view of the world he encountered. In three collections, *Moments Without Proper Names* (1975), *Whispers of Intimate Things* (1971), and *A Poet and His Camera* (1968), Parks matches his images with some of his own poems. The words and images do not necessarily describe the same thing, but they are related by mood or idea. Responding to either of these books, literacy students can describe what they see or how they feel about these evocative photographs, or they might consider why Parks chose to match particular words and images. Parks's photographs and poetry reflect both his worldwide travels and his perspective as a black man who has known intense poverty and discrimination as well as public acclaim. In another book, similar in format but very different in content and effect, photographer Art Gore presents memories of his North Carolina childhood through his pictures and his poetry. In *Images of Yesterday*, photographs display Gore's tender affection for the simple rural life he knew as a boy, but his poetry reveals the pain of those lost years. Comparing the work of these two photographer/poets, new readers would at first be struck by the difference in their perspectives, yet any close examination would reveal common themes.

When first presented with paintings or photographs, most students will see them on a literal level. They will describe what they see, perhaps connect the picture to memories or experiences of their own, and decide whether they like or dislike the picture. Eventually, as they become more familiar with the task of looking carefully at pictures and responding to thoughtful questions posed by teachers, they will begin to see those details that suggest other layers of meaning, to 'see between the lines.' This is the same learning process we hope they will eventually apply to their reading. Developing this more critical and discerning eye is not an easy task, and not all students will be able to do it. But using pictures as a starting point presents students with a familiar and less intimidating media through which they can stretch their powers of observation and understanding beyond the comfortable world of what they already know to consider ideas and perspectives new to them.

A Note to Librarians

There are many ways you can promote the use of art and photography books among new readers. Set up displays of these books near the new readers' collection. Connect the displays to seasonal or topical themes when possible. Consider a library-wide promotion of "picture books for adults" geared to readers at all levels. Have a display of books that are, in themselves, works of art. When selecting new books for the library, be alert to art and photography books that will appeal to new readers as well as other patrons. Remember, too, that many older collections of art and photography still have something to say to our contemporary world. Plan a program for parents that discusses the extraordinary art work that appears in children's books. If possible, invite a book illustrator to give a presentation. Connect book displays with local exhibitions of art and photography in your area. Whenever you go to a librarians' meeting at which publishers distribute posters promoting their books, take home enough to share with local literacy programs. If you give a book talk at a literacy program, be sure to bring a few art or photography collections along. Whenever the opportunity arises, display the powerful connection between the pictures that we see all around us and the words that we need to understand those pictures.

A Note to Literacy Tutors

Make your environment rich with interesting pictures. Hang posters, paintings, and photographs on the walls of the literacy center. Ask your local librarian to share book posters distributed by publishing companies. Display art and photography books in classrooms, student lounges, or reception areas and encourage browsing and spontaneous discussions. Though these books are expensive when new, they are often available in used book stores and sometimes at library book sales at much lower prices. Magazines with many pictures such as *Life* and *National Geographic* are also available at these sales. Invite local artists and photographers to visit your program and discuss their work. Take students to local museum exhibits and build discussions and writing assignments around the experience. Create and display books of photographs that students take, including the students' own annotations if possible. Visit the library and look for art and photography books about subjects or places of interest to the students. At every opportunity, help students to "read" the stories and information presented in the pictures that surround us everyday and to see the connection between these pictures and the words and ideas they will encounter in their reading.

Bibliography

Abe, K. *Jazz Giants: a Visual Retrospective.* New York: Billboard Publications, 1986.

    The photographs in this collection take you behind the scenes with some of the most famous names in the history of jazz. A brief, informative introduction by noted jazz writer Nat Hentoff helps the reader put the pictures into historical perspective.
Adult collection.

Adams, Ansel. *Ansel Adams in Color.* Boston: Little, Brown & Co., 1993.

    Best known for his black-and-white photographs of the western United States, Ansel Adams also produced a small body of work in color. The photographs collected here present the vast and imposing landscape of the American west tinged with delicate color and subtle variations of light. These large vistas are truly awe-inspiring.
Adult collection.

Aldridge, Gwen, and Bret Wills. *Baseball Archaeology: Artifacts from the Great American Pastime.* San Francisco: Chronicle Books, 1993.

    Artifacts from baseball's long and colorful history are presented here: Satchel Paige's shoe with a reinforced steel toe, the ball Roger Maris hit for his record-breaking sixty-first homerun, the Atlanta Braves lineup card for April 8, 1974, the day Hank Aaron passed Babe Ruth's lifetime homerun record, as well as numerous bats, balls, gloves, ticket stubs, and other memorabilia. Browsing through this rich collection of folklore, students will find many items that recall fond memories or spark discussions about the particular magic of baseball.
Adult collection.

Anastos, Philip, and Chris French. *Illegal: Seeking the American Dream.* New York: Rizzoli, 1991.

    Anastos and French were two high school students when they learned about the many unaccompanied minors who enter the United States illegally at the border between Mexico and Texas. Moved by the plight of these children and intrigued by the lure of a new life that leads so many to risk so

much, they embarked on a summer project to photograph the border. The large black-and-white photographs collected in this book present a telling tale of the border and the people that it both separates and unites in a common drama.
Adult collection.

Bachrach, Susan D. *Tell Them We Remember: The Story of the Holocaust.* Boston: Little, Brown & Co., 1994.

Drawn from the collection of photographs and artifacts in the Holocaust Memorial Museum in Washington D.C., this photo-history tells the story of the Holocaust from the perspective of several children who lost family, friends, and the world they knew. The accompanying text is brief and clear, but it is the pictures of an evil witnessed by children that tell the powerful story.
Children's collection.

Benjamin, Tritobia Hayes. *The Life and Art of Lois Mailou Jones.* San Francisco: Pomegranate Artbooks, 1994.

The range of Jones's life experiences and artistic expression are truly stunning. Born into an upperclass black family in Boston in 1905, she travelled extensively in Europe, Africa, and Haiti. Her art reflects the influence of the places she visited and the other artists and movements she encountered, but her unique vision shines through in the vivid colors and strong sense of design that link all her works from the early impressionistic landscapes to the striking portraits, vibrant street scenes, and bold abstract paintings of her later years. Benjamin's commentary helps viewers connect Jones's experiences with her art but never overwhelms the art itself, which makes its own statement about the artistic vision of one remarkable woman.
Adult collection.

Boudaille, Georges. *Jasper Johns.* New York: Rizzoli International Publishers, 1989.

In Johns's paintings, flags, maps, numbers, and other familiar objects are presented in a recognizable but slightly distorted perspective, causing the viewer to look anew at these everyday items. Discussing and writing about this altered perspective may help develop students' ability to describe what

they see as well as their ability to see beyond the obvious. The first thirty pages discuss Johns's life, work, and influences and are followed by color plates, presented one per page with titles only.
Adult collection.

Brettell, Richard R. *French Impressionists.* New York: Harry N. Abrams, Inc. Publishers, 1987.

Impressionist paintings have captured the imagination of viewers for over a century because they evoke such varied responses. Some paintings help us recall veiled memories of distant times and places, others take us to a dreamlike state of contemplation, still others nudge us to look at the way the light creates a mood or an altered perspective leads to a new understanding. The collection here offers new readers a chance to choose particular paintings to react to and write about or to compare the mood or subject matter of several paintings.
Adult collection.

Burn, Barbara, ed. *Masterpieces of the Metropolitan Museum of Art.* New York: Bulfinch Press of Little Brown, 1993.

Carpets and illustrated manuscripts from the Islamic world, artifacts from ancient civilizations in Egypt, Greece, and Rome, religious art of the Renaissance, furniture, coverlets, and historical paintings from colonial America, European masterpieces of the nineteenth century, and an international collection of contemporary art both realistic and abstract are presented in this collection intended to introduce the general reader to the treasures of the Metropolitan. By virtue of its size and diversity, this volume also offers new readers a window into the extraordinary creative power of the human spirit and the many faces of beauty.
Adult collection.

Callahan, Harry. *New Color: Photographs 1978–1987.* Kansas City, MO: Hallmark Cards, Inc., 1988.

The color photographs in this collection were taken in Ireland, North Africa, and various American cities. They capture both the natural and the architectural characteristics of each setting and in the process convey some sense of the cultural differences that define these geographically diverse places.
Adult collection.

Capa, Robert. *Children of War, Children of Peace.* Edited by Cornell Capa and Robert Whelan. Boston: Little, Brown & Co., 1991.

Known as the pre-eminent photographer of war, Robert Capa also took hundreds of pictures of children, some in war-ravaged situations, others in moments of playfulness and peace. This haunting collection of photographs spanning more than twenty years and several continents constitutes an extraordinary statement of hope.
Adult collection.

Cleary, Margot. *Grandma Moses.* New York: Crescent Books, 1991.

Anna Mary Robertson Moses became known as Grandma Moses when, well into her eighties, she was "discovered" by the world of art. Although she always enjoyed drawing, she didn't begin to paint seriously until late in life when she no longer had to devote so much time to her chores as farm wife and mother. "Memory is a painter," she said, and her paintings reflect that belief, vividly recreating scenes from the rural life she knew and obviously loved.
Adult collection.

Clery, Val. *Windows.* New York: Viking Press, 1978.

Looking at this collection of photographs of windows focuses our attention on the particular details of size, style, and placement that we normally overlook when considering objects so common to our everyday life. The windows here are pictured along with quotations from poetry and literature that invite us to consider not just the appearance and function of the windows, but their metaphorical meaning as well.
Adult collection.

Cohen, David, ed. *The Circle of Life: Rituals from the Human Family Album.* New York: HarperCollins, 1991.

Diversity amid universality is the theme of this collection of more than 200 photographs taken at ritual celebrations around the world. The pictures document the similarity of human experience by focusing on the passages which all cultures celebrate through ritual: birth, coming of age, marriage, and death. They also portray the extraordinary diversity of cultural expression seen in the range of ceremonies used to mark these common occurrences in the course of a human life.
Adult collection.

Collins, Charles M., and David Cohen. *The African Americans.* New York: Viking, 1993.

Some of the people pictured in this collection are famous, but many are not. All have made significant contributions to their own community and to American culture. The photographs are grouped around such themes as service to the community, education, the church, and culture and the arts. Brief descriptions of the accomplishments of those pictured provide an introduction to the cultural history of African Americans.

Adult collection.

———

Conner, Patrick. *People at Work.* Looking at Art. New York: Atheneum, 1982.

Although gathered from different times and cultures, all the paintings in this book address the theme of people at work. Brief comments about each picture provide some historical context and focus the viewer's attention on particular details. They also pose some thought-provoking questions. Intended to introduce children to a way of looking at art, all the books in this series group pictures according to theme and provide brief but instructive commentary. In subject and format, they are very appropriate for adults as well. Other titles include *People at Home* and *Faces.*

Children's collection.

———

Corn, Wanda M. *The Art of Andrew Wyeth.* Boston: New York Graphic Society, Little, Brown & Co., 1973.

At first glance, Andrew Wyeth's rather spare paintings of the rocks, water, animals, buildings, farms, and people of his rural Pennsylvania countryside seem ordinary and familiar. Any attempt to describe them, however, reveals the incredible detail with which he has rendered these seemingly common objects, making us consider their significance in the lives of the people who inhabit this landscape.

Adult collection.

———

Cousins, Norman. *The Human Adventure: A Camera Chronicle.* Selection and arrangement by Antony di Gesu. Dallas, TX: Saybrook Publishers, 1986.

In his travels to five continents during his long tenure as editor of the *Saturday Review*, Norman Cousins always carried a camera with his notebook. For this book, photographer di Gesu has selected from among the thousands of pictures Cousins took as well as excerpts from his extensive writing. The resulting collection combines pictures of men and women the

world over at work, at leisure, in quiet contemplation, and in joyful celebration with Cousins's thoughtful commentary about the nature of human beings and the forces that unite us in the face of conflict and diversity.
Adult collection.

Daniel, Pete, and Raymond Smock. *A Talent for Detail: The Photographs of Miss Frances Benjamin Johnston, 1889–1910.* New York: Harmony Books, 1974.
  This book opens with a photographic biography of Miss Johnston, a pioneer both as a photographer and a professional woman. These personal pictures are followed by a collection of Johnston's documentary photographs, including such subjects as working women and the schools of Washington, D.C. Browsing through these photographs offers the viewer an intriguing picture of life in the United States at the turn of the century.
Adult collection.

Davidson, Bruce. *Subway.* Photographs and text by Bruce Davidson. New York: An Aperture Book Published in Association with Floyd A. Yearout, 1986.
  For many New Yorkers, the subway is more than a mode of transportation, it is an integral part of their urban environment. In this collection of photographs, we see the subway from various and sometimes surprising perspectives. We see the face of violence that is an omnipresent threat, but we also see a young man in cap and gown travelling to his graduation in the company of obviously proud parents. We see the weary faces of riders enduring yet another trip to work or school, but we also see a beautiful sunrise, the rivers and bays that define New York's landscape, and the architecture that identifies it throughout the world, all framed by the subway's window. There is much to see on the subway, and these photographs encourage us to look as we have never looked before.
Adult collection.

Dinhofer, Sally Mehlman. *The Art of Baseball: The Great American Game in Painting, Sculpture, and Folk Art.* New York: Harmony Books, 1990.
  Baseball is a fertile subject for artists who combine their own love of the game with keen powers of observation and vivid imaginations. Looking at the works collected in this book, we see baseball through the artist's

lens, adding yet another dimension to the sights, sounds, and history of this part of American culture. Brief commentaries accompany each work of art, describing the work and its connection to baseball.
Adult collection.

Easter, Eric, D. Michael Cheers, and Dudley M. Brooks. *Songs of My People: African Americans: a Self-Portrait.* Introduction by Gordon Parks. Boston: Little, Brown & Co., 1991.

To create this book, fifty-three black photographers spent the Summer and Fall of 1990 photographing African Americans in various settings throughout the United States. The resulting photographs are, in the words of the editors, "stories which speak of our beauty, our achievements, our troubles, our diversity, our African heritage, and our American-ness." The photographs are arranged to explore such themes as religion, the arts, and the family. Four brief but telling essays invite the reader to look beyond the pictures and consider the stories they tell.
Adult collection.

Edey, Maitland. *Great Photographic Essays from* Life. Boston: New York Graphic Society, Little, Brown & Co., 1975.

These photographic essays explore topics outside the realm of hard "news," such as life in a Montana boom town earlier in this century and the anxiety of a young boy meeting his new adoptive family. Each essay includes several black-and-white photographs accompanied by a few paragraphs explaining the event. Collectively, they offer a "slice of life" view of mid-twentieth century America.
Adult collection.

Evans, Walker. *Walker Evans.* Introduction by John Szarkowski. New York: Museum of Modern Art, 1971.

The poet William Carlos Williams said of Walker Evans's photographs, "It is ourselves we see, ourselves lifted up from a parochial setting. We see what we have not . . . realized, ourselves made worthy in our anonymity." The photographs in this collection, many taken during the days of the Great Depression, are an essential part of our national archives. For a more comprehensive collection of the photographs of Walker Evans, see *Walker Evans: The Hungry Eye*, discussed below.
Adult collection.

Failing, Patricia. *Best-Loved Art from American Museums*. New York: Clarkson N. Potter, Inc., 1983.

To create this collection, fifty-seven museums in the United States and Canada were asked to choose the works they considered most popular. The resulting collection includes among its many treasures American, European, and Asian paintings as well as textiles and objects of decorative art. Shown together, they provide an opportunity for new readers to browse the major museums of North America and react to a wide variety of art. *Adult collection.*

Feininger, Andreas. *Feininger's Chicago, 1941*. New York: Dover Publications, 1980.

Originally photographed for *Life* magazine, these pictures portray a black-and-white vision of Carl Sandburg's "city of the big shoulders." Highlighting the architectural features of bridges, buildings, trains, and other structures of strength and steel, the photographs convey the industrial vitality that marked Chicago in the days before World War II. *Adult collection.*

———. *The Mountains of the Mind: A Fantastic Journey into Reality*. New York: The Viking Press, 1977.

This collection of photographs from nature will challenge the viewer's imagination. The fish, rocks, shells, driftwood, and other objects pictured are all positioned, illuminated, and in some cases magnified to display the artistic impact of shapes, lines, contours, and contrasts, often masking the object's true identity. *Adult collection.*

Ferris, Timothy. *Spaceshots: The Beauty of Nature Beyond Earth*. New York: Pantheon Books, 1984.

Taken for scientific purposes by various spacecraft, these photographs of planet Earth and other heavenly bodies nevertheless evoke a sense of awe and wonder. An introductory essay discusses the nature of beauty in the natural world, a discussion that will easily be extended by the photographs themselves. *Adult collection.*

Frank, Robert. *The Americans.* New York: Aperture, Inc., 1959.

In 1955, Robert Frank bought an old car and began a journey across the forty-eight states, photographing what he saw. This now famous collection of photographs offers a sometimes funny, sometimes bleak, but always fascinating view of the American scene in the 1950's.
Adult collection.

Fraser, James. *The American Billboard: 100 Years.* New York: Harry N. Abrams, Inc., 1991.

In a culture that is as dependent on the automobile as ours is, billboards become important indicators of popular culture as well as familiar features of the landscape. A book such as this could spark discussions about clever visual design, the powers of commercial persuasion, and American social history over the last century. Such a discussion in a class with students from other countries might be particularly revealing.
Adult collection.

Freedman, Russell. *Children of the Wild West.* New York: Clarion Books/ Ticknor & Fields, 1983.

We all know that the pioneers who settled the American West suffered great hardships, but viewing the rare nineteenth-century photographs collected in this documentary gives readers a sense of the bleakness of that life that no verbal account could do alone. Combined with a fascinating and readable text, these pictures tell a vivid story of courage, optimism, danger, and sadness, a story that continues to shape our modern view of what it means to be an American and to raise questions that haunt our collective conscience.
Children's collection.

Gore, Art. *Images of Yesterday.* Palo Alto, CA: American West Publishing Co., 1975.

Gore opens this collection of photographs with a brief account of his early life in rural North Carolina, a life filled with physical hardship but tempered by great love for his family and his environment. The photographs reflect that life and Gore's very spiritual response to the beauty and bounty of nature. He invites viewers to "refresh your own perspective on the beauty of the world, to look at the whole apple before you bite into it."
Adult collection.

Graham, David. *Only in America: Some Unexpected Scenery.* New York: Alfred
A. Knopf, 1991.
> Funny, bizarre, and corny are a few of the words that describe these pho-
> tos of dinosaur sculptures, country murals, and commercial ventures that
> decorate American roadsides. This book would elicit some unexpected
> comments in an ESOL class.
> *Adult collection.*

Harlem Renaissance: Art of Black America. New York: Harry N. Abrams, 1987.
> Essentially a photodocumentary of the vibrant cultural life of Harlem dur-
> ing the 1920's and 1930's, this book also includes reproductions of some
> of the paintings and sculpture produced at that time. Collectively, the
> works presented here convey a strong sense of the energy, diversity, and
> quality of the artistic expression of that time and place.
> *Adult collection.*

Higgins, Chester Jr. *Drums of Life: A Photographic Essay on the Black Man in
America.* Text by Orde Coombs. Garden City, NY: Anchor Books, 1974.
> A brief text introduces each section of photographs of black men in four
> stages of the cycle of life: as children, young adults, middle-aged men, and
> elders. The men are not identified, making the pictures particularly evoca-
> tive. The viewer wonders: Who is this person? What is his life like? How
> much is he like me? This photographer and writer team has also produced
> *Black Woman: A Photographic Essay.*
> *Adult collection.*

Hine, Lewis W. *America and Lewis Hine: Photographs 1904–1940.* Millerton,
NY: Aperture Inc., 1977.
> Lewis Hine was a documentary photographer who wanted "to show the
> things that had to be corrected . . . and the things that had to be appreci-
> ated." Most of the pictures in this book document the lives and social con-
> ditions of Americans, particularly poor Americans, living in the first half
> of this century. Many of the photographs show examples of child labor
> and the sometimes appalling conditions in which immigrants lived, two
> subjects for which he is particularly well known. Hine's photographs offer
> a graphic view of particular segments of American history, giving students
> an opportunity to compare the America he pictured with the culture they
> see today.
> *Adult collection.*

————. *Men at Work: Photographic Studies of Modern Men and Machines.* New York: Dover Publications, Inc., 1977.

Originally published in 1932, the photographs in this collection glorify the power of men and machines working together to build the railroads, mines, factories, and skyscrapers that defined industrial America in the twentieth century. This sense of man's power over nature and machine is most stunningly portrayed in Hine's photographs of men working high above ground to build the Empire State Building. It would be interesting for students to compare these photos, which offer an optimistic view of men and machines, with Hine's photographs of children in forced labor collected in the book *Kids at Work: Lewis Hine and the Crusade Against Child Labor*, listed in Chapter 4.

Adult collection.

————. *Women at Work: 153 Photographs by Lewis W. Hine.* New York: Dover Publications, 1981.

Dover Publications has reprinted the works of several well-known photographers, bringing them to the attention of a new generation of viewers, as well as resurrecting their documentary account of the past century. This book and the companion *Men at Work*, listed above, are two good examples. Comparing the two volumes, a far bleaker view emerges from this collection. Taken during the period 1907–1938, these pictures show not only the difficult conditions under which women of the time worked, but also the limited number of jobs available to them. Students might also compare this book with Betty Medsger's work of the same title, listed below, which shows pictures taken some forty years and several social movements later.

Adult collection.

Holden, Donald. *Whistler Landscapes and Seascapes.* New York: Watson-Guptill Publications in cooperation with the Freer Gallery of Art, Smithsonian Institution, Washington, D.C., 1976.

Several of the works included in this book are nocturnes, muted and misty paintings which invite the viewer to consider the more mysterious elements of the real world. Watson-Guptill Publications has produced several collections of the works of various artists which are well suited for use with adult literacy students. All the titles contain a brief discussion of the artist's life and influences along with beautiful reproductions of paintings.

Adult collection.

Hoopes, Donelson F. *Winslow Homer Watercolors*. New York: Watson-Guptill Publications in cooperation with The Brooklyn Museum, New York and The Metropolitan Museum of Art, New York, 1976.

Winslow Homer's paintings portray America in the late nineteenth century with a realism that helps us picture the daily lives of the people who shaped the country we now live in, as well as a kind of fragile beauty that helps us imagine the hopes, dreams, and sorrows they inevitably had. *Adult collection.*

Hubbard, Jim, ed. *Shooting Back: A Photographic View of Life by Homeless Children*. San Francisco: Chronicle Books, 1991.

Shooting Back is a project through which professional photographers volunteer their time and talents to teach homeless children how to use a camera. The numerous pictures from that project presented here show kids on the streets and in shelters doing what kids do: playing, going to school, hanging out with friends, eating meals with their families. They also show things not so common to childhood experience: learning to cope with the mix of people who share their homeless plight and struggling with their parents to create a home in a welfare hotel. Though never sentimental, a child-like innocence shines through these pictures, creating a haunting perspective that will move any adult who encounters this book. *Adult collection.*

Hughes, Langston, Milton Meltzer, C. Eric Lincoln, and Jon Michael Spencer. *A Pictorial History of African Americans: From 1619 to the Present*. Sixth revised edition. New York: Crown Publishers, Inc., 1995.

This is a browsable book first published in 1956 by Hughes and Meltzer, then periodically updated by Meltzer and others. Brief sections cover topics such as slavery, the Civil War, leaders in the arts, religion, and sports, and the Civil Rights Movement of the 1960's and beyond. Not itself an in-depth reference, this book would serve as a good introduction to some of the names and events that have shaped African American history over nearly four centuries. *Adult collection.*

Iooss, Walter. *Baseball*. Text by Roger Angell. New York: Harry N. Abrams, Inc., 1984.

Just as baseball itself moves from high drama to routine play, the color

photographs in this book capture individual players in moments of dramatic tension as well as in more light-hearted times on and off the field.
Adult collection.

————. *Sports People.* Text by Frank Deford. New York: Harry N. Abrams, Inc., 1988.

These stunning photographs capture athletes from a wide range of sports in moments of beauty, grace, courage, determination, and disappointment. Sports photography is commonplace in our culture, but these pictures, accompanied by brief but insightful commentaries that introduce each section, invite the viewer to look beyond the famous name or circumstance to see some part of the universal human drama played out in the athletic arena.
Adult collection.

Jardi, Enric. *Paul Klee.* New York: Rizzoli International Publications, 1990.

Though not specifically part of a series, this is another of the many Rizzoli art books whose format of minimum text and large reproductions makes them appealing for use with new readers. This title presents the work of Paul Klee, an abstract painter whose work is accessible to new readers because his nuances of color and design invite description and his intriguing titles hint at possible interpretations of the work.
Adult collection.

Kaufman, Kenneth. *Of Trees, Leaves, and Ponds: Studies in Photo-Impressionism.* New York: E.P. Dutton, 1981.

Short excerpts from poetry accompany color photographs from nature which are evocative and inspirational. In response to this pairing of words and pictures, students could explain the connection between the poems and photographs, describe places or events the photographs call to mind, or write their own poetic accompaniment to the photographs.
Adult collection.

Kertesz, Andre. *On Reading.* New York: Grossman Publishers, 1975.

People read almost anywhere and anytime: on park benches, in the subway and on buses, on rooftops, at the beach, in elegant reading rooms, in moments of quiet leisure or in the midst of a bustling city, in the glare of

sunlight or in the glow of a small candle. In an intriguing range of settings, Kertesz, an internationally acclaimed photographer, has captured the very private nature of this often public activity.
Adult collection.

Kunhardt, Philip B., Jr. *Life Smiles Back.* New York: Simon and Schuster, 1987.

For many years, *Life* magazine closed each issue with a single photograph that could be of anything so long as it was funny. The pictures captured people and animals in what were, in most cases, unintentionally amusing circumstances. Taken over a span of thirty years from the 1930's to the 1960's, these photographs offer an interesting perspective on social change. What might have been funny in the 1940's, a man standing before a judge in his boxer shorts, for example, hardly raises a chuckle in the very informal 1990's when people routinely exercise on city streets in clothes that look like underwear. What makes us laugh is sometimes timeless, sometimes not, and realizing the difference shows us much about the society in which we live.
Adult collection.

Lanker, Brian. *I Dream a World: Portraits of Black Women Who Changed America.* New York: Stewart, Tabori & Chang, 1989.

Stunning photographs of seventy-five black women who made significant contributions to American culture, particularly in the worlds of politics and the arts, are accompanied by segments of interviews in which each woman talks about her struggles, triumphs, and hopes for the future. There is a nobility in these photographs that is echoed in the stories the women tell.
Adult collection.

Lauber, Patricia. *Seeing Earth from Space.* New York: Orchard Books, 1990.

Photographs and illustrations from NASA show us the Earth as seen from space, a perspective that alters our understanding of our physical world and gives us clues to our evolutionary past and uncertain environmental future.
Adult collection/children's collection.

Lawrence, Jacob. *Jacob Lawrence: The Migration Series.* Edited by Elizabeth Hutton Turner. Washington, D.C.: The Rappahannock Press in association with the Phillips Collection, 1993.

In much of his work, Lawrence is both painter and storyteller. The sixty panels in this series tell the story of the migration of American blacks from the rural South to the industrial North after World War I. Brief captions, written by the artist, explain the content of each picture. With bold colors and a slightly distorted perspective, Lawrence's paintings captivate viewers and draw them directly into the heart of the subject. Alone, each painting is a powerful work of art. Together, they dramatize a vivid and important story in American history. A children's book, *The Migration Series,* also reproduces these paintings and is listed in Chapter 6.
Adult collection.

Lieberman, Archie. *Neighbors: A Forty-Year Portrait of an American Farm Community.* San Francisco: Collins Publishers, 1993.

In the 1950's, on assignment from *This Week Magazine,* Lieberman photographed a particular farm family in northwest Illinois. He became fascinated by this family and the farming life, coming back over several decades to photograph them, their neighbors, and the inevitable changes that affected them all.
Adult collection.

Loengard, John. *Life Classic Photographs: A Personal Interpretation.* Boston: Little, Brown & Co., 1988.

For this collection, Loengard has chosen more than 100 of the photographs he considers the best of what *Life* magazine had to offer. These are photographs which "stick in the mind and become classics." Some depict important events of their day, others tell human interest stories. A brief description of the event pictured accompanies each photograph.
Adult collection.

Lopes, Sal. *The Wall: Images and Offerings from the Vietnam Veterans Memorial.* New York: HarperCollins, 1987.

Visitors to the Vietnam Veterans Memorial touch and kiss the names on the wall, leave letters and pictures for loved ones, introduce children to the dead, and come in all seasons and at all times of day to reflect on the

names and the meaning of this most-visited of war memorials. The pictures in this book are exquisite and poignant.
Adult collection.

Lowe, Jacques. *JFK Remembered: An Intimate Portrait by His Personal Photographer.* New York: Random House, 1993.

Although a young and inexperienced photographer when he began to cover the presidential primaries of 1960, Lowe won the confidence and trust of John Kennedy who asked him to "hang around" the White House, recording the new administration. Given access to virtually all political and family gatherings, Lowe witnessed the events of the early sixties from an extraordinary vantage point, and he has given us some of the most memorable pictures of those years. His brief but insightful commentary adds information as well as a personal perspective on the lives of the Kennedy family and the people with whom they worked. In an earlier book, *The Kennedy Legacy: A Generation Later*, Lowe reproduces many of the same pictures, but focuses somewhat more on political events.
Adult collection.

McCabe, Constance, and Neal McCabe. *Baseball's Golden Age: The Photographs of Charles M. Conlon.* New York: Harry N. Abrams, Inc., 1993.

Between 1904 and 1942, Charles M. Conlon photographed the characters and events that made baseball a major American attraction. Many of his most famous photographs are presented here, accompanied by brief commentaries which relate some of the colorful anecdotes and personal stories that are as much a part of baseball as its huge body of statistics. The result is a very browsable book which will remind viewers of the men and times that made baseball but also give them a sense of the mythic quality that helps account for the sport's hold on the American imagination.
Adult collection.

Margaret Walker's "For My People": A Tribute. Photographs by Roland L. Freeman. Jackson, MS: University Press of Mississippi, 1992.

When Margaret Walker's poem "For My People" was published in 1942, its strong affirmation of the spirit of black people made it a standard within the African American community. On the fiftieth anniversary of the poem's

publication, photographer Freeman pays tribute to Walker by publishing the poem with thirty-eight photographs which he believes portray that same beauty and tenacity of spirit that Walker captured in words.
Adult collection.

Marling, Karal Ann. *Edward Hopper*. Rizzoli Art Series. New York: Rizzoli International Publications, Inc., 1992.

Whether they depict individual persons or a particular landscape, Edward Hopper's paintings touch deep emotional chords. Asked to discuss or write about one of his paintings, students will inevitably be drawn into the emotional content of the work, perhaps recalling times and places long past, perhaps gaining new perspective on current circumstances. The books in this Rizzoli Art Series are particularly suitable for use with adult literacy students. All paperbacks, they have pages large enough to accommodate beautiful reproductions but are thin enough to be easy to handle. Brief introductions discuss the artist and his or her time and work, followed by color plates which offer a representative sampling of the artist's major work. The series covers a wide range of art history, including Michelangelo and The Sistine Chapel, European masters Monet and Degas, American realists Hopper and Winslow Homer, and American modernist Roy Lichtenstein. Tutors may wish to choose individual artists whose work will appeal to their students, or they may wish to present several books at once, offering students the chance to compare styles, themes, and subjects across a wide spectrum of human history.
Adult collection.

Medsger, Betty. *Women at Work: A Photodocumentary*. New York: Sheed and Ward, Inc., 1975.

Although now twenty years old, this collection of more than 100 black-and-white photographs of women engaged in jobs ranging from the traditional to the unusual will still spark discussion on the question of women's work. Several of the women pictured offer statements describing their jobs and feelings about them.
Adult collection.

Melvin, Betsy, and Tom Melvin. *Robert Frost Country*. Garden City, NY: Doubleday, Inc., 1977.

The authors have matched color photographs of New England in differ-

ent seasons with excerpts from Robert Frost's poetry. Beautiful in themselves, the photographs gain an added dimension when paired with the poetry.
Adult collection.

Memories of Childhood: Award Winning Quilts Created for the Great American Quilt Festival 2. New York: E.P. Dutton in association with the Museum of American Folk Art, 1989.

"Memories of Childhood" was the theme of this second quilt festival sponsored by the Museum of American Folk Art. Highly imaginative and varied creations, these quilts are also household items meant to record and preserve very personal memories. Viewing many together in a book such as this offers students a chance to compare styles and methods as well as subject matter. The quilts may also inspire students to recall memories of their own which they can record in writing or in oral history collections, perhaps with a visual accompaniment for those so inclined.
Adult collection.

Menashe, Abraham. *The Face of Prayer.* New York: Alfred A. Knopf, 1983.

Menashe collected these photographs in part to honor his "commitment to images that affirm life, provide refuge, and offer healing." The universal need to address the spiritual is apparent in these photographs showing people from around the world and from many different faiths and traditions gathered together to pray.
Adult collection.

Meyerowitz, Joel. *A Summer's Day.* New York: Times Books, 1985.

According to Meyerowitz, "summer is a time for remembering, a time for taking in." His lush and beautiful color photographs invite us to do just that as we follow a summer's day from dawn to twilight.
Adult collection.

Monk, Lorraine. *Photographs that Changed the World.* New York: Doubleday, 1989.

A photograph from 1826, one of the earliest in existence, is among the fifty-one included in this collection of pictures that mark an extraordinary progression of events occurring over the last century and a half. Among others are Abraham Lincoln meeting with his generals, the flag raising at Iwo Jima, and an earthrise as seen by the astronauts aboard *Apollo 8*. *Adult collection.*

Mora, Gilles, and John T. Hill. *Walker Evans: The Hungry Eye*. New York: Harry N. Abrams, Inc., 1993.

Photographer Walker Evans "specialized in the life of the street—carefully observed views of architecture, the American roadside, and the people who lived in the nation's cities, towns, and villages." His broad range of interests is evident in this comprehensive collection which includes his photographs of New York in the 1920's and 1930's, the Great Depression as seen in the faces and landscape of rural America, surreptitious "portraits" taken on the New York subway and in other places, and numerous architectural photos of America's small towns. For a simpler introduction to this important photographer's work, see listing under Walker Evans above. *Adult collection.*

Myers, Walter Dean. *Brown Angels: An Album of Pictures and Verse*. New York: HarperCollins Publishers, 1993.

Over the years, novelist Myers has collected turn-of-the-century photographs of African American children, mostly formal portraits of well-scrubbed faces dressed in Sunday best clothing. The photographs inspired him to write poems about the joys of childhood and the love and delight that adults lavish on the children in their lives. The poems are good, but the pictures tell the real story. Although published for children, this book will be truly appreciated by adults who know how it feels to look in the face of a special child. *Children's collection.*

O'Keeffe, Georgia. *Georgia O'Keeffe: One Hundred Flowers*. Edited by Nicholas Calloway. New York: Alfred A. Knopf, 1989.

Georgia O'Keeffe painted these flowers, and indeed many other natural objects from her New Mexico environment, in such vivid and extravagant detail that, though real, they appear almost magical. Describing them, whether orally or in writing, requires close observation and may inspire some imaginative associations as well. *Adult collection.*

O'Kelley, Mattie Lou. *From the Hills of Georgia: An Autobiography in Painting*. Boston: Little, Brown & Co., 1983.

O'Kelley is a folk artist whose work was discovered by the world outside her rural Georgia home when she was already well into her sixties. The paintings in this book depict scenes from her early life rendered in a rich and colorful style reminiscent of quilting or mosaic tile. Each picture could stand on its own, but this collection of several paintings, each accompanied by brief descriptive text, tells an engaging story of life in rural Georgia in the early twentieth century.
Adult collection/children's collection.

———. *Mattie Lou O'Kelley: Folk Artist*. Introduction by Robert Bishop. Boston: Little, Brown & Co., 1989.

In his introduction, Robert Bishop, director of the Museum of American Folk Art in New York City, describes O'Kelley as "an exquisite recorder of time and place." The paintings included here mostly depict O'Kelley's rural Georgia home, which she rarely left until she was "discovered" by Bishop and began to travel into the wider world. There are no stories attached to the pictures here as there are in *From the Hills of Rural Georgia: An Autobiography in Paintings*, but the paintings themselves reveal much about the times and places in which she has lived.
Adult collection.

Parks, Gordon. *Gordon Parks: Whispers of Intimate Things*. Introduction by Philip B. Kunhardt, Jr. New York: Viking Press, 1971.

There are more poems in this collection from photographer and poet Parks than in his later work, *Moments Without Proper Names*, listed below. It is the photographs, however, that carry the burden of meaning, strengthened and extended by the poems but never overshadowed by them. "Reading" both together, new readers will be challenged to connect the words and pictures and consider ways in which they support and stretch each other. An earlier book, *A Poet and His Camera*, published in 1968, is similar.
Adult collection.

———. *Moments Without Proper Names*. New York: The Viking Press, 1975.

Known mostly as a photographer, including several years on the staff of *Life* magazine, Parks is also an accomplished poet. To this collection of pictures covering three decades, several countries and a range of moods,

Parks has added a few of his poems which reflect the haunting, questioning quality of many of the photographs.
Adult collection.

Perry, Regenia A. *Free Within Ourselves: African American Artists in the Collection of the National Museum of American Art.* Washington, D.C.: National Museum of American Art, Smithsonian Institution in association with Pomegranate Artbooks, Petaluma, CA, 1992.

Thirty-one African American artists whose works hang in the Smithsonian are presented alphabetically in a format that combines two or three of their works with a brief explanation of their lives and artistic aspirations. This collection provides a wonderful introduction to the range and quality of work produced by these artists, many of whom are not well known among the general public.
Adult collection.

Pfahl, John. *Picture Windows.* Boston: Little, Brown & Co., 1987.

We look at art for connections to and clues about real life. In these pictures, that process is given a subtle twist as real life is presented as art, framed by a picture window. The scenes vary from a construction grid in New York City, to suburban back yards, to a Spanish tile roof in California, but in all the pictures the limited view focuses our attention on the scene within the border and asks us to imagine how it fits into a larger context.
Adult collection.

Pippin, Horace. *Horace Pippin.* With an essay by Romare Bearden. Washington, D.C.: The Phillips Collection, 1977.

Although his arm was damaged in World War I, Pippin nevertheless struggled to continue the artistic career he had begun before the war. He painted searing memories from the war, scenes from the lives of black Americans, and pictures which considered religious themes as well as historical events and social conditions. Called a primitive or folk artist, Pippin's work reveals both the strength of character and clarity of perspective that adversity can bring. This is a simple book, one picture per page with a minimum of text, but it speaks volumes. For a more comprehensive presentation of this artist's life and work, see *I Tell My Heart: The Art of Horace Pippin,* discussed below.
Adult collection.

Plowden, David. *Small Town America.* Introduction by David McCullough. New York: Harry N. Abrams, Inc., 1994.

Photographer Plowden has set a mission for himself: documenting the look of America's small towns which seem to be vanishing as the twenty-first century approaches. In doing so, he has conferred "a certain kind of immortality on certain aspects of American civilization." Viewing these intriguing black-and-white photographs of the main streets, gas pumps, barbershops, general stores, and other artifacts of small town life, students may consider what has been lost as well as gained by the inevitable march of progress.
Adult collection.

Porter, Eliot. *The West.* Boston: Little, Brown & Co., 1988.

These extraordinary photographs of the desert in bloom, magnificently colored canyons, and towering mountains of the American West are truly awe-inspiring. Porter also provides a brief history of the geology and the course of human habitation of these majestic lands.
Adult collection.

Rajs, Jake. *America.* Foreword by James A. Michener. New York: Rizzoli International Publications, 1990.

Everything about this book is on a grand scale: the photographs, the book itself, the country it celebrates, and the very idea of freedom that inspired Rajs's father to immigrate here. The range of the pictures—from wilderness to roadways, farmland to shoreline, small towns to great cities—reflects the many faces of American geography and culture.
Adult collection.

Read-Miller, Cynthia. *Main Street, U.S.A in Early Photographs.* New York: Dover Publications, Inc., 1988.

These 113 photographs were taken early in the twentieth century by the Detroit Publishing Company and kept by the Henry Ford Museum expressly to preserve a visual record of the vanishing commercial districts of America's small towns. To look at these photographs is to remember—or to learn—what came before us and to consider the progress, or lack of it, that we have made.
Adult collection.

Rice, Leland. *Up Against It: Photographs of the Berlin Wall.* Albuquerque, NM: University of New Mexico Press, 1991.

When it divided Germany's largest city, the Berlin Wall was an obvious symbol of oppression, but in some ways it became a symbol of hope and resistance as well, especially in the hundreds of statements and messages scrawled on its western face. In his photographs, Rice preserved many of those messages which were lost when the wall came down, and they still speak across all barriers.

Adult collection.

Ritter, Lawrence S. *The Babe: A Life in Pictures.* Picture research by Mark Rucker. New York: Ticknor & Fields, 1988.

Ritter is both a fan and scholar of baseball, and the text he provides for this picture biography is engaging and informative. The illustrations tell an equally detailed and captivating story. Using photographs, news-clippings, old posters, baseball cards, and other memorabilia of one of baseball's greatest stars, the book presents the complex life of Babe Ruth with humor, honesty, and compassion.

Adult collection.

Roalf, Peggy. *Looking at Paintings: Children.* Looking at Pictures series. New York: Hyperion Books for Children, 1993.

All the books in this series present paintings focused on a particular theme such as families, flowers, cats, or, in the case of this title, children. Each color plate is accompanied by a brief text discussing the artist as well as salient features of the painting. This format stimulates discussions about the art among adults. It is also a good title to recommend for family literacy because the text is intended to help adults and children look at and talk about the art together.

Children's collection.

Robeson, Susan. *The Whole World in His Hands: A Pictorial Biography of Paul Robeson.* Secaucus, NJ: Citadel Press, 1981.

Written and compiled by his granddaughter, this picture biography tells the extraordinary life story of Paul Robeson, grandson of a slave, athlete, scholar, actor, singer, and internationally-renowned Civil Rights leader. Some of Paul Robeson's own words are interspersed with Susan Robeson's commentary.

Adult collection.

Rockwell, Norman. *102 Favorite Paintings.* Introduction by Christopher Finch. New York: Crown Publishers, Inc., 1977.

For some, Norman Rockwell's paintings depict American life in the mid-twentieth century with humor, charm, and a comfortable nostalgia. Others see his work as narrow and overly optimistic. Despite these varied opinions however, Rockwell's paintings are a significant part of American culture, and this collection offers students a chance to voice their own opinions about the people and the life he depicted so memorably.
Adult collection.

Sandler, Martin. *Cowboys: A Library of Congress Book.* New York: Harper-Collins, 1994.

Many Americans probably do not realize that, in addition to its vast collection of books, the Library of Congress contains historical photographs, posters, paintings, and artifacts that vividly portray this country's history. This book is an attractive photographic history of cowboys and the cowboy life, including pictures from the nineteenth century to the present.

This title is one of the first in this series intended to "make the riches of the Library even more available" to a wider range of Americans. Another title, *Pioneers*, is also available.
Children's collection.

Schapiro, Meyer. *Vincent Van Gogh.* New York: Harry N. Abrams, Inc., 1983.

A Dutch painter who lived in France at the end of the nineteenth century, Van Gogh gave his paintings an emotional power that seems to cross all borders of time and place. While there are many collections of Van Gogh's works, this one is particularly accessible to literacy students because it presents forty-seven of his well-known pictures in large plates, one per page, accompanied by a brief, one page description. Students and teachers who want to learn more about this compelling artist can read the brief but informative discussion of Van Gogh's life and work which opens the book.
Adult collection.

Schick, Ron, and Julia Van Haaften. *The View from Space: American Astronaut Photography 1962–1972.* New York: Clarkson N. Potter, Inc., 1988.

The photographs in this collection were taken by several different astronauts during various missions into space. They show planet Earth from

the viewpoint of outer space, a perspective that was entirely new in the 1960's. The book also includes several pictures taken within the spacecrafts, pictures which amuse for their novelty but also serve to remind us of the extraordinary accomplishments of the last half century.
Adult collection.

Schulke, Flip. *He Had a Dream: Martin Luther King, Jr. and the Civil Rights Movement.* New York: W.W. Norton & Co., 1995.

Schulke was a photographer for *Life* magazine when assigned to cover Dr. King and the Civil Rights struggle in the late 1950's. His photographs of the protest marches, the confrontations, and the power of the people—both black and white—who were determined to bring change helped tell the movement's story to the nation and the world. In the process, Schulke also became a friend of King, so many photographs in this collection show us Martin Luther King the man as well as the public figure.
Adult collection.

Sinatra, Frank. *A Man and His Art.* Introduction by Tina Sinatra. New York: Random House, 1991.

Until recently, well-known singer Frank Sinatra never shared his painting beyond a small circle of family and friends. According to his daughter Tina, Sinatra, who is basically self-taught, interprets art in much the same way he interprets song. He sees something he likes and then creates not an imitation but an interpretation based on the original. With bold colors and vivid designs, these abstract paintings could inspire both discussion and creative writing.
Adult collection.

Smolan, Rick, and David Cohen, eds. *A Day in the Life of America.* New York: Collins Publishers, 1986.

Two hundred photographers were sent on assignment to take pictures anywhere in the United States during the twenty-four hours of May 2, 1986. The resulting montage of photographs published here captures the amazing diversity of land, people, and lifestyles that defines the United States in the late twentieth century. Brief annotations identify places and events pictured. Collins has also published similar books about other countries.
Adult collection.

Stein, Judith, ed. *I Tell My Heart: The Art of Horace Pippin.* Philadelphia: The Pennsylvania Academy of Fine Arts, 1993.

This volume accompanied a major exhibition of Pippin's works across the country, becoming perhaps the greatest recognition this black artist has received to date. Beautiful color plates show the range and power of his paintings while a comprehensive text discusses his life, influences, and work. Considered a folk artist, Pippin gives his work an immediacy that compels the viewer to examine the picture and consider its meaning. For a simpler introduction to the work of Horace Pippin, see *Horace Pippin*, discussed above.

Adult collection.

Strickland, William. *Malcolm X: Make it Plain.* Oral histories selected and edited by Cheryll Y. Greene. New York: Viking, 1994.

In this photographic biography, oral histories and remembrances from those who knew and worked with Malcolm X are interspersed among photographs which follow his life. Author Strickland has also contributed brief biographical passages, but it is the pictures which carry the powerful story of Malcolm's rise from petty criminal to international leader.

Adult collection.

Stryker, Roy, and Nancy Wood. *In This Proud Land: America 1935-1943 As Seen in the FSA Photographs.* Greenwich, CT: New York Graphic Society, Ltd., 1973.

A part of President Roosevelt's attempt to reverse the hardships of the Great Depression, the FSA, or Farm Security Administration, hired photographers to document the living conditions of people in America's small towns and rural areas. Several great photographers began their serious work under Roy Stryker, and their pictures, as collected in this book, are as much a testament to the power of photography to effect change as they are to the difficulty of the lives they immortalized.

Adult collection.

Suares, J. C., and J. Spencer Beck. *Uncommon Grace: Reminiscences and Photographs of Jacqueline Bouvier Kennedy Onassis.* Charlottesville, VA: Thomasson-Grant, 1994.

Jacqueline Kennedy Onassis was one of the world's most photographed women, so there are numerous pictorial biographies of her life. This book

offers a broad view of that life, including many pictures and remembrances from her childhood and life before she met Jack Kennedy, as well as an intriguing glimpse of her life in the years after her husband's assassination when she was a working mother and editor for a major New York publishing house. Of course, the White House years are here too, when Jacqueline Kennedy was at the center of history for such a brief but memorable time. This book may help readers, especially those born after 1963, understand why she remained so central in American culture for all the remaining years of her life.
Adult collection.

Sullivan, Charles, ed. *Children of Promise: African-American Literature and Art for Young People.* New York: Harry N. Abrams, Inc., 1991.

The words and images presented in this collection depict slavery, emancipation, life in the South, and the rise of black culture in twentieth-century Harlem, providing an overview of the history of African Americans as well as beautiful and dramatic images to consider and respond to. Intended to introduce children to the literature and art of black America, this collection will do the same for adults unfamiliar with this powerful body of artistic expression.
Children's collection.

———. *Here is My Kingdom: Hispanic-American Literature and Art for Young People.* New York: Harry N. Abrams, Inc., 1994.

In the paintings, photographs, prose, and poetry presented here, the themes of crossing borders, searching for home, and the place of language inform the artistic expression of a wide range of Latino writers and artists. As with editor Sullivan's earlier collection *Children of Promise*, discussed above, this book was intended to introduce children to the art of Latino culture, and it will do the same for adults wishing to explore this diverse and vibrant culture.
Children's collection.

Westwater, James. *Ohio.* Text by Richard McCutcheon. Portland, OR: Graphic Arts Center Publishing Co., 1982.

Stunning color photographs of small town bandstands, covered bridges, glacial rock formations, and bustling modern cities accompanied by brief captions which place each picture in historical, cultural, and geographic context make this a particularly good example of the many books which feature photographs of a particular state or region of the country. *Adult collection.*

Wheat, Ellen Harkins. *Jacob Lawrence: The Frederick Douglass and Harriet Tubman Series of 1938-40.* Hampton, VA: Hampton University Museum in association with the University of Washington Press, Seattle, 1991.

As an artist, Jacob Lawrence is best known for his series paintings which depict historical events or movements. (See *Jacob Lawrence: The Migration Series*). In the two series presented here, Lawrence tells the stories of two black leaders of the anti-slavery movement, Frederick Douglass and Harriet Tubman. As Lawrence has said of his work, "When the subjects are strong, I believe simplicity is the best way of treating them." The simplicity of these paintings makes them readily accessible to any viewer, but the strength of the characters and their influence over events of their times comes shining through.
Adult collection.

Willis-Braithwaite, Deborah. *VanDerZee: Photographer, 1886-1983.* New York: Harry N. Abrams Inc. in association with the National Portrait Gallery, Smithsonian Institution, 1993.

James VanDerZee, who may have been the first well-known black photographer, was also one of the masters of the profession in this century. Known particularly for his photographs of Harlem between the wars and his formal portraits, including many taken when the subject was dead, VanDerZee created a vivid and lasting record of his time and place. To browse through this book is to remember that Harlem was once a thriving and successful community of black professionals and middle class families.
Adult collection.

Winter. With essays by Donald Hall and Clifton C. Olds. Hanover, NH: Hood Museum of Art, Dartmouth College, distributed by University Press of New England, 1986.

A thematic collection such as this one provides students with an opportunity to compare pictures which present different views of the same phenomenon, in this case, the season of Winter. Describing the various scenes pictured, colors used, and emotions evoked could help students stretch

their vocabulary as well as their powers of observation. Teachers may choose to read to students from the thoughtful essays which open the book to add other viewpoints to the discussion created by the students' own reactions.
Adult collection.

Wyeth, Jamie. *Jamie Wyeth*. Boston: Houghton Mifflin Co., 1980.
Jamie Wyeth's paintings are realistic images of people, nature, and common objects, but their simplicity is deceptive. Looking at Wyeth's paintings, the viewer lingers and finds a depth and beauty not apparent at first glance. Describing or writing about one of his paintings will enhance students' opportunities to see the richness and potential meaning in these works of art.
Adult collection.

Young, Mahonri Sharp. *The Paintings of George Bellows*. New York: Watson-Guptill Publications, 1973.
Bellows was a member of the "Ashcan School," a group of painters who found inspiration in the streets, at the construction sites, and from the sporting events of ordinary people in early twentieth-century America. His paintings are realistic, yet they suggest many questions about the quality of the life depicted.
Adult collection.

Notes

1. John Loengard, *Life Classic Photographs: A Personal Interpretation*, (Boston: New York Graphic Society Books, Little, Brown & Co., 1988), 8.

Chapter 2

Wisdom and Delight:
Poetry for Adult New Readers

Poetry begins in delight and ends in wisdom.
—Robert Frost[1]

Certain language characteristics—rhyme, repetition, short sentences, simple words—are commonly found in books written for adults learning to read. Many of these same elements characterize some poetry as well, poetry that was written for a general adult audience but happens to be relatively simple. Here the comparison ends, however; while material written specifically for the new reader audience is intended to be easy to read, poetry seeks to convey an image or an idea in a memorable way. Good poetry offers new readers so much more than just words to learn to read. It offers words that engage the ear and heart with powerful rhythms, words that strike a chord of memory, words that startle readers into a new way of seeing the familiar, words that amuse and delight, words that, even when simple, change the way we look at our lives.

Using Poetry with New Readers

Poetry can also be a powerful resource for classroom instruction in specific subject areas. For example, some poetry draws its inspiration from historical events, but in describing those events it combines the power of language with the poet's keen observations to reveal deeper truths than a mere recitation of facts could ever do. Students learning about the American Civil Rights movement of the 1950's and 1960's could read the poems collected in Langston Hughes's *The Panther and the Lash* in conjunction with *Rosa Parks: My Story*, an autobiography of the Civil Rights activist written with Jim Haskins (listed in the anthology in Chapter 4). The autobiography recounts the events of the Civil Rights movement in which Parks was a prominent figure, but

Hughes's poetry probes the deeper significance of those events and creates vivid images that will become a permanent part of the reader's understanding of that time and place.

The many variations of language and meaning make poetry a particularly rich resource for adult literacy students. Poems which are short, use simple language, speak directly to the reader, and talk about subjects familiar to students are particularly good to use when introducing poetry to students, because the students will be able to read and understand them with relative ease. Take, for example, Langston Hughes's poem "Winter Moon" from *The Dream Keeper*.

> How thin and sharp is the moon tonight!
> How thin and sharp and ghostly white
> Is the slim curved crook of the moon tonight!

Using rhyme, rhythm, repetition, and alliteration, yet very simple words, Hughes has created an exact and memorable description of a winter moon. In one-on-one tutoring situations, tutors can read poems such as "Winter Moon" to their students, invite them to react to its sounds and ideas as well as to the feelings it evokes, then help the students read the poems on their own. Teachers can also take full advantage of poetry's ability to stretch and challenge the reader's way of looking at the world by introducing poems that examine events, ideas, and feelings that are universally recognized but set in times, places, and cultures different from our own. Reading these poems, students can root themselves in familiar circumstances and feelings but can still be carried to a new perspective by the language.

Reading poetry can also encourage students to write poetry of their own. In his poem, "Young Woman at a Window" (*The Complete Collected Works of William Carlos Williams*), William Carlos Williams uses just twenty-three words to convey a striking image of how a particular woman looks and even to suggest how she feels:

> She sits with
> tears on
>
> her cheek
> her cheek on
>
> her hand
> the child

in her lap
his nose
pressed
to the glass

After reading this poem, students might try to create a vivid word picture of a scene from their own memory or imagination.

Metaphor and vivid imagery are two of the elements that make poetry such a memorable and cogent form of expression, so it is also important to introduce poetry that will help students read and interpret a more sophisticated kind of language. These poems will help new readers look beyond the literal and begin to see how words can convey meaning on several levels. This is an important step in developing those critical thinking skills so necessary not just to reading but to living an informed and participatory life in our increasingly complex society. Poetry is written in many forms and covers virtually any subject matter imaginable. There are poems that tell stories, poems that make clever use of language, poems that create vivid word pictures, poems which sing in memorable rhymes and rhythms that capture the ear and the imagination, poems which recall memories both bitter and sweet, poems which cry out against pain and injustice, poems which celebrate laughter and living, poems which express our deepest fears and longings—poems, in short, which communicate across the spectrum of human experience.

The Bibliography

The bibliography in this chapter offers a broad sampling of poetry. Most of the poets included are American, but some of the anthologies listed include writers from other countries. Of course, the very term *American* conjures up a veritable mosaic of images, and the poems reflect that national diversity. Some poems describe vibrant urban scenes while others take the reader to quiet moments in America's small towns and countryside. The voices that speak in these poems come from men and women, as well as from blacks, whites, Latinos, Native Americans, and others. They offer glimpses of life seen by writers who are still young as well as from elder poets reflecting with the perspective of long lives. The great majority of the poems were written in this century, although some anthologies include earlier works.

Many of the titles listed in the bibliography are general anthologies that include the works of several different poets. In some cases, the poems were collected around a theme such as Lillian Morrison's collection of sports poems, *Rhythm Road: Poems to Move to*. For her anthology *Peeling the Onion*, on the other hand, Ruth Gordon chose poems for the clarity of their insight rather than for any thematic similarity. Most of these anthologies will be found in the children's collection in the library, although in almost every instance the poems within these anthologies were originally written for adults. Whatever their intended audience, however, all of the poetry collections listed in this bibliography are, by virtue of their format and appearance as well as their content, appropriate for adult students.

In some instances, books marketed for children seem even more appropriate for adults. Cynthia Rylant's *Something Permanent*, for example, is a collection of poems which Rylant wrote in response to the Depression-era photographs of Walker Evans. The poems are easy to read and might well appeal to middle school children, but the depth of insight they reveal can best be appreciated by adults whose own lives have known the sting of hardship and the renewing power of family. Lee Bennett Hopkins's two anthologies *A Song in Stone: City Poems* and *On Our Way: Poems of Pride and Love* are both commonly found in the children's section of the public library as well as in college libraries. Both these anthologies match simple but evocative poems with equally compelling photographs to create images that children will understand but adults will find inspiring.

Publishers and educators work to introduce the poems of prominent American writers to children, so you will find collections of the works of writers such as Robert Frost, Emily Dickinson, and Carl Sandburg among the many anthologies in the children's section of the library. Here too, most if not all of the individual poems were originally written for adults; several of these anthologies are highly appropriate for adult literacy students. *You Come, Too*, a collection of Robert Frost's poems, *Rainbow are Made*, Lee Bennett Hopkins's anthology of the works of Carl Sandburg, and Helen Plotz's *Poems of Emily Dickinson* are three good examples of collections that will appeal to adult students.

All poets write in their own unique style which derives from their experiences and influences, their subject matter, and their particular way of speaking. The style and language of some poets make their works particularly suited to literacy students, many of whom will be new to poetry as well as to reading. Langston Hughes, William Carlos Williams, and Lucille Clifton are three good examples. Hughes used the rhythms of Negro spirituals, jazz, and the blues to write about his experience as a black American and citizen of the world. In their simplicity, his poems sing with memorable rhythms and reveal stunning insights that quickly embed themselves in the reader's mind and heart. Read Langston Hughes, hear the rhythm of his phrases, and wonder how such simple words can engage a reader so completely. *The Dream Keeper* and *The Panther and the Lash* are two collections of Hughes's poetry that are suitable for adult new readers. In addition, many of his individual poems are included in other anthologies.

William Carlos Williams was a world-renowned poet who also happened to be a practicing family doctor in New Jersey. Williams wrote hundreds of poems, many inspired by the ordinary people he encountered in his daily rounds tending to the births, illnesses, and deaths of the working people who were both his neighbors and his patients. As with Hughes, many of Williams's poems are short and simple, but never simplistic. Indeed, they are so precise in their use of words and phrases that they create memorable word pictures. His poems will be found in many of the anthologies listed in this chapter's bibliography. *The Complete Collected Poems of William Carlos Williams*, a comprehensive anthology of his work, and the shorter collection, *Selected Poems*, are also listed.

Writing in the language of kitchens and families and the company of women, Lucille Clifton examines the human condition in a way that draws readers in as if they were invited to a family gathering. Collections of her poetry, such as *Good Woman: Poems and a Memoir 1969–1980*, will introduce the reader to Clifton's perspective on life as grandmother, wife, mother, daughter, sister, and black woman in America.

In a few cases, the bibliography lists comprehensive anthologies which address important themes. While each of these anthologies includes many short and accessible poems, inevitably they also contain some long or difficult poems likely to be beyond the reach of most literacy students. Teachers and tutors can pick and choose poems from these anthologies that they consider appropriate for their students. Two examples are *Every Shut Eye Ain't Asleep: An Anthology of Poetry by African Americans Since 1945* which presents many new voices who speak with power and eloquence about life in the latter half of the twentieth century and *No More Masks,* an anthology which offers hundreds of voices of women, some famous but many unknown, speaking about their experiences as daughters, mothers, wives, workers, and participants in historical and cultural events.

Two additional titles require special mention because, although they are relatively difficult texts, they are also potentially important ones for literacy students. In his book *What Work Is,* Philip Levine, who once labored in the auto industry, gives us poems which examine the experiences of those whose lives are consumed in manual labor. *What Work Is* contains many poems that may be difficult for students to read on their own. Given the opportunity to hear the poems read aloud and to discuss them with teachers and perhaps with colleagues at work and in the literacy program, students will find a voice which speaks in solidarity with workers in factories, warehouses, and other places where monotony and physical labor are a common currency.

Rita Dove is the first black writer, and only the second woman, to be named Poet Laureate of the United States. Writing about the personal history of her family, and by extension of her race and country, she speaks to all Americans about the power of family and the burden of responsibility we must all share for our common future. Her poetry is sometimes difficult, yet just listening to her beautifully crafted language, even without comprehending its meaning, gives one a sense of how language can be used to evoke feelings and to create images in the mind of the listener. Sometimes the pleasure of the sound, the intensity of the feeling, or the clarity of the image are all that come, but still, that is enough. Sometimes, though, the words and images also plant ideas which may not become apparent until later readings, or until a discussion with teachers and other students sparks a deeper understanding. For teachers and students willing to be challenged by this kind of language, *Selected Poems* contains many works from Dove's earlier collections as well as the text of the Pulitzer Prize-winning *Thomas and Beulah*, which is based on the life of her grandparents.

A Note to Librarians

Look for ways to make your poetry collection attractive and accessible to literacy students and their teachers. Identify poetry anthologies from the children's collection that will be suitable for adults. Consider labelling them to indicate their appeal to a wider audience. If your library maintains a separate collection for new readers, consider shelving duplicate copies with that collection. Train librarians who purchase poetry books to recognize collections that will appeal to new readers so they can purchase second copies for the literacy collection. Give book talks highlighting poetry at local literacy programs. Sponsor poetry readings and invite staff and students from the literacy programs. Seek funding for poets-in-residence to offer writing workshops and public readings. In all your activities on behalf of poetry and literacy in general, be sure to include the tutors and students from local schools and literacy programs.

A Note to Tutors

The bibliography that follows is just a starting point. With your students, explore the many faces of poetry. Identify particular poets you like and find examples of their poems. Read poetry to your students and encourage them to read poems they like to you. With your students, memorize poems and recite them to each other. Use resources such as *The Columbia Granger's Index to Poetry*, available in the reference section of any library, to find poems about particular topics. Consult your local librarians for assistance in finding anthologies suitable for adult students. As you and your students find poems or books that excite you, share this information with other students. Poetry readings are growing in number and popularity in many cities. Consider organizing a group outing to such an event in your area. Have your students write reviews of books or individual poems to share with other students and even with other programs. Personalize the bibliography in this book by adding titles found by you and your students. Poetry is a rich source of words, ideas, and compelling images. Help your students discover and explore this resource to its fullest.

Bibliography

Adoff, Arnold, ed. *Black Out Loud: An Anthology of Modern Poems by Black Americans.* Illustrated by Alvin Hollingsworth. New York: The Macmillan Co., 1970.
> Gathered for "brothers and sisters of all races," the poems in this anthology describe the feelings and reflect on the history of black Americans in the mid-twentieth century. A simple one-poem-per-page layout is enhanced by occasional line drawings.
> *Beginning new reader/adult collection/children's collection.*

———. *Celebrations: A New Anthology of Black American Poetry.* Chicago: Follett Publishing Co., 1977.
> The theme of celebration—past and present, heroes and heroines, ordinary people who inspire us, and the strength of survival—runs through the 240 poems in this excellent collection of works written in the twentieth century. Adoff is also the editor of the earlier collection *I am the Darker Brother* which also contains many poems suitable for new readers.
> *Intermediate new reader/adult collection/children's collection.*

—————————. *My Black Me: A Beginning Book of Black Poetry.* Rev. ed. New York: E.P. Dutton, 1994.

> The poems in this collection, written by Langston Hughes, Nikki Giovanni, and Lucille Clifton among others, speak directly to the reader about experiences and feelings recognizable to us all. Chosen for beginning readers and for readers new to poetry, the poems were all originally written for adults and are presented in a simple, appealing format. Brief biographies of each poet add to the book's interest and value.

Beginning new reader/children's collection.

Adoff, Arnold. *Sports Pages.* Illustrated by Steve Kuzma. New York: Harper-Collins Publishers, 1985.

> Adoff's thirty-seven poems describe the pleasures of playing a game well and the pain of injury and defeat in soccer, baseball, gymnastics and other sports. The playfulness in the language, and the unusual arrangement of lines on the page will intrigue some readers but may confuse others. Black-and-white sketches convey a breezy feeling that matches the text, making this book best suited for younger students and those particularly interested in sports.

Beginning-intermediate new reader/children's collection.

—————————. *Tornado!* Illustrated by Ronald Himler. New York: Delacorte Press, 1976.

> Written in response to the 1974 tornado in Xenia, Ohio, these poems describe the fear, wonder, sadness, and relief experienced by a family and a town. The black-and-white illustrations and bold type face suggest the darkness of the impending storm. An epilogue recounts factual details of a rash of storms that struck the Midwest that day.

Intermediate new reader/children's collection.

Angelou, Maya. *I Shall Not Be Moved.* New York: Random House, 1990.

> The rhythm and musical quality of Angelou's poetic voice carry her powerful words and vivid images right into the reader's heart. Whether she is speaking of ordinary circumstances or historical events, she reveals an extraordinary understanding of the ways in which human beings struggle to live and love, and she teaches us to look at our own circumstances with a sharpened eye. This short, rich volume is particularly appropriate for the

new reader audience. Other collections of her poetry are *And Still I Rise* (1978), *Oh Pray My Wings are Gonna Fit Me Well* (1975), *Just Give Me a Cool Drink of Water 'Fore I Diiie* (1971), and *Shaker Why Don't You Sing* (1983).
Intermediate new reader/young adult collection/adult collection.

Atwood, Ann. *My Own Rhythm: An Approach to Haiku.* Photographs by the author. New York: Charles Scribner's Sons, 1973.

Sometimes imposing the discipline of a strict formula upon writing can help focus students' ideas as well as their choice of language. In this book, poet and photographer Atwood introduces readers to haiku, a kind of poetry that attempts to express the essence of an idea or an experience in seventeen syllables. She first presents selections from three Japanese masters of the form, then offers her own haiku, each accompanied by a photograph. Her particularly detailed subjects are most frequently taken from nature. Though definitely not a textbook, this collection of poetry and photography offers teachers and students a very helpful introduction to the reading and writing of haiku, and, indeed, to any kind of poetry.
Beginning-intermediate new reader/children's collection.

Brooks, Gwendolyn. *Selected Poems.* New York: Harper & Row Publishers, 1963.

Brooks writes about the ordinary people she knows from the streets and stores, the churches and pool halls of her South Side Chicago neighborhood. She celebrates humanity as she questions the decisions we make as individuals and as a society. The power of her poetry compels the reader to do the same.
Intermediate-advanced new reader/adult collection.

Bruchac, Joseph. *The Light From Another Country: Poetry from American Prisons.* Greenfield Center, NY: The Greenfield Review Press, 1984.

The poems collected here, written while the authors were imprisoned, express deep feelings, sometimes with language of surprising hope and beauty, sometimes in strong language that will not be to every reader's taste. A personal statement from each prisoner explains his involvement in writing workshops and the inspiration for his poetry.
Intermediate-advanced new reader/adult collection.

Carlson, Lori M., ed. *Cool Salsa: Bilingual Poems on Growing Up Latino in the United States.* New York: Henry Holt & Co., 1994.

> All the poems in this collection are presented in English and in Spanish, or are written in English with a generous sprinkling of Spanish words. Intended for a young adult audience, they address issues of prejudice, assimilation, cultural differences, and individual identity, issues which matter very much to all students who must forge their place in a multicultural world, regardless of their age or origin.
>
> *Intermediate new reader/young adult collection.*

Carson, Jo. *Stories I Ain't Told Nobody Yet: Selections from the People Pieces.* New York: Orchard Books, 1989.

> Carson calls herself an eavesdropper, and in these poems she tells stories heard over the back fence, in the grocery store, and in other familar places. Written in the Appalachian dialect of east Tennessee, these stories are funny and wise, folksy and profound, and honed to the incisive clarity of poetry. Wonderful to read, they may also inspire students to write some of their own stories. Carson's model of good story telling and clear writing is an excellent one for new readers and writers.
>
> *Intermediate new reader/children's collection.*

Cisneros, Sandra. *My Wicked Wicked Ways.* New York: Turtle Bay Books, 1993.

> The poems collected here are brief, the language familiar, and the one-poem-per-page format attractive, but these works are harder to read than they appear. The book is included in this bibliography because Cisneros's imagery is beautiful, even startling at times, and her subjects of male/female relationships, family ties, and life in the barrio and beyond will appeal to a contemporary audience. Reading these poems will require some work on the part of the teacher as well as the student, but the example set of teachers and students reading and struggling together with a beautiful and profound work of art will be well worth the effort.
>
> *Advanced new reader/adult collection.*

Clifton, Lucille. *Good Woman: Poems and a Memoir 1969-1980.* Brockport, NY: BOA Editions, Ltd., 1987.

> With stunning insight and masterful use of the language of everyday life, Clifton writes as daughter, wife, mother, grandmother, and black woman

in America. This volume also contains a short memoir of her family.
Beginning-intermediate new reader/adult collection.

―――. *Next: New Poems.* Brockport, NY: BOA Editions, Ltd., 1987.
To read Clifton's poems is to meet her family and feel invited into her
kitchen for intimate conversation among ordinary women, causing all readers to look more deeply into the everyday events of their own lives.
Beginning-intermediate new reader/adult collection.

―――. *An Ordinary Woman.* New York: Random House, 1974.
Clifton writes about the life of an ordinary woman with extraordinary perception and vivid imagery. Her poems are short and use familiar language,
making them ideal for beginning new readers. *Good Times* (1969) is another similar collection.
Beginning-intermediate new reader/adult collection.

Cole, William, ed. *Eight Lines and Under.* New York: The Macmillan Co.,
1971.
Writing short, incisive poems can be more difficult than it seems, but the
short poems in this collection hit the mark. The same editor has also produced *Poetry Brief.*
Beginning-intermediate new reader/adult collection.

Coles, Robert. *A Festering Sweetness: Poems of American People.* Pittsburgh,
PA: University of Pittsburgh Press, 1978.
For twenty years, child psychiatrist Coles worked amid people who struggle:
blacks in a desegregating South, rural families in Appalachia, migrant workers in the vineyards of America. Trained as he was by his mentor, the poet
William Carlos Williams, to hear the poetry in everyday speech, Coles has
taken the words of the people he studied and turned them into poetry in
this unique and moving book.
Intermediate new reader/adult collection.

Cornish, Sam. *Folks Like Me.* Cambridge, MA: Zoland Books, Inc., 1993.
The poems in this collection present "a political portrait" of the African
American community in the twentieth century. Cornish recalls his own

experiences and expresses his own views, incorporating the voices of others as well, including influential figures such as Paul Robeson and James Baldwin. Although most of the poems are short, many new readers will need help understanding the historical references they contain. A glossary provides background information about the places, persons, and events referred to in the poems. Having students read these poems in conjunction with the reading of factual accounts of history or personal memoirs will further enhance their understanding of the events and ideas discussed. *Advanced new reader/adult collection.*

Cullen, Countee, ed. *Caroling Dusk: An Anthology of Verse by Black Poets of the Twenties.* New York: Citadel, 1993.

Originally published in 1927 and first reissued in 1955, this collection is of historical as well as literary value. The works of major black writers such as W.E.B. DuBois, James Weldon Johnson, Paul Lawrence Dunbar, and Countee Cullen are included as well as poems by writers whose names are unknown today. Their poetry offers a perspective on life in the earlier part of the twentieth century that resonates with life in the modern world yet stands in sharp contrast to it. Each poet's work is preceded by a brief biographical statement, sometimes written by the poet himself. The range of topics, style, length, and difficulty is great, but many poems will be accessible to adult new readers, even those at beginning stages. *Beginning-advanced new reader/adult collection.*

Doggerel: Great Poets on Remarkable Dogs. Linocuts by Martha Paulos. San Francisco: Chronicle Books, 1990.

Eighteen well-known poets present "light and literary" verse to describe the many ways in which our canine companions cheer and change our lives. Striking black-and-white linocuts complement the whimsical verse. *Intermediate new reader/adult collection.*

Dove, Rita. *Selected Poems.* New York: Vintage Books, 1993.

In writing about her life, her family, and her African American heritage, Poet Laureate Dove draws lines that connect all of us to our personal and national history. Her poetry is not easy, but it is rich with metaphor, sonorous language, and layers of meaning. For students eager to stretch their minds and prepare for continuing education, reading or listening to these

poems will spark lively discussions as well as a deeper appreciation for the power of the written word.
Advanced new reader/adult collection.

Dunning, Stephen, Edward Lueders, and Hugh Smith, eds. *Reflections on a Gift of Watermelon Pickle and Other Modern Verse.* New York: Lothrop, Lee, & Shepard Co., 1967.

Believing that poetry books for children placed too much emphasis on "bunnies and galoshes," the compilers of this collection selected poems that were simple but stimulating. Most of the poems were originally written for adults and, even after twenty-five years, this remains a vital collection.
Intermediate new reader/children's collection.

Elkind, Sue Saniel. *Another Language.* Photographs by Lori Burkhalter-Lackey. Watsonville, CA: Papier Mache Press, 1988.

Growing old in America is the theme of this collection. The poems are written in spare, direct language, many in the form of a story, making them very accessible to readers new to poetry. Photographs of elderly persons, while not directly related to the poems, extend the emotional impact of the words.
Intermediate-advanced new reader/adult collection.

Evans, Mari. *I Am a Black Woman.* New York: William Morrow & Co., 1970.

These brief poems recall the joys and the anguish the writer has experienced as a black woman. Lyrical and penetrating, they go directly to the heart of the message and the reader. Some poems refer to historical events or persons, so students may need additional information to understand the references, offering opportunities for a review of historical events in conjunction with the poetry they inspired.
Intermediate new reader/adult collection.

Farrell, Kate, ed. *Art and Love: an Illustrated Anthology of Love Poetry.* New York: Metropolitan Museum of Art in conjunction with Bulfinch Press, Boston, 1990.

In this collection, poems expressing love in its many manifestations are matched with works of art chosen from the collection of the Metropolitan

Museum of Art in New York. The matches are never literal; sometimes poem and picture are related by theme or subject, sometimes by mood. The pairings offer opportunities for discussion about common theme or mood, style, and interpretation. They also offer students the opportunity to write their own responses to the pictures or the poetry. The poems and pictures collected here cross borders of country, culture, century, and style.
Intermediate-advanced new reader/adult collection.

Feelings, Tom. *Soul Looks Back in Wonder.* New York: Dial Books, 1993.
To create this unique book, Feelings, who is an artist not a poet, selected sketches of black people made over many years of travel in Africa, South America, and the United States. He reworked his original sketches with colored pencils and paper cut-outs to create stunning collages then asked several black poets to contribute poems to reflect and extend his images. Adults will respond to the beauty and passion of the words and pictures and want to share them with the young people in their lives.
Intermediate new reader/children's collection.

Fleming, Alice, ed. *America is Not All Traffic Lights: Poems of the Midwest.* Boston: Little, Brown & Co., 1976.
Images, moods, and memories of life in the Midwest are captured in these poems. Black-and-white photographs depicting life on farms and in small towns complement the thoughtful mood of the words.
Intermediate new reader/adult collection/children's collection.

Frost, Robert. *You Come, Too.* Wood engravings by Thomas W. Nason. New York: Holt, Rinehart and Winston, 1959.
Though collected for children, all these poems were originally written for adults. They offer a wonderful introduction to the work of one of America's most well-known poets. Frost was a genius at finding insight in nature or in the lives of his New England neighbors. Many poems frequently referred to in our common culture are included here such as "The Road Not Taken" and "Stopping by Woods on a Snowy Evening."
Intermediate-advanced new reader/children's collection.

Gillan, Maria Mazziotti, and Jennifer Gillan, eds. *Unsettling America: An Anthology of Contemporary Multicultural Poetry*. New York: Penguin, 1994.

Within the covers of this book, readers will discover a richly-colored and many-faceted portrayal of life in contemporary America. While all the poems explore the themes of cultural identity within a multicultural world, the range of experience, sentiment, writing style, and ethnic background of the authors is as diverse as America itself.

Intermediate-advanced new reader/adult collection.

Giovanni, Nikki. *Cotton Candy on a Rainy Day*. New York: William Morrow & Co., 1978.

In these poems, ordinary moments common to all our lives are captured by a particularly insightful poet. Giovanni talks of loneliness and regret, love and tenderness, anger and hope, always questioning what is or what could be.

Intermediate-advanced new reader/adult collection/children's collection.

———. *My House*. New York: William Morrow & Co., 1983.

In relatively short and direct poems, Giovanni speaks of love and family commitment. She writes passionately of her experience as a black woman, but her message is universal.

Intermediate-advanced new reader/adult collection.

———. *Spin a Soft Black Song*. Rev. ed. Illustrated by George Martins. New York: Hill & Wang, 1985.

This is a book best appreciated by adults and children reading together. Written in the voice of a child speaking to adults, these poems tell of activities, perceptions, and dreams that all children will easily recognize. Adult readers will also recognize the wistfulness born in the conjunction of joy and melancholy that inevitably accompanies thoughts about our children. Black-and-white pencil drawings match the emotional tension of the words.

Beginning-intermediate new reader/children's collection.

———. *Those Who Ride the Night Winds*. New York: William Morrow & Co., 1983.

Giovanni speaks as a perceptive and passionate witness to our society. In these poems, called "her most accessible collection to date," she writes

about people who tried to change things. The unusual format—phrases separated by ellipses—enhances the direct, conversational tone of the words.
Intermediate-advanced new reader/adult collection.

———. *The Women and the Men.* New York: William Morrow & Co., 1975.
Relationships between and among men and women are discussed in these descriptive and powerful poems.
Intermediate-advanced new reader/adult collection/children's collection.

Gordon, Ruth, ed. *Peeling the Onion: An Anthology of Poems.* New York: HarperCollins Publishers, 1992.
The introductory section, "A Note to Readers," explains the title of this collection: "Like the onion, poetry is a constant discovery. Peel the onion, layer after layer, until its very heart is reached." The words in these poems are relatively easy, but the meaning is not always obvious. This union of easy words with probing thoughts, plus a very attractive and readable one-poem-per-page layout in larger-than-usual type makes this anthology collected for children particularly suitable for adult new readers.
Beginning-intermediate new readers/children's collection.

———. *Time Is the Longest Distance.* New York: HarperCollins Publishers, 1991.
Poets from around the globe and across the ages speak in many voices of the element which measures us all: time. Although recommended for junior high students and above, the poems will be appreciated by adults who have felt the pangs of time's passing more acutely.
Intermediate-advanced new reader/children's collection.

———. *Under All Silences: Shades of Love.* New York: Harper & Row, Publishers, 1987.
In this collection, poets from around the globe give voice to common but inexpressible feelings, "the love that is the voice under all silences." One poem per page and generous spacing make this book attractive to the eye as well as the heart.
Intermediate-advanced new reader/adult collection.

Harper, Michael S., and Anthony Walton, eds. *Every Shut Eye Ain't Asleep: An Anthology of Poetry by African Americans Since 1945*. Boston: Little, Brown & Co., 1994.

Thirty-five poets writing since the end of WW II, some well known but most unfamiliar, offer poetry that responds to the creative influences of jazz and the blues while also chronicling the struggles of blacks in contemporary America. This is a large, comprehensive collection that contains poems covering a range of difficulty. Some may be beyond new readers, but many will be accessible and stimulating to those who have attained basic literacy and need to stretch their minds and their skills.
Advanced new reader/adult collection.

Hearne, Betsy. *Love Lines: Poetry in Person*. New York: Margaret K. McElderry Books, 1987.

Poems in the first section of this book speak about love and loss; those in the second about love within the family. Hearne finds inspiration in ordinary experiences and objects, and her poems reveal an uncommon insight into the nature of the familiar world.
Intermediate new reader/children's collection.

————. *Polaroid and Other Poems of View*. Photographs by Peter Kiar. New York: Margaret K. McElderry Books, 1991.

Hearne says that "Poetry allows a second look at what may seem, at first glance, too simple to notice or too complex to understand." These poems offer a second, and deeper, look into the everyday world. The few black-and-white photographs present striking visual images as counterpoint to Hearne's verbal ones.
Intermediate new reader/children's collection.

Hopkins, Lee Bennett, ed. *On Our Way: Poems of Pride and Love*. New York: Alfred A. Knopf, 1974.

Each poem in this collection of works by black writers is accompanied by a black-and-white photograph that helps elucidate and extend the poem. The combination of short poems arranged with photographs makes this a very accessible collection for beginning new readers.
Beginning-intermediate new reader/children's collection/adult collection.

————. *A Song in Stone: City Poems.* Photographs by Anna Held Audette. New York: Thomas Y. Crowell, 1982.

> The vitality of city life comes sharply into focus in this brief collection of twenty poems matched with photographs that are themselves evocative works of art. A simple but lovely book.
> *Beginning new reader/children's collection/adult collection.*

Hopkins, Lee Bennett. *To Look at Any Thing.* Photographs by John Earl. New York: Harcourt Brace Jovanovitch, 1978.

> The photographs presented in this book show familiar objects in a way that makes the viewer question what he is seeing. There is a tree trunk, for example, that looks like an elephant's trunk and a piece of driftwood that looks like a broken-winged bird. Hopkins, best known as an anthologist, was so fascinated by the photos that he was inspired to write poems of his own to match them.
> *Beginning-intermediate new reader/children's collection.*

Howe, Florence, ed. *No More Masks!: An Anthology of Twentieth Century American Women Poets.* Rev. ed. New York: HarperCollins Publishers, 1993.

> Poets from the generation of Edna St. Vincent Millay to those actively writing today are included in this revised and expanded anthology. Their poetry addresses the inherent joys and fundamental contradictions experienced by all women in our complex culture. The poems are presented chronologically, with a brief biographical statement about each poet preceding her work. A comprehensive collection such as this contains poems which cover a range of topics as well as reading difficulty, including many wonderful poems which new readers, both male and female, will find challenging and stimulating.
> *Intermediate-advanced new reader/adult collection.*

Hughes, Langston. *The Collected Poems of Langston Hughes.* Edited by Arnold Rampersad and David Roessel. New York: Alfred A. Knopf, 1994.

> Readers who have discovered the poetry of Langston Hughes in the many anthologies in which it appears now have the opportunity to explore his work in depth in this newly-published edition of his collected poems. More advanced readers might be interested in the editors' succinct but informative introduction which discusses Hughes's development as an individual writer and a force in American letters. Teachers will find many poems in

this large anthology whose vivid and captivating language, used in celebration of the lives of ordinary folks, will entice students to discover the beauty and power of poetry.
Beginning-advanced new reader/adult collection.

———. *The Dream Keeper*. New York: Knopf, 1994.
Sometimes the most extraordinary poetry is that which sounds simple yet rings so true that phrases, rhythms, and images remain long after the reading is over. Langston Hughes was a master of such poetry. He could draw from the pulsing rhythms of jazz, the melancholy of the blues, the soul-stirring sounds of black spirituals, the yearnings of the young, the dreams of country folk, and the vitality of urban life and distill this rich mix into a quintessential American voice. This collection of poems, written for adults but simple enough for children, was first published in 1937 with woodcuts by Helen Sewell, then reissued in 1986. The newer edition cited here contains scratchboard illustrations by Brian Pinckney. In both these recent editions, the illustrations capture the subtlety and sensitivity of the language beautifully. New readers will treasure either book.
Beginning-intermediate new reader/adult collection/children's collect.

———. *The Panther and the Lash*. New York: Alfred A. Knopf, 1987.
While much of Langston Hughes's poetry speaks of universal themes, the poems collected here refer more specifically to the experience of being black in America and to particular events in the Civil Rights struggle. The poems are relatively easy to read, but some historical references may require explanation. This book would make an excellent companion to any study of American history and the movement for racial equality.
Beginning-intermediate new reader/adult new reader.

Janeczko, Paul B., ed. *Don't Forget to Fly: A Cycle of Modern Poems*. Scarsdale, NY: Bradbury Press, 1981.
Paul Janeczko is a poet and prolific anthologist who has compiled many books of poetry intended for young adults which are also appropriate for adult literacy students. Several are discussed below. The poems collected here are described on the book's jacket as "one melodious hymn to being human," poetry that reminds us of our nature and of our possibilities.
Intermediate new reader/adult collection/children's collection.

———. *Going Over to Your Place.* New York: Bradbury Press, 1987.
The mysterious and indefinable yearnings expressed in poetry and in our own hearts thematically link the poems collected here.
Intermediate-advanced new reader/adult collection/children's collection.

———. *Pocket Poems.* New York: Bradbury Press, 1985.
In this small volume are one hundred twenty brief poems that provide a moment's inspiration or glimpse into the deeper meaning of a seemingly ordinary experience.
Beginning-intermediate new reader/children's collection.

———. *Poetspeak: In Their Work, About Their Work.* Scarsdale, New York: Bradbury Press, 1983.
The poets whose writings are collected in this book also speak about what inspires them and what is important to them. Many of the entries are deeply personal and may inspire students to write as well as to read.
Intermediate-advanced new reader/children's collection.

———. *Postcard Poems: a Collection of Poetry for Sharing.* Scarsdale, NY: Bradbury Press, 1979.
Poems that are short enough to fit on a postcard yet powerful enough to convey an insight, image, or impression in a memorable word picture are collected in this anthology.
Beginning-intermediate new reader/adult collection.

———. *Strings: A Gathering of Family Poems.* Scarsdale, New York: Bradbury Press, 1984.
The theme of family connections makes these poems highly appropriate for adults. The poems are alternately funny, sad, wise, or joyful, and they offer a rich perspective on the many ways, some obvious and some subtle, in which we are affected by our families.
Intermediate new reader/children's collection.

———. *This Delicious Day: 65 Poems.* New York: Orchard Books, 1987.
Crisp images and morsels of insight are crystallized into short poems in this sometimes clever, sometimes funny collection.
Beginning-intermediate new reader/children's collection.

Johnson, James Weldon. *God's Trombones: Seven Negro Sermons in Verse.* Illustrated by Aaron Douglas. New York: Penguin, 1990.

As a child growing up in the deep South early in this century, Johnson heard "folk sermons" that were passed from one preacher to another. These sermons told the familiar stories of Christianity—the Prodigal Son, the story of Noah, the Creation—in a style that echoed the rhythm and power of Negro spirituals. In this book, Johnson recreates those sermons in lyrical verse that propels the narrative with the same driving force the originals had.

Beginning-intermediate new reader/adult collection.

Jones, Hettie. *The Trees Stand Shining: Poetry of the North American Indians.* Paintings by Robert Andrew Parker. New York: Dial Press, 1993.

Originally published in 1971, the poems collected here might also be described as songs, stories, lullabies, and war chants that tell how the Indians of various tribes looked upon their land and their lives. The paintings are impressionistic yet powerful images that convey the beauty, fragility, and impermanence of the land and the way of life they recall.

Beginning new reader/children's collection.

Jordan, June. *Passion: New Poems, 1977-1980.* Boston: Beacon Press, 1980.

In her preface, Jordan counts herself among the descendants of Walt Whitman, committed to celebrate the American experience and to write "nothing obscure, nothing contrived, nothing an ordinary straphanger in the subway would be puzzled by." Her poems speak of the passions of life, both dark and uplifting, in the voice of a black woman unafraid to tell us what she sees.

Intermediate-advanced new reader/adult collection.

———. *Who Look at Me.* New York: Thomas Y. Crowell Co., 1969.

Jordan has written a poem to accompany twenty-seven paintings of African Americans from the days of slavery through the twentieth century. The powerful, rhythmic poem could stand alone, and the paintings themselves tell a haunting tale of resilience, love, and triumph. Together, poem and paintings draw strength and insight from each other, resulting in a brilliant tapestry.

Intermediate-advanced new reader/adult collection.

Jordan, June, ed. *Soulscript: Afro-American Poetry*. Garden City, NY: Doubleday & Co., Inc., 1970.

> For this collection, poet Jordan selects poems from other African American poets whose work, while giving voice to the experiences of black people, speaks of the aspirations and yearning, the pains and pleasures of all who share this life. Brief biographies of all poets are included.
> *Intermediate new reader/adult collection/children's collection.*

Kavanaugh, James. *Walk Easy on the Earth*. New York: E.P. Dutton, 1979.

> Kavanaugh's poetry confronts spiritual issues: a search for God and meaning, love or the lack of it, how to be truly human in this world. He doesn't claim to know the answers, but in language that is contemporary and very readable, he invites the reader to examine the same questions.
> *Intermediate new reader/adult collection.*

Knudson, R. R., and May Swenson, eds. *American Sports Poems*. New York: Orchard Books, 1988.

> Playing sports, watching others play sports, or dreaming about games that could be or might have been fill countless hours and spark endless conversations in modern American life. These poems are part of that national conversation. Some are light-hearted and playful, others probing and eloquent. This large collection includes poems about many different sports which will appeal to new readers, whether they are players, spectators, or dreamers.
> *Intermediate-advanced new reader/children's collection.*

Lansky, Bruce, ed. *If We'd Wanted Quiet, We Would Have Raised Goldfish: Poems for Parents*. Deephaven MN: Meadowbrook Press, 1994.

> After compiling two anthologies of poetry for children, Lansky decided that adults also need collections of poetry that are easy to read and speak to the important issues of their lives. In this collection, parents respond with awe, joy, confusion, humor, and doubt to the unfolding lives of their children. In several poems, grown-up children confront the task of becoming parents to their aging mothers and fathers. The poems are very accessible and more insightful than the flippant title might suggest.
> *Beginning-intermediate new reader/adult collection.*

Larrick, Nancy, ed. *Cats are Cats*. Drawings by Ed Young. New York: Philomel Books, 1988.

These forty-two poems describe dainty, grumbling, curious, snarling, proud, demanding, lovable cats. The charcoal and pastel drawings capture the mystery and grace of these favorite pets.
Intermediate new reader/children's collection.

———. *Crazy to be Alive in Such a Strange World*. Photographs by Alexander L. Crosby. New York: M. Evans & Co., 1977.

The poems and accompanying black-and-white photographs in this collection reveal a fascinating variety among the people with whom we share this life. As is the case in several of Larrick's anthologies, the poems were selected with the help of her young students, but they were all originally written for adults and the collection remains one that adults will enjoy.
Intermediate new reader/adult collection/children's collection.

———. *The Night of the Whippoorwill*. Illustrated by David Ray. New York: Philomel Books, 1992.

The night, with its inevitable themes of solitude and mystery, is the subject of all the poems in this collection. The misty blues and greys of the acrylic illustrations suit the moods expressed in the poetry.
Intermediate new reader/children's collection.

———. *On City Streets: An Anthology of Poetry*. Photographs by David Sagarin. New York: Bantam Books, 1968.

The many voices of urban life speak through these poems, showing us the city in all its magic, excitement, and loneliness. The black-and-white photographs match and extend the words.
Beginning-intermediate new reader/children's collection.

———. *Room for Me and a Mountain Lion*. New York: M. Evans & Co., 1974.

In this collection, Larrick offers poetry about living in or being inspired by open spaces.
Beginning-intermediate new reader/adult collection/children's collection.

Levine, Philip. *What Work Is*. New York: Alfred A. Knopf, 1991.

Levine, once a factory worker himself, uses poetry to examine the experiences and lives of the men and women whose labor produces the goods of our common culture. These poems are not easy, but their quality, honesty, and subject matter make them excellent material to read aloud and to discuss with adult literacy students, many of whom also labor in difficult and unappreciated circumstances.

Advanced new reader/adult collection.

Livingston, Myra Cohn. *Light and Shadow*. Photographs by Barbara Rogasky. New York: Holiday House, 1992.

Light is the first word in all these poems: light in nature, light in the city, light as it illuminates various times of day, light creating shadows. The poetry is relatively simple, but it makes you want to look anew at the light in your own world. The striking color photographs suggest additional views of light.

Intermediate new reader/children's collection.

———. *No Way of Knowing: Dallas Poems*. New York: Atheneum, 1980.

From 1952 through 1964, Livingston, who is white, lived in a Dallas community that was mostly black. Years later, she began writing poems to remember and honor her many friends there. The voices that speak through these poems are of that community. As they tell about their everyday lives, they also reveal the sources of their strength and love.

Beginning new reader/adult collection.

Livingston, Myra Cohn, ed. *One Little Room, an Everywhere: Poems of Love*. Woodcuts by Antonio Frasconi. New York: Atheneum, 1975.

Most of poet Livingston's anthologies have been collected for young people, yet several are very suitable for adults. This collection and the two listed above are good examples of anthologies that will appeal to adult students. Here, the subject is love across the ages, from the early Greeks and Romans to Biblical times to contemporary America.

Intermediate new reader/children's collection.

―――――. ed. *A Time to Talk: Poems of Friendship*. New York: Macmillan, 1992.
The human need for friendship is a universal theme expressed in these
poems collected from across the ages and oceans.
Intermediate new reader/children's collection.

―――――. *A Tune Beyond Us*. Illustrated by James J. Spanfeller. New York:
Harcourt, Brace & World, Inc., 1968.
Livingston says that the poems in this collection take us to "a tune be-
yond us," a place we may not immediately recognize, yet we learn some-
thing about ourselves by going there.
Intermediate new reader/children's collection.

Lueders, Edward, and Primus St. John, eds. *Zero Makes Me Hungry*. Illustrated by John Reuter-Pacyna. New York: Lothrop, Lee and Shepard Co.,
1976.
A sequel to *Reflections on a Gift of Watermelon Pickle* (Dunning, Lueders,
and Smith), the poems in this international collection are alternately wry,
explosive, or quietly reflective. Bold designs in primary colors complement
the poetry.
Beginning-intermediate new reader/children's collection.

McCullough, Frances, ed. *Earth, Air, Fire, and Water*. New York: Harper &
Row, Publishers, 1987.
Exploring the fundamental mysteries of nature inevitably leads to a simi-
lar quest in search of an understanding of the human heart. These poems
take us on that journey.
Intermediate-advanced new reader/adult collection/children's collection.

Macioci, R. Nikolas. *Cafes of Childhood*. Desert Hot Springs, CA: Event Horizon Press, 1992.
Macioci's poems were called "beautifully harrowing" by the judges of the
1991 Pearl Chapbook Contest, which this book won. They deal with child
abuse, a difficult subject treated here with honesty and without self-pity.
For those interested in the topic, these poems show one person's triumph
over painful memories.
Advanced new reader/adult collection.

Marcus, Leonard S. *Lifelines: A Poetry Anthology Patterned on the Stages of Life*. New York: Dutton, 1994.

The four sections of this book correspond to four stages of life: growing up, coming of age, accepting responsibility, and facing mortality. Marketed for young adults, these poems will have greater impact on adults who, being somewhere in the middle of the lifeline, have a better view of both ends.

Intermediate new reader/children's collection.

Merriam, Eve. *The Inner City Mother Goose*. Visuals by Lawrence Ratzkin. New York: Simon & Schuster, 1969.

Merriam has taken words and rhythms from common nursery rhymes and turned them into biting statements of social protest. Written in the late 1960's, the poems clearly reflect the raucous, irreverent tenor of those times, but the questions they raise remain relevant. Not for everyone's taste, but many who feel disaffected or disenfranchised will find resonance here.

Intermediate new reader/adult collection.

————. *Rainbow Writing*. New York: Atheneum, 1976.

Clever word plays and a wry sense of humor color the ordinary moments of life in these funny yet poignant poems. Merriam is a prolific poet who writes for adults and children.

Beginning-intermediate new reader/adult collection/children's collection.

Millay, Edna St. Vincent. *Edna St. Vincent Millay's Poems Selected for Young People*. Illustrated by Ronald Keller. New York: Harper & Row, 1979.

Edna St. Vincent Millay is one of the major American poets of this century whose work will be appealing and accessible to many adult new readers. Despite this book's title, the poetry it presents deals with very adult issues of conflict, loss, and the yearnings of the human heart. The blue-tinted woodcut illustrations add a haunting quality which enhances the book's appeal.

Intermediate new reader/children's collection.

Mitchell, Stephen, ed. *The Enlightened Heart: An Anthology of Sacred Poetry*. New York: Harper & Row, 1989.

Selections from the Book of Psalms, the Bhagavad Gita, and other sacred

texts, along with inspirational poems from contemporary poets, all speak to the human need to ask and to understand.
Intermediate-advanced new reader/adult collection.

Montez, Susan. *Radio Free Queens.* New York: George Braziller, 1994.
Montez says that she wants to "write poems that people other than poets would read." At times brash and street smart, at times lyrical and inspired, her poetry moves with the staccato rhythm of the city—New York—she both suffers and celebrates.
Advanced new reader/adult collection.

Moore, Lilian. *I Thought I Heard the City.* Illustrated by Mary Jane Dunton. New York: Atheneum, 1969.
Moore offers simple poems that speak of bridges, pigeons, rooftops, and other common sights that define city life. Color collages complement the poems.
Beginning new reader/children's collection.

Moore, Lilian ed. *Go With the Poem.* New York: McGraw Hill Book Co., 1979.
Contemporary in spirit, these poems were collected for "middle graders" but the appearance of the book and the content of the poems are quite suitable for adults. Many well-known poets are included, and the poems cover a range of topics, style, and level of difficulty.
Beginning-intermediate new reader/children's collection.

Moore, Lilian, and Judith Thurman, eds. *To See the World Afresh.* New York: Atheneum, 1974.
Believing that the need "to see the world afresh" is an urgent one in our difficult times, the compilers have chosen poems they hope will help readers see the ordinary and familiar with new eyes.
Intermediate new reader/children's collection.

Morrison, Lillian. *The Break Dance Kids.* New York: Lothrop, Lee & Shepard Books, 1985.
Using rhythm and word play, these snappy, clever poems about a variety of sports will appeal to teens and young adults who jive with the rhythm of modern urban life.
Beginning-intermediate new reader/children's collection.

————. *Sidewalk Racer and Other Poems of Sports and Motion.* New York: Lothrop, Lee and Shepard, 1977.

Morrison's collection of poems celebrates the enjoyment and beauty to be found in sports and movement of various kinds. The poems range from clever to reflective and will appeal to older teens and students interested in sports.

Beginning-intermediate new reader/children's collection.

Morrison, Lillian, ed. *At the Crack of the Bat: Baseball Poems.* Illustrated by Steve Cieslawski. New York: Hyperion Books for Children, 1992.

These poems reflect the many faces of baseball: the kid's game that grown-ups love to play, the remembered game of times and places long gone, the game that crosses lines of class and generation, the game that feeds our fascination with numbers, comparisons, and "what if's," and the game that has inspired innumerable artists and writers.

Beginning-intermediate new reader/children's collection.

————. *Rhythm Road: Poems to Move to.* New York: Lothrop, Lee and Shepard Books, 1988.

Morrison says that feeling the rhythm and sounds of poetry adds "another level to our pleasure and excitement." For many of the poems included here, the rhythm and music of the language convey meaning as much as the words do.

Beginning-intermediate new reader/children's collection.

Niatum, Duane, ed. *Carriers of the Dream Wheel: Contemporary Native American Poetry.* New York: Harper & Row Publishers, 1975.

The fifth in a series of collections of Native American poetry, these poems represent a rich and diverse cultural heritage. Brief biographical statements about each writer help place the poetry in context.

Intermediate-advanced new reader/adult collection.

Nye, Naomi Shihab, ed. *This Same Sky: A Collection of Poems from Around the World.* New York: Four Winds Press, 1992.

Believing that poetry helps us "feel or imagine faraway worlds from the inside," Nye has gathered poems from sixty-eight countries to help readers cross the political borders that the human imagination must always challenge. The poems selected cross generational as well as geographical

lines and would be particularly appropriate in classes with students from many age groups and cultures.
Intermediate-advanced new reader/children's collection.

Oresick, Peter, and Nicholas Coles, eds. *Working Classics: Poems on Industrial Life.* Urbana, IL: University of Illinois Press, 1990.

There is a gritty quality to these poems that tell stories of men and women who spend their days in hard and often monotonous physical labor. They speak of loneliness and lost dreams but also of hope and survival. These poems are not easy and would be best read aloud, but they will spark a lively and thoughtful discussion about a subject that is central not only to our survival but to our very sense of who we are.
Advanced new reader/adult collection.

Parks, Gordon. *Gordon Parks: A Poet and His Camera.* New York: Viking Press, 1968.

A highly regarded photographer for *Life* magazine, Parks has also achieved prominence as a poet. For this collection he selected highly evocative photographs that match the spirit if not necessarily the words of the poem. The combination yields haunting and beautiful images that make this a wonderful book for stimulating group discussions.
Intermediate-advanced new reader/adult collection.

Plotz, Helen, ed. *The Gift Outright.* New York: Greenwillow Books, 1977.

America is a geographic place, but it is also an idea and a dream. The poems collected here reflect many views of America. Some focus on individuals, both famous and unknown, some describe historical events, and some offer personal reflections on life in America. The title poem was read by Robert Frost at the inauguration of President John F. Kennedy.
Intermediate-advanced new reader/children's collection.

———. *Poems of Emily Dickinson.* Drawings by Robert Kipniss. New York: Thomas Y. Crowell, 1964.

There are numerous anthologies of the works of Emily Dickinson whose brief, sometimes cryptic poetry will appeal to many new readers. The choice of poems and the appealing artwork in this book make it a collection particularly suitable for adult literacy students.
Beginning-intermediate new reader/children's collection.

Rylant, Cynthia. *Soda Jerk.* New York: Orchard Books, 1990.

From his vantage point as the soda jerk in a small town drug store, the teenage narrator of these rhythmic but unrhymed poems finds clues for his own future in the daily lives and changing moods of his customers. As he reflects on his own prospects, he searches for a balance between acceptance and change, hope and regret.
Intermediate-advanced new reader/children's collection.

————. *Something Permanent.* Photographs by Walker Evans. San Diego: Harcourt Brace & Co., 1994.

Walker Evans's photographs of the ravages of the Great Depression as portrayed in the faces and circumstances of its many victims are permanently etched in our historical memory. For each photograph presented here, Cynthia Rylant has written a poem which imagines the lives of the people and places pictured. The result is a marriage of two art forms which deepens our understanding not just of a particular place and time, but also of the humanity we all share, regardless of circumstance.
Intermediate new reader/adult collection/children's collection.

Sanchez, Sonia. *Love Poems.* Illustrated by Bennie Arrington. New York: The Third Press, 1973.

Love in all its glory, pain, and uncertainty is the theme of this collection. Sanchez writes as a woman who is wary of the potentially overwhelming power of men. The collection includes several haiku, short and trenchant poems which will appeal to adult literacy students.
Intermediate new reader/adult collection.

Sandburg, Carl. *Honey and Salt.* New York: Harcourt, Brace, Jovanovich, 1963.

Although some poems in this collection are difficult, many short and accessible poems in which Sandburg muses about love and the meaning of life are also included. The long and prayer-like "Timesweep," which ends the collection, will also appeal to many new readers.
Beginning-advanced new reader/adult collection.

————. *Rainbows are Made.* Selected by Lee Bennett Hopkins. Wood engravings by Fritz Eichenberg. San Diego, CA: Harcourt Brace Jovanovich, 1982.

Sandburg wrote of the prairies, people, and growing cities of mid-century middle America without sentimentality, often with the sting of wit and social protest. The bold woodcuts complement Sandburg's clear and potent voice and enhance its poetic mystery as well. Although intended for children, this is an appealing anthology for adults.

Beginning-intermediate new reader/children's collection.

————. *Selected Poems.* New York: Gramercy Books, 1992.

This is a new collection of the poems upon which Sandburg's reputation is built. It includes the Chicago poems, which celebrate working men and women in their own language, and the war poems, written from 1914 to 1915, which speak not just of glory but of death and loss as well. The one-poem-per-page format makes this an appealing and accessible collection for adult literacy students.

Beginning-intermediate new reader/adult collection.

————. *Wind Song.* Illustrated by William A. Smith. New York: Harcourt, Brace and World, Inc., 1960.

Sandburg himself selected these poems for an anthology for young people. Reflecting his delight in the sounds of words as well as his playful and imaginative spirit, these poems will find a receptive audience among adults as well.

Intermediate new reader/children's collection.

Smith, William Jay, ed. *A Green Place: Modern Poems.* Illustrated by Jacques Hnizdovsky. New York: Delacorte Press, 1982.

Anthologist and poet Smith says poetry offers us a place that is "eternally green, made up of parts of our world, but wholly new and different." This substantial collection of modern poems, often used as an introduction to poetry in college classes, contains many works which are short and relatively simple but never simplistic.

Intermediate-advanced new reader/adult collection.

Soto, Gary. *A Fire in My Hands: A Book of Poems.* Illustrated by James M. Cardillo. New York: Scholastic Inc., 1990.

Whether he is recalling an incident from his childhood in California's San Joaquin Valley or reflecting on the experience of being a modern day husband and father, Soto is a thoughtful observer, constantly examining but always enjoying those small moments that are the essence of our daily lives.
Intermediate new reader/children's collection.

—————. *Neighborhood Odes.* Illustrated by David Diaz. San Diego, CA: Harcourt Brace Jovanovich, 1992.

Soto celebrates the neighborhood of his youth: snow cones and water sprinklers, family weddings, the library, the tortilla, and all those seemingly insignificant little things that hold our memories and bind us to a particular place and time. A few Spanish words are interspersed, but they do not make the poems inaccessible to non-Spanish speakers. The memories may be specific to Soto's experience, but they will spark recognition in all readers, wherever their childhood neighborhoods may have been.
Intermediate new reader/children's collection.

Stafford, William. *Learning to Live in the World: Earth Poems.* San Diego, CA: Harcourt Brace & Co., 1994.

Reflecting on life's ordinary moments and their impact on the natural world as well as on the individuals who inhabit that world, Stafford writes in a casual and appealing voice. His poems are often found in anthologies for young readers, but their message and style will appeal to adults as well.
Intermediate new reader/children's collection.

Walker, Alice. *Good Night, Willie Lee, I'll See You in the Morning.* New York: The Dial Press, 1979.

Walker's poetry celebrates and explores her experiences as a black woman. She writes of strength and weakness, of seeking love and giving it, of accepting circumstances and fighting for change. Her words are blunt and passionate, at times angry, always searching. Her poetry can spur lively and heartfelt discussion.
Intermediate-advanced new reader/adult collection.

―――. *Horses Make a Landscape Look More Beautiful.* San Diego, CA: Harcourt Brace Jovanovich, 1984.

With vivid language and compelling rhythm, Walker captures moments in the lives of ordinary people that reveal what it means to be a human being.

Intermediate-advanced new reader/adult collection.

―――. *Revolutionary Petunias and Other Poems.* New York: Harcourt, Brace, Jovanovich, 1973.

This collection includes vivid portraits of people in the rural Georgia community where Walker grew up, as well as many autobiographical poems.

Intermediate-advanced new reader/adult collection.

Whitman, Walt. *Voyages: Poems by Walt Whitman.* Selected by Lee Bennett Hopkins. Illustrated by Charles Mikolaycak. San Diego, CA: Harcourt Brace Jovanovich, 1988.

Walt Whitman's poetry celebrates the human spirit, the life force and beauty that lives in all of us. This thoughtful selection of Whitman's work includes poems from his youth on Long Island, poems which chronicle his wanderings about the country discovering himself and his vision of humanity, poems that describe his work with the wounded during the Civil War and his admiration for President Lincoln, and poems which reckon with old age and death. Although prepared for young readers, this book will introduce adults to an important American literary figure whose powerful words strike a very spiritual chord.

Intermediate new reader/children's collection.

Wilbur, Richard. *More Opposites: Poems and Drawings.* New York: Harcourt Brace Jovanovich, Publishers, 1991.

The opposite of duck is . . . getting hit, at least in a snowball fight. That is the spirit of these clever, original poems written by Pulitzer Prize-winning Wilbur. Good for a laugh, the poems can also lead to all sorts of lessons about the multiple meanings of words. An earlier collection, *Opposites,* is also available.

Intermediate new reader/adult collection.

Williams, William Carlos. *The Collected Poems of William Carlos Williams. Volume I 1909-1939. Volume II 1939-1962.* Volume I edited by A. Walton Litz and Christopher MacGowan; Volume II edited by Christopher MacGowan. New York: New Directions Books, 1986.

This is the latest edition of Williams's *Collected Poems,* first published in 1939. Although not all of his poems are short or readily understandable, Williams is a true master at crystallizing, in a few carefully selected words, a feeling or an insight gleaned from everyday objects and experiences. It is these poems which are particularly suitable to new readers. This is the complete source for this master.

Beginning-advanced new reader/adult collection.

———. *Selected Poems.* Edited with an Introduction by Charles Tomlinson. New York: New Directions Books, 1985.

First published in 1976, this selection includes many of the poems which are brief but powerful word pictures accessible to new readers and inspiring to new writers.

Beginning-advanced new reader/adult collection.

Worth, Valerie. *Small Poems.* New York: Farrar, Straus, 1972.

Simple observations of ordinary things originally written for children, these poems speak with a gentle eloquence that will appeal to adults as well. They are direct, surprising, witty, insightful, and never cute or cloying. Similar collections are *More Small Poems* (1976) and *Still More Small Poems* (1978).

Beginning new reader/children's collection.

Yolen, Jane, ed. *Weather Report.* Illustrated by Annie Gusman. Honesdale, PA: Wordsong, Boyds Mills Press, 1993.

The weather and how it affects us is the theme of this collection which includes the works of many famous poets such as Robert Frost, Langston Hughes, and Carl Sandburg.

Beginning-intermediate new reader/children's collection.

Notes

1. Robert Frost, *The Road Not Taken: A Selection of Robert Frost's Poems*, Louis Untermeyer, sel. (New York: Henry Holt & Co.).

Chapter 3

Stories from the Human Family: Sharing Works of Literature with Adult New Readers

> . . . Coke bottles were the best because they had a shape
> like a body. You could tell the bottom from the top.
> —Hattie, a literacy student

Hattie, an adult literacy student with whom I once worked, was a middle-aged, African American woman who grew up in the rural South. She had known poverty, discrimination, and despair, as well as the hope born of close family and religious ties. In response to a writing assignment asking her to recall a particular memory from childhood, she wrote a vivid and amusing story about making dolls out of Coke bottles. Her story reminded me of some of the stories in Maya Angelou's memoir, *I Know Why the Caged Bird Sings*. When I told Hattie my reaction, I was startled to realize that she had never heard of Maya Angelou. It seemed no less than a tragedy to me that Hattie—and so many others like her—might never enjoy the thrill of reading about experiences so similar to her own written by a writer whose language captivates readers and carries them along on a fascinating journey through the mind and heart of another human being.

People crave stories. Stories tell us who we are as individuals and as members of families, social groups, and nations. The sacred stories of the ancient Hebrews in the Old Testament, the parables of Jesus in the New Testament, and the stories of the Koran and other religious books guide our spiritual and moral journey through life. Children the world over are instinctively drawn to the fairy tales and legends of their culture, because these stories address the many fears and questions that children have but cannot articulate: the fear of losing a parent and one's secure place in the world, the desire to exercise power over the darker elements of life, the need to leave home to find one's own way in the world.

In ancient times, poets and storytellers such as Homer and the griots of Africa recited long and complex tales that recounted the stories and legends of their ancestors. Using rhyme, meter, repetitive verse, and recurring images to aid their memory as well as paint a vivid picture, these early historians were revered in their communities because of their skill in captivating an audience. They were the living repositories of communal history.

Stories are still important today, but the formats in which they are presented vary. We find today's descendants of Homer and the African griots in blues and folk singers and most recently rap singers, who use those same rhetorical devices of meter, rhyme, and repetition to tell personal as well as communal stories. We find our continuing need for stories reflected in the rise and popularity of the novel, a story form which serves a literate and mobile society. From classic novels such as James Fenimore Cooper's *The Last of the Mohicans*, still meaningful enough to be recently made into a popular film, to the burgeoning collection of romance novels found in most book stores and libraries, we find evidence of our need to share stories about people just like ourselves, about the people we might wish we were, and about people living in distant times and places.

Television and movies have the extraordinary power to bring the same story into millions of homes and affect the way an entire culture understands its personal as well as national history. In the late 1970's, the televised version of Alex Haley's book *Roots* was broadcast over several nights. *Roots* traced the story of Haley's ancestors back many generations to a young African boy who was captured and taken to America as a slave. *Roots* also told the story of how Haley researched that history by travelling to many places to search for documents and talk to people who might have information that would lead to other sources. The book and television show inspired millions of Americans, both black and white, to trace their roots and learn their own family stories, creating in the process a new depth of understanding of America as a land of immigrants.

In the early 1990s, another television program captured the imagination of millions of Americans rather unexpectedly. Critics could not have predicted that Ken Burns's series *The Civil War*, an eleven-hour documentary based on still photographs, commentary from historians, and letters from people long dead, would have gained such a wide and faithful audience. It did so because Burns presented that conflict not as textbook history but as a story. *The Civil War* told the story of a nation coming to grips with the darker side of its own idealistic promise as well as the story of individuals confronted with extraordinary choices, from General Robert E. Lee's decision that loyalty to his state took precedence over allegiance to his country to decisions made by soldiers on the line, crystallized in the letter that Major Sullivan Ballou wrote to his wife explaining why he believed in the rightness of the cause of maintaining the Union, even though he knew he might have to pay the heartbreaking cost of never seeing his sons "grown up to honorable manhood." For many who knew little more about the Civil War than the names Lee, Grant, and Gettysburg, *The Civil War* made that historical event a story that millions of Americans came to understand as part of their own personal and national heritage.

It is the literature of any culture that tells its stories. Whether they are fiction, folktales, essays, memoirs, letters, or true life accounts, these are the stories that we need to bring to Hattie and to other literacy students. While it is true that selected stories are easily told to us as movies and television programs, it is equally true that the great wealth of stories exist in written form, waiting to be brought alive, time and time again, to individuals who relive them through the pleasure and power of reading. How can we do this? Aren't most of these books and stories too difficult for literacy students to read? Some are, but many are not, particularly if students have tutors and teachers read the stories aloud or assist them in their own reading. A method for doing so is discussed below, along with some examples.

Introducing New Readers to Literature

How can we bring these stories to adult literacy students? An answer lies in three practices found with increasing frequency in elementary school reading programs: teachers reading aloud to students, a literature-based approach to reading instruction, and whole language. Let's look at each of these three methodologies.

Both research and common experience show that reading aloud to young children greatly enhances their initial reading success as well as the possibility that they will grow into eager and mature readers. Reading aloud to children immerses them in the language of the written word and teaches them to use context, illustrations, and their own imaginations to understand the story, even if they don't recognize all the words. Reading aloud also stimulates discussions about the events, characters, and language of the stories, as well as personal experiences, memories, and deeply-rooted feelings that the story evokes.

In many of today's elementary school classrooms, there is a movement to incorporate the practice of reading aloud from children's literature and institute a new way of teaching reading called the literature-based approach. Teachers use works of children's literature as the primary reading texts, rather than traditional basal readers. Basal readers contain stories written with a strictly-controlled vocabulary, intended to teach children to read certain words. In contrast, works of children's literature are written to tell a captivating story or convey certain information in a manner that makes the story or the information, not the words used, primary.

The whole language concept of teaching reading recognizes that learning to read is just one aspect of learning to use language; it cannot be separated from the other language skills of listening, speaking, writing, and, ultimately, thinking. In classrooms where literature and whole language prevail, teachers not only engage the children in listening to an interesting story, they also create opportunities to involve them in the many language activities that connect the words on the page to the children's own attempts to express themselves. For example, a teacher might read Eric Carle's *The Very Hungry Caterpillar*, a picture book that details all the things a caterpillar eats before turning into a butterfly, then ask students to create a class list of all the things they ate for breakfast that morning or ask them to bring in food ads from home, cut out pictures of certain foods, prepare labels for them, then display them all around the classroom. A teacher might read the folktale *Stone Soup*, a story about a clever trio of hungry soldiers who trick the townspeople into sharing food with them, then plan a classroom version of stone soup, asking each child to bring one ingredient—a carrot, an onion, and of course, a stone—to contribute. In these examples, teachers use literature as the starting point then involve students in a variety of language-related activities: discussing the characters, events, and language of the stories; drawing pictures suggested by the story; imagining themselves in similar circumstances; writing sentences and stories of their own; creating language experience stories as a class; writing their own sentences and stories in response to the images and ideas in the story; investigating the lives and other books of favorite authors; and acting out scenes from the stories. In other words, teachers involve students in the intellectual activities of discussing, analyzing, comparing, applying, and evaluating a story, skills they will eventually apply to words they read and write on their own.

This is the model we need to adopt in our adult literacy classrooms and tutoring sessions. We need to create the opportunity for students to experience an inspired response to the written word, to learn to read from stories that have something to say about how we live our lives. Although the books and materials we read will obviously be different from those used in the elementary classroom (with some possible exceptions, as discussed in Chapter 6), adult literacy teachers can apply the principles of whole language and literature-based reading. Many books available in the public library will support such an approach. There are numerous books that contain the stories of the human family in various contexts and formats, including fiction, folktales, collections of newspaper columns, letters, essays, memoirs, and true stories that will be suitable for use with literacy students. What follows is an outline of a procedure that tutors or classroom teachers can follow when using works of literature with adult literacy students, one sample lesson, a few additional examples of books that are suitable, and a bibliography of additional titles.

General Procedure
1. **Reading/Listening.** The teacher chooses a short story, letter, essay, newspaper column or an excerpt from a longer work and reads aloud to the students, who follow along with individual printed copies.

2. **General Discussion.** The teacher and students discuss the selection. The teacher tries to elicit initial reactions by asking questions such as, "Did you like the reading or not?" "Why or why not?" "What did it make you think of?" "How did it make you feel?" "Does it sound believable to you?" "What's your first response to this story?"

3. **Critical Thinking.** The teacher asks more specific questions that require students to check the text to find the words, phrases, or sentences that locate factual information, reveal the tone or purpose of the writer, and support inferences and opinions. The questions are intended to probe as well as push the students' level of understanding. Teachers may choose to have students respond to these questions orally or in writing, depending on their abilities.

4. **Vocabulary.** The teacher selects words that students may not be familiar with and asks them to guess the meaning, using context clues. Students then check the dictionary to confirm definitions.

5. **Writing.** The teacher gives the students a writing assignment which uses the reading selection as a stimulus.

6. **Sharing Writing.** If students are willing, they can read drafts to the class. Teachers comment by finding something positive to say about the piece: a nice phrase, a different insight, a vivid description, etc. Students are particularly helpful and encouraging to each other because they act as a real audience, helping writers see whether or not they have conveyed

the intended message. Comments from the teacher on technical elements, such as fragments or run-on sentences, can be saved for later.

7. **Revising**. The teacher collects the writing samples, reads them, and makes notes suggesting possible revisions. It is here, in the revision process, that teachers can deal with mechanics by noting particular skills students need to work on. In the following class, the teacher distributes the reviewed work and meets briefly with each student to discuss revisions and suggest skill-building exercises. At each stage of the revision process, students can read their revised work aloud to an audience of other students. When the students feel they have completed a piece of writing, they enter it into a computer and create a printed copy.

Sample Lesson

This sample lesson was used with a group of literacy students ranging from middle to advanced new reader levels. Julia Alvarez's story "Snow" is a chapter from her novel *How the Garcia Girls Lost Their Accents*, which also appears in slightly altered form in the story collection *Listening to Ourselves: More Stories from the Sound of Writing*, edited by Alan Cheuse and listed in the bibliography.

Snow
by Julia Alvarez

Our first year in New York we rented a small apartment with a Catholic school nearby, taught by the Sisters of Charity, hefty women in long black gowns and bonnets that made them look peculiar, like dolls in mourning. I liked them a lot, especially my grandmotherly fourth-grade teacher, Sister Zoe. I had a lovely name, she said, and she had me teach the whole class how to pronounce it: "Yo-lan-da." As the only immigrant in my class, I was put in a special seat in the first row by the window, apart from the other children so that Sister Zoe could tutor me without disturbing them. Slowly, she enunciated the new words I was to repeat: *laundromat, corn flakes, subway, snow.*

Soon I picked up enough English to understand holocaust was in the air. Sister Zoe explained to a wide-eyed classroom what was happening in Cuba. Russian missiles were being assembled, trained supposedly on New York City. President Kennedy, looking worried too, was on the television at home, explaining we might have to go to war against the Communists.

At school, we had air-raid drills: an ominous bell would go off and we'd file into the hall, fall to the floor, cover our heads with our coats, and imagine our hair falling out, the bones in our arms going soft. At home, my mother and my sisters and I said a rosary for world peace. I heard new vocabulary: *nuclear bomb, radioactive fallout, bomb shelter.* Sister Zoe explained how it would happen. She drew a picture of a mushroom on the blackboard and dotted a flurry of chalk marks for the dusty fallout that would kill us all.

The months grew cold, November, December. It was dark when I got up in the morning, frosty when I followed my breath to school. One morning as I sat at my desk daydreaming out the window, I saw dots in the air like the ones Sister Zoe had drawn—random at first, then lots and lots. I shrieked, "Bomb! Bomb!" Sister Zoe jerked around, her full black skirt ballooning as she hurried to my side. A few girls began to cry.

But then Sister Zoe's shocked look faded. "Why, Yolanda dear, that's snow!" She laughed. "Snow."

"Snow," I repeated. I looked out the window warily. All my life I had heard about the white crystals that fell out of American skies in the winter. From my desk I watched the fine powder dust the sidewalk and parked cars below. Each flake was different, Sister Zoe had said, like a person, irreplaceable and beautiful.

Questions from the story
1. Who were the Sisters of Charity?

2. Would you describe the author's family as religious? Why?

3. The author says she came to understand that "holocaust was in the air." What is she referring to?

4. Why was the author afraid when she saw her first snow?

5. How do you think the author felt as the only immigrant in her class? How would you feel in such a situation?

6. Explain the word in bold type in each of the phrases below:

   "**trained** supposedly on New York"
   "an **ominous** bell would go off"
   "**random** at first, then lots and lots"

7. Writing Assignment

Recall a particular incident from your childhood that stands out in your memory. As you describe it, give as many details as possible so that anyone who reads your story will get a vivid mental picture.

A Few Suggested Titles

There are hundreds of books in the public library that will give new readers a chance to respond to stories such as "Snow." A few additional examples are discussed below, and titles are suggested in the bibliography at the end of this chapter. Some of the books recommended contain short pieces—short stories, letters, newspaper columns—which can be read aloud and discussed within a class session. Others are longer works, memoirs and novels for instance, which can also be read in excerpts or in entirety by those advanced new readers developing the habit of reading complete books. All of the books recommended at the advanced new reader level are suitable for readers new to the experience of reading complete books.

Newspaper columns are a good place to start. They are short enough to be read aloud in one class or tutoring session, but they tell a whole story or state an opinion and support it with facts. Any public library will have collections of syndicated newspaper columnists. The collected columns of Bob Greene are a case in point. Greene has an uncanny knack for finding that "man or woman in the street" with an interesting story. In collections of his columns such as *He Was a Midwestern Boy on His Own* you'll find characters such as a washroom attendant at a fancy night club who always wanted to be a professional singer and can belt out a song with extraordinary talent and presence, but only does so when there's no one in the club except the piano player, or the woman who organized and promoted a convention for women named "Linda" (no "Lyndas" were allowed). Ellen Goodman's work is collected in several books, the latest being *Value Judgments.* Goodman addresses the major issues of the day such as abortion, working women, education, and government responsibility to disadvantaged citizens. She connects these issues to ordinary people, citing examples of how friends, family members, and others are affected by the conditions of contemporary society. Reading her columns, students can see their own lives reflected in her discussion of the pressing issues of the day.

Robert Fulghum writes brief and readable essays on the joys and dilemmas of everyday life. The former minister's stories often read like parables, helping us see the larger meaning in the routine events of life. In *It Was on Fire When I Lay Down on It*, Fulghum tells about his "Box of Good Stuff" which contains odd fragments from past years and times in his life that matter to him and no one else: letters, pictures, pieces of old toys. As we read his description of each item and the connection it has to some time or person in his life, we also learn what he considers to be the things in life worth preserving.

Spiritual concerns are important motivators for many students who might initially come to a reading program to learn to read the Bible and other religious texts. James Washington's *Conversations with God* and W.E.B. DuBois's *Prayers of Dark People*, two wide ranging collections of prayers, may appeal to students with religious needs for improved literacy.

Memoirs are popular with readers at all levels: their narrative style and personal intimacy offer new readers an easy entry into the world of literature. Many recent memoirs describe how their authors overcame various forms of personal and societal adversity. Several of these will be accessible to new readers. Collections of short pieces are particularly good for reading aloud or for introducing students to silent reading. A good example is Judith Ortiz-Cofer's *Latin Deli*, a collection of poems, essays, and short stories in which she talks about growing up in the island culture of her Puerto Rican parents and the American culture she encounters in her school and neighborhood in Paterson, New Jersey. A longer work with an accessible narrative style is *Having Our Say: The Delany Sisters' First 100 Years,* written by Sadie and Bessie Delany with the assistance of journalist Amy Hill Hearth. The lives of these two black women are extraordinary not just because of their length but because of their observation of profound social change. Born in the South before Jim Crow laws were enacted, they later lived in Harlem during its flowering as an artistic center. They succeeded in their careers, one as a teacher and the other as a dentist, at a time when few women, and even fewer black women, were accepted in professional circles. The Delany sisters' memoir is funny, folksy, and uplifting. Others can be deeply moving and disturbing. In *Girl, Interrupted*, for example, Susan Kaysen recalls the two years she spent as a patient in a mental hospital. In *The Big Lie: A True Story*, a book published for children, Isabella Leitner looks back on a truly horrifying childhood when she and her family were rousted out of their homes in a small Hungarian town and transported to Auschwitz. In spare prose she helps us feel the loss of those who perished as well as the determination of the survivors not to let their story die.

Oral histories offer a conversational style that will appeal to new readers. Studs Terkel is a master of this form, having compiled several oral histories around issues of social importance, such as *Working*, a collection of interviews about what people do for a living and how they feel about their work, *Hard*

Times, an oral history of the Great Depression, and his most recent book *Race: How Blacks and Whites Feel About the American Obsession.* The format in each of these oral histories is similar. Most of the speakers are ordinary people, although a few famous names appear as well. All the entries are relatively brief, appropriate for reading aloud in a class session or as silent reading exercises with follow-up questions. Most importantly, all look beyond the facts of an historical event or era to reveal the human story behind it. The *Foxfire* series, of which *Foxfire 10* is the most recent, is another excellent example of oral history. These books grew out of an assignment that teacher Eliot Wigginton gave to his rural Georgia high school students, sending them out into the hills and hollows of their countryside to collect the stories, folklore, songs, recipes, and lifetime wisdom of the people who had lived in that country all their lives. The students created their own magazine with the stories they collected. The experience of collecting and publishing the stories helped the students integrate the realities of their life and community with the skills they were learning at school. *Foxfire* is a good source of reading material for literacy students and a shining example of what students can do to mine the treasures of their own community, creating their own reading material in the process.

Collections of historical documents also tell stories about our nation's development. Diane Ravitch's *The American Reader: Words that Moved a Nation,* for example, presents letters, speeches, posters, poems, songs, and other documents, each of which recounts some part of the history of the United States as it grew from a loosely-connected set of colonies to a major world power.

The stories in the books just mentioned are true. Of course, many stories we read are not true but are the fictional renderings of the imagination of the writer. They still, however, reveal some truth about the way we live our human lives. Many works of fiction published for middle school readers and young adults have themes and settings that make them appealing to older adults. In Cynthia Rylant's *I Had Seen Castles,* an elderly man recalls the year in which he turned eighteen, fell in love, went to war, and saw his whole world change around him. Teenagers will identify with the turmoil felt by the young lovers torn between duty and desire, but older readers will recognize the voice of the old man looking back with a mixture of joy, sadness, and more than a tinge of regret. Robert Lipsyte's classic young adult novel *The Contender* is almost thirty years old, but the power with which it tells the story of a seventeen-year-old high school dropout who learns the lesson of the boxing ring—the effort to be a contender matters more than being a champion—transcends any limitations of time or the age of the reader. Angela Johnson's *Toning the Sweep* is a contemporary novel for teens with strong adult characters that will appeal to readers of all ages. In this story, three generations of women confront the fact that the oldest of them is dying of cancer. When the daughter and granddaughter come to take the grandmother home to live with them, all three share memories and sadness. As the grandmother teaches them a lesson in the art of dying, the daughter and granddaughter recognize their responsibility of remembering.

Historical fiction is a popular genre for young adults, and several titles will be of interest to adults as well. Good historical fiction not only engages us with a story, it also teaches us about history by helping us imagine what it was like to live in particular times and places. One particularly appealing title is Paul Fleischman's *Bull Run* which takes us to the Civil War battle in the company of sixteen different people, eight on each side of the war, whose lives were profoundly affected by that battle.

There are adult contemporary novels which are suitable for students at the advanced new reader level, especially if they do so with a tutor or in a book discussion group. Two excellent and very accessible examples are Sandra Cisneros's *The House on Mango Street*, a series of brief vignettes based on the vivid and engrossing memories of the narrator's childhood in a Latino section of Chicago, and Alice Walker's *The Color Purple*, a prize-winning novel written in the form of brief letters that a forsaken black girl sends to her sister and to God in the hope of finding a way out of her misery. This book offers the added advantage of a movie version that students could watch before or after reading the book.

As literacy students move through the stages of intermediate and advanced new reader, they gain the confidence and skill in reading that they need for their jobs or family responsibilities. This is the point where they are mastering the skills of reading but have not necessarily become *readers*. It is a crucial juncture in their literacy development, because it is the point at which reading can make a profound difference in their lives. Their increasing level of literacy can lead to job promotions or entrance into a job training program, increased responsibilities in the community, completion of a diploma or GED, and perhaps entry into a community college. If students at this level can begin to see reading as a source of pleasure, entertainment, and even inspiration, as well as a source of information, then their chances of getting hooked on the reading habit—of becoming readers and ultimately lifelong learners—are greatly enhanced. Introducing students to stories from the human family found in the vast collection of literature available at any public library will bring them many possibilities of enjoyment, growth, and personal fulfillment.

A Note to Librarians

Consider the many forms of literature in the library that may be accessible to adult new readers: collections of short works such as letters, newspaper columns, and short stories; memoirs, especially those of people who are well-known or have prevailed over adversity and tell their story in a readable, narrative style; young adult fiction that will also appeal to adults; adult fiction that is relatively easy to read, including genre fiction such as romance novels. Find ways to display and promote these materials to a range of patrons, including those from literacy programs. Feature a display of books that have been made into movies or books which are available in audio format. Sponsor author visits and invite participants in the literacy program. In conjunction with the local literacy program, organize book discussion groups for new readers. Sponsor oral history projects in your community and invite new readers as well as the general public to contribute interesting stories about the history of the area, a particular immigrant group, or any other topic that is appropriate. In whatever ways possible, promote the telling of, the writing of, and the reading of stories from the human family.

A Note to Tutors

Read aloud to your students at every tutoring session if possible. Read a story for discussion and follow-up exercises or read a short story or novel for short periods at the end of the session. Encourage your students to write about the stories in their own lives and the stories they see around them, including those they might see on television. Ask the young adult librarian in your library to recommend titles appropriate for older adults. Choose a book on tape that you and your student can listen to between tutoring sessions then discuss the book when you've finished. Read books with your students that have been made into movies then watch the movies and discuss the quality of the stories as well as the faithfulness of the movies to the books. Work with your local library and other community agencies to sponsor oral history projects encouraging the people of the community to tell their stories. The literacy program can be responsible for writing the stories, collecting them, and distributing them within the community as well as to other literacy programs. In every way possible, remind students that books tell stories that enrich our lives and connect us to those who have gone before as well as to those who will follow in the paths we are creating.

Bibliography

Memoirs/Collections

Alexander, Sally Hobart. *Taking Hold: My Journey into Blindness*. New York: Macmillan, 1994.

> Sally Hobart was a healthy, young third grade teacher when a little black line began creeping across her field of vision. After numerous hospital stays and visits with specialists, she was forced to come to grips with impending blindness and its assault on her emotional stability as well as her everyday life. Her harrowing experience reads like a suspense novel, and teachers might well consider reading it aloud over several days, to be followed up by the picture book *Mom Can't See Me*, which Sally Hobart Alexander, now married and a mother, wrote with her nine-year-old daughter.

Intermediate-advanced new reader/children's collection.

Allen, Steve. *Reflections*. Amherst, NY: Prometheus Books, 1994.

> Well-known as a comedian, actor, and musician, Steve Allen is also a prolific writer and keen observer of the modern world. In this collection he offers his reflections, alternately funny, insightful, and challenging, on a variety of issues affecting American culture. Arranged alphabetically, the entries range from a few lines to several pages, making this book attractive for browsing.

Intermediate-advanced new reader/adult collection.

Angelou, Maya. *I Know Why the Caged Bird Sings*. New York: Random House, 1970.

> Just a glance at the titles of Angelou's extraordinary five-volume autobiography, of which this is the first, convinces readers that they are in the hands of a writer who knows how to use the compelling musicality of language. The content of these books is no less powerful. Angelou has risen from the racism and material poverty of small town Arkansas to acclaim as one of America's great writers. Along the way, she has experienced life as a struggling single mother, an entertainer in some of the seedier sections of American cities as well as on some of Europe's most famous stages, and an African American woman searching for her place in the wider world. Angelou tells her story with vivid, sometimes searing, prose that immerses readers in the unique experience of one life while sharing the

universality of all human experience. Subsequent titles are *Gather Together in My Name* (1974), *Singin' and Swingin' and Gettin' Merry Like Christmas* (1976), *The Heart of a Woman* (1981), and *All God's Children Need Travelin' Shoes* (1986).
Intermediate-advanced new reader/adult collection/young adult collection.

———. *Wouldn't Take Nothing for My Journey Now.* New York: Random House, 1993.

Angelou's poetic voice rings through these brief essays in which she offers some of the wisdom and understanding she has gleaned from her extraordinary life. She speaks of spirituality and sensuality, kindness and responsibility, and caring for ourselves as well as others.
Intermediate new reader/adult collection.

Aparicio, Frances R., ed. *Latino Voices.* Brookfield, CT: The Millbrook Press, 1994.

Well-known Latino writers such as Sandra Cisneros and Julia Alvarez, as well as immigrants still struggling to find their place within the wider culture, speak about their experiences. An arrangement that links entries of similar themes with thoughtful introductions and brief biographies helps the reader place each writer's voice within a context of time, place, and perspective.
Intermediate-advanced new reader/young adult collection.

Archer, Chalmers Jr. *Growing Up Black in Rural Mississippi: Memories of a Family, Heritage of a Place.* New York: Walker & Co., 1992.

Now a professor at Northern Virginia Community College, Archer recalls growing up in a large and loving extended family shaped by the demands of a farming life and the spiritual comfort of a strong church community. Stories from Archer's childhood are interwoven with the memories of other family members to create a vivid, easy-to-read text. Individual chapters can stand alone and would provide a good introduction to silent reading for students new to reading on their own. More advanced readers will enjoy following the fortunes of the many fascinating characters.
Intermediate-advanced new reader/adult collection.

Bach, Alice, and J. Cheryl Exum. *Miriam's Well: Stories About Women in the Bible*. New York: Delacorte Press, 1991.

The names of Miriam, Rebekah, Leah, Delilah, and other women in the Bible may be familiar, but their stories are less so. Bach and Exum have examined Biblical texts and other religious source documents to find the stories of these women and tell them for modern readers.
Advanced new reader/children's collection.

Banks, Ann, ed. *First Person America*. New York: Alfred A. Knopf, 1980.

Gathered by writers working for the Federal Writers' Project during the Depression, these oral histories give brief accounts of the lives of pioneers, miners, meat packers, factory workers, and other laborers. The short pieces are good for reading aloud and for sparking discussions about the conditions of working people then and now.
Intermediate-advanced new reader/adult collection.

Beals, Melba Pattillo. *Warriors Don't Cry: A Searing Memoir of the Battle to Integrate Little Rock's Central High*. New York: Washington Square Press, 1994.

In 1957, Beals and eight other black students confronted a hostile state government and decades of separatist tradition when they integrated Central High School in Little Rock, Arkansas under the protection of the 101st Airborne Division of the United States Army. In a clear and highly readable voice, she talks about the fear and hatred she faced, not only in 1957 but in the years that followed.
Advanced new reader/adult collection.

Bell-Scott, Patricia. *Life Notes: Personal Writings by Contemporary Black Women*. New York: W.W. Norton & Co., 1994.

Forty-nine black women writers, some well-known and some not, have contributed excerpts from their journals and other writings to create this intensely personal and compelling collection. As Ann Gillespie notes in the forward, the work included is "unedited, uncensored womantalk." Some segments are brief, others several pages; some are brash and angry, others reflective and probing. Interesting in themselves, these selections may also inspire students to keep their own journals, not only as a way of improving their writing but also as a means to exploring their deeper selves.
Intermediate-advanced new reader/adult collection.

Bode, Janet. *New Kids on the Block: Oral Histories of Immigrant Teens.* New York: Franklin Watts, 1989.

In their own words, teenage immigrants from Asia, Latin America, and the Middle East tell how it feels to be uprooted from familiar surroundings to come to the strange and sometimes hostile United States. They speak of fear and loss, humiliation and adjustment, and pride and hope. The short narrative entries are easy to read and will generate much discussion, especially among students who are themselves immigrants.
Intermediate new reader/children's collection.

Bolden, Tonya. *Rites of Passage: Stories About Growing Up by Black Writers from Around the World.* New York: Hyperion, 1994.

Black writers from Africa, Britain, the Caribbean, Central America, and the United States recall experiences from their early lives. The collection is aimed at young adult readers, but it will appeal to older readers as well, because most pieces are written in the voice of an adult looking back on the events and circumstances of his or her youth. The international cast of writers emphasizes the universal character of the events recalled.
Advanced new reader/young adult collection.

Boswell, Thomas. *Cracking the Show.* New York: Doubleday, 1994.

A syndicated sports columnist for *The Washington Post,* Boswell writes mostly about baseball. In the columns collected here, he writes not from the perspective of an authority on the game, although he certainly is one, but rather as a fan who can talk as easily to stadium ushers as to college professors.
Intermediate-advanced new reader/adult collection.

Brant, Beth, ed. *A Gathering of Spirit: Writing and Art by North American Indian Women.* 2nd ed., expanded. Rockland, ME: Sinister Wisdom Books, 1984.

The stories, poems, photographs, and original art work collected here offer readers a glimpse into the life experiences and cultural influences of contemporary North American Indian women.
Intermediate-advanced new reader/adult collection.

Breslin, Jimmy. *The World According to Breslin.* New York: Ticknor & Fields, 1984.

Whether he is writing about street kids, celebrities, or the vagaries of big city life, Breslin's straightforward narrative carries the force of humor, compassion, and truth. The columns collected here were all written for *The New York Daily News.*

Intermediate new reader/adult collection.

Bruchac, Joseph, ed. *Returning the Gift: Poetry and Prose from the First North American Native Writers Festival.* Tucson, AZ: University of Arizona Press, 1994.

Writers from many different tribes in Mexico, Central America, Canada, and the United States gathered together to "return the gift," that is, to share the poetry and fiction they had created from stories heard from their ancestral people. The selections cover a wide range of style and subject; more than half are poems, and the stories are one to three pages long, making them ideal for reading aloud within a class setting.

Advanced new reader/adult collection.

Capote, Truman. *I Remember Grandpa.* Illustrated by Barry Moser. Atlanta, GA: Peachtree Publishers, Ltd., 1985.

While still a young man, Capote wrote this story as a gift for an aunt who had cared for him, and it was she who published it after his death. It tells of a young boy who, at the age of six, must leave his Appalachian homeland and his beloved grandparents to accompany his parents to a place where he can attend school and learn about the world "on the other side of the hills." The haunting watercolor illustrations complement this sad but loving recollection.

Intermediate new reader/adult collection.

Carawan, Guy, and Candie Carawan, eds. *Sing for Freedom: The Story of the Civil Rights Movement Through Its Songs.* Bethlehem, PA: Sing Out Corporation, 1990.

Singing was an integral part of the Civil Rights Movement of the 1960's. Many folk songs and spirituals were adapted to fit the issues and events of that time. The songs collected here, along with newspaper accounts of various events, recollections of participants, and numerous photographs,

document the grass roots character of this tumultuous time in America's history.
Intermediate new reader/Adult collection.

Cataldi, Ann. *Letters from Sarajevo: Voices of a Besieged City.* Translated by Avril Bardoni. Rockport, MA: Element, Inc., 1994.

Citizens of Sarajevo who endured the 1992–1993 siege of their city wrote these letters as a cry for help from friends, family, and the world press. They recount events in the war, describe people's attempts to survive, and add names to the growing list of casualties. Arranged by season, these letters expose the horrific contrast between the cyclical and expected events of nature and the wholly unexpected carnage and privation that occurred in that city.
Intermediate new reader/adult collection.

Coca-Cola Culture: Icons of Pop. Icarus World Issues Series. New York: The Rosen Publishing Group, Inc, 1993.

How the products of American culture, from blue jeans to Disney World, affect the cultures of other nations and create perceptions of the United States is a fascinating topic for discussion, especially among ESOL students or in GED classes with students from other countries. The nine essays and one work of fiction in this collection, a volume in the Icarus World Issues Series, focus on issues such as the movie industry and the depiction of Native Americans in advertising. Marketed for a high school audience, these essays will challenge all readers to view familiar aspects of American culture from a different perspective.
Advanced new reader/young adult collection.

Cormier, Robert. *I Have Words to Spend: Reflections of a Small-Town Editor.* New York: Delacorte Press, 1991.

Best known as an author of novels for young adults, Cormier also wrote a column for his local newspaper, *The Fitchburg Sentinel and Enterprise*, as well as articles for other publications. The pieces collected here include memories of growing up, observations on being a father and a son, and reflections on small town life and the larger American culture. Although some articles were written in the 1970's, the topics discussed are not bound by place or time.
Intermediate new reader/young adult collection.

Cosby, Bill. *Fatherhood.* Garden City, NY: Doubleday & Co., 1986.

Actor, comedian, and educator Cosby shares the many lessons he has learned from raising five children. His stories are short, easy-to-read, and funny, but the messages about love and responsibility are never too far from the surface. In another book, *Time Flies* (1987), Cosby turns his insightful wit to the topic of growing old.

Intermediate new reader/adult collection.

David, Jay, ed. *Growing Up Black: From Slave Days to the Present—25 African Americans Reveal the Trials and Triumphs of Their Childhoods.* Rev. ed. New York: Avon Books, 1992.

First published in 1968, this volume has been revised and expanded to include more recent voices. The writing spans American history from the days of slavery to a final essay by Nathan McCall on the devastation wrought by contemporary inner city life on many young black males. These excerpts from longer works of some of our best African American writers may draw students to the complete books. Individual pieces offer glimpses into particular lives shaped by particular circumstances; taken as a whole, the book offers a broad perspective on the lives of African Americans in the United States.

Advanced new reader/young adult collection.

de Vinck, Christopher. *Only the Heart Knows How to Find Them.* New York: Viking, 1991.

Given that de Vinck's essays appear in magazines and newspapers such as the *Wall Street Journal,* their content comes as a surprise. Inspired by nature as well as by everyday events, de Vinck tells stories—some remembered from childhood and days past, others from his present life—through which he searches for the true meaning of life. Never heavy or preachy, these essays strike a spiritual chord amidst the frenzy of our modern world.

Intermediate-advanced new reader/adult collection.

———. *Songs of Innocence and Experience: Essays in Celebration of the Ordinary.* New York: Viking, 1994.

In this second collection of essays, de Vinck again explores the meaning in the ordinary events of life, especially those related to his family.

Intermediate-advanced new reader/adult collection.

Delany, Sarah, and A. Elizabeth Delany. *The Delany Sisters' Book of Everyday Wisdom*. With Amy Hill Hearth. New York: Kodansha International, 1994.

The extraordinary popularity of the Delany sisters' memoir, *Having Our Say: The Delany Sisters' First Hundred Years*, discussed below, generated thousands of "fan letters" to these two centenarian black ladies, asking for the secrets of their long, productive, and happy lives. Not able to answer all the letters personally, the sisters decided to collect their common wisdom into a book with the help of journalist Amy Hill Hearth. Short sections offer succinct, earthy wisdom about family, religion, education, and civility in a chatty, highly readable format.
Intermediate new reader/adult collection.

———. *Having Our Say: The Delany Sisters' First 100 Years*. With Amy Hill Hearth. New York: Kodansha International, 1993.

Sadie and Bessie Delany were 104 and 102 years old when the remarkable story of their lives became a surprise bestseller. Born in the South before the establishment of Jim Crow laws, their personal history parallels the history of blacks in America in the twentieth century. Their father was born a slave but became an Episcopal bishop and an advocate for quality education. The sisters learned to survive in a culture hostile to their success, drawing strength from their faith and family. They lived in Harlem after World War I, a time of burgeoning artistic expression. They had pioneering careers as, respectively, home economics teacher and dentist. They met many of the leaders of the early Civil Rights Movement, and they were among the first blacks to integrate the suburbs in the 1950's. Told in voices that are alternately feisty and quietly determined, funny and reflective, the Delany sisters' story has been transcribed and organized by journalist Hearth into a highly readable and fascinating American saga.
Intermediate new reader/adult collection.

Douglass, Frederick. *Escape from Slavery: The Boyhood of Frederick Douglass in His Own Words*. Edited and illustrated by Michael McCurdy. New York: Alfred A. Knopf, 1994.

Born a slave and forbidden to learn to read, Douglass nevertheless taught himself to read, to write, and ultimately to speak against slavery and all forms of oppression with an eloquence that moved others to sympathy and to action. McCurdy has taken excerpts from Douglass's autobiogra-

phy to introduce new readers to an extraordinary American life. His black-and-white scratchboard illustrations underscore the depth of struggle and power that characterized Douglass's life. Many students may want to continue the story by reading *The Narrative of the Life of Frederick Douglass.*
Intermediate new reader/children's collection.

Du Bois, W. E. B. *Prayers for Dark People.* Amherst, MA: University of Massachusetts Press, 1980.

In this collection of short prayers, including some quotations from the Bible, noted historian and author Du Bois offers his religious beliefs as well as his hopes for the spiritual growth of the African American people and all of American society.
Intermediate new reader/adult collection.

Edelman, Marian Wright. *The Measure of Our Success: A Letter to My Children and Yours.* New York: HarperCollins, 1992.

A long time advocate for children, Edelman offers her perspectives on the importance of family and responsibility. She first recalls her own close family ties and the lessons she learned from her parents and others then lists the twenty-five "Lessons for Life" that she wanted to impart to her three sons as they moved into adulthood. Begun as a family letter, her simple but inspiring ideas have found a wide and receptive audience.
Intermediate-advanced new reader/adult collection.

Elliot, Jeffrey, ed. *Conversations with Maya Angelou.* Jackson, MS: University Press of Mississippi, 1989.

Through her many autobiographical writings, Maya Angelou has inspired millions of readers from all races and walks of life. This collection of interviews with Angelou and articles about her spans the time from 1971-1987, a time when she lived in several places and experienced many changes in her personal world as well as in the world around her. Through setbacks as well as successes, she maintains an indomitable optimism. Students and teachers who admire her writing will enjoy learning more about this enormously talented woman.
Advanced new reader/adult collection.

Foreman, Michael. *War Boy: A Country Childhood.* Written and Illustrated by Michael Foreman. New York: Arcade Publishing, 1989.

Foreman, who grew up in England during World War II, draws his own illustrations to accompany his memories of a bomb coming through his roof, of the great excitement generated among the boys and young ladies of his small town when the "Yanks" arrived, and of the "war games" he and his friends delighted in playing, even after a terrifying night in the air raid shelter. Although classed as children's literature, the funny, touching, and sometimes irreverent stories in this memoir of a child caught in a horrifying yet fascinating time and place will easily appeal to adults.
Intermediate new reader/children's collection.

Frank, Anne. *Anne Frank: The Diary of a Young Girl.* The Definitive Edition. Translated by Susan Massotty. New York: Doubleday, 1994.

This is the classic story of the young Dutch girl who lived in hiding from the Nazis for two years before being captured. In the nearly fifty years since this book was first published, Anne's adolescent yearnings and indomitable spirit have captured the minds and hearts of readers like no other book in the history of that well-documented war. Although the voice and feelings are those of an adolescent girl, the circumstances in which she lived render that voice meaningful beyond its years.
Intermediate-advanced new reader/adult collection/children's collection.

Fulghum, Robert. *Maybe (Maybe Not): Second Thoughts from a Secret Life.* New York: Villard Books, 1993.

Fulghum has a gift for seeing those little twists and oddities that turn seemingly mundane events into a good story. Given that he is a former minister, his stories often carry an implied lesson as well, making them good reading for students who need to sharpen their critical thinking skills. Don't be deterred by fear of a sermon, however; the stories are funny, wise, and full of concern for our common fate as fellow travellers in this life. Previous titles, which are similar in content and style, include *Uh-Oh* (1991), *It Was On Fire When I Lay Down on It* (1989), and his first best seller, *All I Really Need to Know I Learned in Kindergarten* (1988).
Intermediate new reader/adult collection.

Gates, Henry Louis. *Colored People.* New York: Knopf, 1994.

The small town of Piedmont, West Virginia is the setting for this memoir of growing up black with little material benefit but a rich cultural heritage in which the author felt loved and secure. As the Civil Rights Movement progressed and Gates reached his own adolescence, he came to understand that the turmoil of the wider world also existed within his own. His book is a lyrical, easy-to-read memoir that offers a rare glimpse into a vanishing part of this country which still has many lessons to teach about the value of family and community.

Advanced new reader/adult collection.

––––––––––

Giovanni, Nikki. *Racism 101.* New York: William Morrow & Co., Inc, 1994.

In these essays, poet Giovanni offers her opinions about some difficult social issues facing our society, particularly those affecting the lives of black Americans. She speaks about education, the role of writers and artists, crime and violence, and other topics in a style that is both cogent and accessible to new readers.

Intermediate-advanced new reader/adult collection.

––––––––––

–––––––. *Sacred Cows . . . and Other Edibles.* New York: William Morrow & Co., Inc., 1988.

Here Giovanni writes about topics ranging from the Miss America pageant to parenthood to life as a black woman and poet. Her keen observations, wry wit, and over-the-kitchen-table writing style invite lively responses.

Advanced new reader/adult collection.

––––––––––

Giovanni, Nikki, ed. *Grand Mothers: Poems, Reminiscences, and Short Stories about the Keepers of Our Traditions.* New York: Henry Holt and Co., 1994.

Remembering the love and influence of her own grandmother, Giovanni invited a number of friends to share stories of their grandmothers. She also included reminiscences from the grandmothers she works with at a local senior citizens center. The result is a warm-hearted collection of family stories by professional and non-professional writers that could well spark literacy students to write stories of their own family memories.

Intermediate-advanced new reader/adult collection.

––––––––––

Goodman, Ellen. *Value Judgments.* New York: Farrar, Straus, and Giroux, 1993.

As a columnist for the *Boston Globe*, Goodman writes about a range of political and social topics. What sets her apart from other commentators is her willingness to allow her perspective as working woman and mother, as well as professional journalist, to inform her understanding of world events. Reading Goodman, we better understand why and how the issues of our time matter not just as stories on the nightly news but as events that shape the way we live our everyday lives. Other collections of her columns include *Keeping in Touch* (1985) and *At Large* (1981).
Advanced new reader/adult collection.

Gore, Art. *Speak Softly to the Echoes.* Flagstaff, AZ: Northland Press, 1978.

A professional photographer, Gore uses his pictures to illustrate this memoir of his early life in rural North Carolina. Though not direct matches, both stories and pictures convey the pain of loss as well as the joy of fulfillment he has felt at various times in his life. In another book, *Images of Yesterday*, reviewed in Chapter 1, Gore relies more completely on his photographs to recall his life as a young boy.
Intermediate new reader/adult collection.

Greene, Bob. *He Was a Midwestern Boy on His Own.* New York: Atheneum, 1991.

Traveling around America, Greene met ordinary people with fascinating stories to tell and famous people who told him things other reporters never mention. In this collection of newspaper columns and magazine articles, we meet a handicapped young man entering a contest to become a sports commentator, registrants at a convention of "Lindas," and David Eisenhower talking about his father-in-law, whom he always addressed, even in family gatherings, as Mr. Nixon. Other collections of his columns include *American Beat* (1983) and *Cheeseburgers* (1986).
Intermediate-advanced new reader/adult collection.

Greenfeld, Howard. *The Hidden Children.* New York: Ticknor & Fields, 1993.

The "hidden children" of the title speak in this book as adults, now in their fifties and sixties, recalling their memories of being hidden from the Gestapo during World War II. Photographs taken both then and now add poignancy to memories that were initially etched on the minds of chil-

dren but have been brought to vivid completion by the adults who have carried them through all the other experiences of their lives.
Intermediate new reader/children's collection.

Greenfield, Eloise, and Lessie Jones Little. *Childtimes: A Three-Generation Memoir.* Illustrated by Jerry Pinkney. New York: HarperCollins Publishers, 1979.

Children's author Greenfield gathered the written diaries of her grandmother and then collaborated with her mother, Lessie Jones Little, to create this memoir of three childhoods, spanning a time from the late nineteenth century into the middle of the twentieth. Though not greatly detailed, each woman's memories recall those moments of childhood whose significance becomes apparent only with the insight gained through time and experience. Jerry Pinckney's black and white drawings join with family photographs to convey the warmth as well as the extraordinary change that marked the lives of black women in the rural South. Adults can appreciate this book on a deeper level than the children with whom they might share it.
Intermediate new reader/children's collection.

Grizzard, Lewis. *Don't Forget to Call Your Mama . . . I Wish I Could Call Mine.* Atlanta, GA: Longstreet Press, 1992.

An only child whose father left the scene early, Grizzard was very close to his mother. This memoir recalls their rural life in Georgia with a downhome humor that is entertaining and easy to read.
Intermediate new reader/adult collection.

Haizlip, Shirlee Taylor. *The Sweeter the Juice: A Family Memoir in Black and White.* New York: Simon & Schuster, 1994.

As Haizlip explains, her family tree has "roots in many gardens." She grew up black in a family with strong and loving relatives on her father's side, but only mystery and unspoken sorrow on her mother's. Eventually, Haizlip came to understand that her mother was born into a mixed race family in which most of the members could and did pass for white, abandoning their darker sister to a black world. With compelling narrative force, Haizlip describes her search for her mother's lost relatives and the ultimate triumph of reuniting her mother with one sister, both old women in their eighties. This is not an easy book, but its powerful story is told in

many short passages, accommodating the teacher who would read it aloud or inexperienced readers still unsure of their ability to handle longer books. In either case, the fascinating story and the questions that it raises about the nature of color and identity make it well worth the effort.
Advanced new reader/adult collection.

Halliburton, Warren J. *Historic Speeches of African Americans.* New York: Franklin Watts, 1993.

The stirring words of black leaders from Sojourner Truth and Frederick Douglass to Angela Davis and Jesse Jackson offer a survey of African American history as well as eloquent testimony to the power of the spoken word. Themes of enduring hardship, survival, hope, and ultimate redemption ring from these speeches, many of which were originally sermons or derived from sermons.
Advanced new reader/children's collection.

Harvey, Paul. *More of Paul Harvey's The Rest of the Story.* Edited and compiled by Lynne Harvey. New York: William Morrow & Co., Inc., 1980.

Particularly good for fostering listening skills, each brief anecdote in this collection tells a little-known part of the story of someone famous, living or dead, whose identity is not revealed until the end. Once students get the pattern, they will enjoy trying to figure out who the subject is. Other editions with similar content have also been published.
Beginning-intermediate new reader/adult collection.

Harvey, Paul Jr., ed. *Paul Harvey's For What It's Worth.* Illustrated by Scott Harris. New York: Bantam Books, 1991.

Radio broadcaster Paul Harvey often ends his program with short items from the "for what it's worth" category, stories sent to him by listeners about strange, often embarrassing, things that happen to them. These pieces range from five or six lines to one page in length. Read in sequence, they would become tedious, but as a short and light ending to a tutoring session or as a lead into writing they could prove very useful, especially with beginning level students.
Beginning-intermediate new reader/adult collection.

Hinojosa, Maria. *Crews: Gang Members Talk to Maria Hinojosa.* Photographs by German Perez. San Diego, CA: Harcourt Brace & Co., 1995.

This book grew out of an assignment that sent National Public Radio correspondent Hinojosa to interview young people who hang out in New York City "crews," the members' preferred word for gangs. Her original broadcast is included, but most of the book consists of extended interviews in which gang members discuss their attitude toward violence and the appeal of the crews, which function almost as an extended family. The anger and callousness of these kids is shocking, but some also reveal an aching vulnerability beneath their tough street demeanor. The photographs have been altered to disguise actual faces, increasing the reader's unease at the faceless violence that stalks our city streets. Clearly not for everyone, this book will move some readers to anger and rejection, others to compassion, and some to both. No reader will be unaffected by the questions the book raises about the deepest problems affecting our society.
Intermediate new reader/adult collection.

Hong, Maria, ed. *Growing Up Asian American: An Anthology.* New York: William Morrow & Co., 1993.

Another in Morrow's "Growing Up" series, this anthology includes the works of Amy Tan, Maxine Hong Kingston, and other Asian American writers. Most of the selections are excerpts from longer works in which the writers describe the varied circumstances but common problems of growing up in a culture vastly different from that of one's parents.
Advanced new reader/adult collection.

Hughes, Langston. *The Return of Simple.* New York: Hill & Wang, 1994.

In the 1940's, Langston Hughes created the character of Jesse B. Semple, know as Simple, and included stories about his life in his regular column for *The Chicago Defender.* Simple was a black man from rural Virginia who managed to survive in the urban world of Harlem. In every story, he talks to an unidentified but clearly better educated friend who asks questions and makes comments, all designed to get Simple to speak his mind about the changing world he lives in. Given that the stories continued into the 1960's, Simple had much to reflect on and react to. This collection brings the tales of Simple back for the contemporary reader to consider.
Intermediate-advanced new reader/adult collection.

Hurston, Zora Neale. *Dust Tracks on a Road.* New forward by Maya Angelou. New York: HarperCollins Publishers, 1991.

Originally published in 1942, this is the autobiography of a black woman who was born into poverty in rural Florida, became a major writer during Harlem's Renaissance of the 1920's and 1930's, then died in virtual obscurity in the 1960's. As Hurston herself put it, "I have been in Sorrow's kitchen and licked out all the pots. Then I have stood on the peaky mountain wrapped in rainbows with a harp and a sword in my hands." Hurston's extraordinary story is matched by her vivid and lyrical manner of telling it. For an easier introduction to Hurston's life, see Mary Lyons's biography for young readers, *Sorrow's Kitchen: The Life and Folklore of Zora Neale Hurston,* listed below.
Advanced new reader/adult collection.

Kaysen, Susanna. *Girl, Interrupted.* New York: Turtle Bay Books, 1993.

For two harrowing years in her late adolescence, Kaysen was confined to a mental institution. She tells her story with vivid clarity and insight, describing several of the characters who shared her fate as well as her own reactions to the experience. The topic is heavy, but the writing is clear and accessible, inviting readers to consider the mysteries of the human mind.
Advanced new reader/adult collection.

Keyes, Ralph, ed. *Sons on Fathers: A Book of Men's Writing.* New York: HarperCollins Publishers, 1992.

From nostalgic adulation for "Daddy," to the need to distance oneself from "The Old Man," to the understanding that comes, if they're lucky, when sons become fathers themselves, this collection explores the complicated relationship of men with their fathers. Poems such as Robert Hayden's "Those Winter Sundays" and Theodore Roethke's "My Papa's Waltz," and Larry L. King's classic essay, "The Old Man," are among the extraordinarily moving pieces included in this collection. If your students are interested in exploring what it means to be a father or a son, these works will open much conversation and personal reflection.
Intermediate-advanced new reader/adult collection.

Leitner, Isabella. *The Big Lie: A True Story.* Illustrated by Judy Pedersen. New York: Scholastic, 1992.

In 1944 the Nazis invaded Leitner's small Hungarian town and sent all the Jews in cattle trains to Auschwitz. She, along with her father, two sis-

ters, and a brother, survived. Her mother and two other sisters did not. In simple, spare language Leitner describes the horror she experienced. Pedersen's charcoal sketches deepen the haunting sense of loss. This book was intended to serve as an introduction to the Holocaust for children.
Intermediate new reader/children's collection.

Levine, Ellen. *Freedom's Children: Young Civil Rights Activists Tell Their Own Story.* New York: G. P. Putnam's Sons, 1993.

The adults telling these stories were teenagers during the 1950's and 1960's when they became involved in Civil Rights demonstrations. Looking back, they recall vivid memories made more powerful by the accumulation of understanding, pain, and joy that they and their communities have experienced in the days since that pivotal era.
Intermediate new reader/children's collection.

Lewin, Ted. *I Was a Teenage Professional Wrestler.* New York: Orchard Books, 1993.

Now an established author/illustrator of children's books, Lewin became a professional wrestler at the age of seventeen. This memoir recalls that time of his life with vivid stories, photographs, and paintings from the young Lewin who was, even then, honing his artistic skills. It is that strange juxtaposition of wrestling and art, as well as the unusual characters and settings, that accounts for the fascination even those who claim to hate wrestling will find in this memoir.
Intermediate new reader/children's collection.

Litoff, Judy Barrett, and David C. Smith, eds. *We're in This War, Too: World War II Letters from American Women in Uniform.* New York: Oxford University Press, 1994.

Woven together with brief explanatory narratives, these letters create a vivid picture of the women's experiences of the horrors and the exhilaration of participating in the major military event of this century. While individual letters may not be long or detailed enough to support a whole lesson, they could provide a useful supplement to other readings and discussions about the changing roles of women. See, for example, Betty Medsger's *Women at Work* (Chapter 1) and the poetry anthology *No More Masks* (Chapter 2).
Intermediate-advanced new reader/adult collection.

Lopez, Tiffany Ana, ed. *Growing Up Chicana/o*. New York: William Morrow & Co., Inc, 1993.

In this collection, twenty contemporary Latino writers, including Rudolfo Anaya and Sandra Cisneros, recall growing up. The pieces cover a range of styles, but the common themes of finding home and finding one's place in the wider world prevail.
Intermediate-advanced new reader/adult collection.

Lyons, Mary E. *Sorrow's Kitchen: The Life and Folklore of Zora Neale Hurston*. New York: Charles Scribner's Sons, 1990.

A prominent writer during the Harlem Renaissance, Hurston died in obscurity in the 1960's. Fortunately, her work has again been recognized, largely through the efforts of writer Alice Walker. Hurston was both novelist and anthropologist, and she mined the folklore of her black ancestors to create her fiction. Lyons emphasizes this point by interspersing biographical segments with excerpts from Hurston's writing, showing the strong connection between her life and work. For more advanced students, consider Hurston's own autobiography, *Dust Tracks on a Road*, listed above.
Intermediate-advanced new reader/children's collection.

McCall, Nathan. *Makes Me Wanna Holler: A Young Black Man in America*. New York: Random House, 1994.

McCall came from a stable family, did well in school, and lived in a working class neighborhood in Portsmouth, VA. Still, growing into adolescence, he became alienated from the culture his parents worked to maintain, got into drugs, crime and, eventually, prison. There he began a serious reading program that changed his life. Today, McCall is a journalist working for *The Washington Post*. His story is a frightening picture of what happens to young people who feel angry and trapped, but it is also a hopeful account of the transforming power of books and knowledge that may inspire others. McCall tells his story in a narrative style that will accommodate teachers who wish to read it aloud in segments or advanced new readers capable of reading on their own.
Advanced new reader/adult collection.

Martz, Sandra, ed. *If I Had a Hammer: Women's Work in Poetry, Fiction and Photographs*. Watsonville, CA: Papier-Mache Press, 1990.

Papier-Mache Press has published several collections of poems and essays by writers who may be prolific but whose work has never reached a large

audience. In this very personal and accessible collection, women write about work, creative achievement, and the particular challenges working women face. The next three entries discuss similar collections built around different topics.
Intermediate new reader/adult collection.

———. *If I Had My Life to Live Over I Would Pick More Daisies.* Watsonville, CA: Papier-Mache Press, 1992.

In stories, poems, and personal recollections, women of various ages talk about the choices they've made. Some pieces share lessons learned, others raise questions still not answered. These pieces have the cozy feel of a kitchen conversation.
Advanced new reader/adult collection.

———. *The Tie That Binds: A Collection of Writing About Fathers and Daughters, Mothers and Sons.* Watsonville, CA: Papier-Mache Press, 1992.

The relationship between a parent and child of the opposite sex is examined in this collection. Writers at both ends of this life-long union recall its joys and sorrows.
Intermediate new reader/adult collection.

———. *When I Am an Old Woman I Shall Wear Purple.* Watsonville, CA: Papier-Mache Press, 1991.

Writers talk frankly about growing and being old.
Advanced new reader/adult collection.

Mazer, Anne, ed. *Going Where I'm Coming From: Memoirs of American Youth.* New York: Persea Books, 1995.

The writers in this collection recall incidents and experiences from their growing up that helped define their sense of home, identity, and purpose. The range of settings, circumstances, and cultures is wide, but the common theme of finding one's own place connects the stories to each other as well as to readers from all backgrounds.
Intermediate new reader/young adult collection.

Michelson, Maureen R., ed. *Women & Work: In Their Own Words.* Troutdale, OR: New Sage Press, 1994.

The subject of women's work remains crucial in our society's ongoing

discussion of economics, opportunity, and quality of life. In this book, more than fifty women speak about their jobs which range from the traditional to the unusual. Pictures accompany all the interviews, but here the words predominate, unlike Betty Medsger's *Women at Work*, reviewed in Chapter 1, where pictures tell the story.
Intermediate new reader/adult collection.

Mullane, Deirdre, ed. *Crossing the Danger Water: 300 Years of African American Writing.* New York: Doubleday, 1993.

As much a history of blacks in America as it is a collection of writings by and about them, this comprehensive anthology includes letters, speeches, newspaper accounts, fiction, memoirs, poetry, and songs. Beginning with an early slave narrative and ending with the Senate testimony of Congresswoman Maxine Waters regarding the Los Angeles riots, this collection offers a rich diversity of form and voice from which teachers can select readings to suit a range of students as well as interests.
Intermediate-advanced new reader/adult collection.

Nauen, Elinor, ed. *Diamonds Are a Girl's Best Friend: Women Writers on Baseball.* Boston: Faber and Faber, 1993.

Women who love baseball and women who don't offer their particular views of the American sport. Poetry, family reminiscences, and essays all present an original "take" on this mostly male sport.
Intermediate-advanced new reader/adult collection.

O'Kelley, Mattie Lou. *From the Hills of Georgia: An Autobiography in Paintings.* Boston: Little, Brown & Co., 1983.

Each page of this autobiography presents a painting and a verbal remembrance of a specific event in O'Kelley's childhood. The text is simple but evocative; the paintings are richly-colored and detailed in a style that is reminiscent of story quilts or mosaic tile. Together, the words and paintings create a lyrical portrait of life in rural Georgia in the early twentieth century.
Intermediate new reader/children's collection.

Ortiz-Cofer, Judith. *Latin Deli.* Athens, GA: University of Georgia Press, 1993.

These autobiographical essays and poems look back on an American girlhood affected at every turn by questions of class, race, gender, and culture. The daughter of Puerto Rican parents, Ortiz-Cofer conveys the conflict of identity she feels when balancing visits to her parents' island homeland with life in "el building," the New Jersey apartment house in which she confronts the particular difficulties of growing up in urban America. An earlier collection, *Silent Dancing: A Partial Remembrance of a Puerto Rican Childhood,* is also available.
Advanced new reader/adult collection.

Paley, Grace. *Long Walks and Intimate Talks.* Illustrated by Vera B. Williams. New York: The Feminist Press at the City University of New York, 1991.

The first in a series called Women and Peace, this book is a protest against all forms of oppression and a celebration of the day which, as Paley says, "is its own reason for peace." Paley's "intimate talks" are stories that read like conversations or oral histories, discussing the important issues of the day by examining their effects on the lives of ordinary people. Vera B. Williams, known for her illustrations of children's books, illustrates Paley's stories with a mixture of whimsy and bold color that enhances the conversational, kitchen-table tone of the book.
Advanced new reader/adult collection.

Peet, Bill. *Bill Peet: An Autobiography.* Boston: Houghton Mifflin Co., 1989.

An artist who worked for many years in the Disney studios creating such characters as Dumbo the Elephant, Bill Peet talks about his early interest in drawing, his time in the army, his struggle with rejection, and his ultimate success in creating animated films. He also gives us a glimpse of life working for a demanding but creative genius like Walt Disney. Peet illustrates the book with his own early sketches, original story boards for various Disney films, and reproductions from the many children's books he has produced since leaving the Disney studios. This is an honest but affectionate memoir of one of America's most well-known and influential institutions.
Intermediate new reader/children's collection.

Powell, Kevin, and Res Baraka, eds. *In the Tradition: An Anthology of Young Black Writers.* New York: Harlem River Press, 1992.

Wishing to continue the literary tradition of the Harlem Renaissance and the Black Power Movement, the editors have collected the writings of several African Americans born in the 1960's or later. Their strong voices talk about hip-hop and other cultural developments of recent years, focusing in particular on how black Americans have shaped and been shaped by that culture.

Advanced new reader/adult collection.

Raspberry, William. *Looking Backward at Us.* Jackson, MS: University of Mississippi Press, 1991.

Saying that he is neither liberal nor conservative, columnist Raspberry offers his analysis of contemporary political and social events. He takes a common sense approach that connects the issues of the day to those who may not be able to shape them but who will certainly be affected by them.

Intermediate new reader/adult collection.

Ravitch, Diane, ed. *The American Reader: Words that Moved a Nation.* New York: HarperCollins Publishers, 1990.

In this informative collection of speeches, poems, songs, illustrations, and other historical documents, we find the well-known words of figures such as Abraham Lincoln alongside the writings of people whose names we may never have known but whose words and actions altered the flow of history. Chosen for their readability and historical significance, these selections review American history and literature from our earliest settlers into the 1980's. Most entries are short and can easily be read aloud.

Intermediate-advanced new reader/adult collection.

Reynolds, George P., ed. *Foxfire 10.* New York: Doubleday, 1992.

The Foxfire series began twenty years ago when teacher Eliot Wigginton sent his high school students out into their rural Georgia county to interview its residents and record their personal stories. The result of that first attempt was a nationally-acclaimed book and an educational movement that inspired thousands of other teachers and students. This tenth volume in the series is similar in format and quality to the others: a rich collection of history, folklore, pictures, personal narrative, recipes, and other literary artifacts of a way of life that remains vital in the hills of central Georgia.

Intermediate-advanced new reader/adult collection.

Rideau, Wilbert, and Ron Wikberg. *Life Sentences: Rage and Survival Behind Bars.* New York: Times Books, 1992.

Since 1975, Rideau has been Editor-in-chief of *The Angolite*, a magazine published at Angola, the Louisiana State Penitentiary, where he is also serving a life sentence. Wikberg was an Associate Editor of the magazine prior to his release. Both editors have won journalism and humanitarian awards for their reporting on life behind bars. The pieces in this collection speak of the hardship and violence of prison life, but they also offer compelling testimony to the power of books and the exchange of ideas they foster, even within the isolating confines of a prison cell.

Intermediate-advanced new reader/adult collection.

Rochman, Hazel, and Darlene Z. McCampbell, eds. *Who Do You Think You Are? Stories of Friends and Enemies.* Boston: Little, Brown and Co., 1993.

The editors ask, "Is it friend or enemy who exposes you to a dark corner inside yourself? Friends make you brave and help you know who you are." Although this collection is marketed for young adults coping with the conflicts of individual and group identity, the authors are all telling stories or looking back on their own lives from the vantage point of years of experience, both joyful and painful. This adult perspective, coupled with the quality of the writing, makes this an appropriate selection for adult new readers.

Advanced new reader/young adult collection.

Rollins, Charlemae Hill, ed. *Christmas Gif': An Anthology of Christmas Poems, Songs, and Stories.* Illustrated by Ashley Bryan. New York: William Morrow and Co., 1993.

Librarian Rollins first compiled this anthology in 1963 to offer children an opportunity to learn about Christmas traditions within the African American community, many of which had their roots in the days of slavery. Included here are stories passed down through the centuries as well as more contemporary memories, Negro spirituals sung at Christmas, poetry, and a final section of special Christmas recipes from "the Big House and the Cabin." In this beautiful new edition, illustrator Bryan's black-and-white linoleum prints convey the simplicity of the celebrations even as they hint of the complexity of the lives of the slaves and their descendants navigating in a white world.

Beginning-intermediate new reader/children's collection.

Rooney, Andy. *Pieces of My Mind.* New York: Atheneum, 1984.
As the quirky commentator for television's *60 Minutes,* Rooney looks at the mundane aspects of everyday life with a wry sense of humor. This collection comes from his newspaper columns, which have a similar ability to make us laugh at those frustrating moments we all must suffer from time to time.
Intermediate new reader/adult collection.

Rylant, Cynthia. *But I'll Be Back Again.* New York: Orchard Books, 1989.
Rylant is a prolific, award-winning author of books for children and young adults. In this slim autobiography, she recalls the circumstances in which she was raised by her extended family in Appalachian West Virginia. She speaks of her confusion about her father's absence and her mother's long exile at school, her teenage devotion to the Beatles, and her growing sense that a different world existed beyond the confines of the surrounding hills. She also speaks about dealing with awakening sexuality with a humor that only years of living, loving, and making one's share of mistakes can impart.
Intermediate-advanced new reader/children's collection.

Santiago, Esmeralda. *When I was Puerto Rican.* Reading, MA: Addison-Wesley, 1993.
As she recalls her experiences growing up, first in Puerto Rico then in an American barrio, Santiago reveals the strength she derived from her family while enduring the conflicts of a child of two cultures searching for a place to be at home.
Advanced new reader/adult collection.

Segal, Lore, and Leonard Baskin. *The Book of Adam to Moses.* New York: Alfred A. Knopf, 1987.
Stories from the first five books of the Bible are translated and presented with black and white illustrations. While the language has been simplified from the King James Version, it maintains much of the poetic beauty of the original.
Intermediate-advanced new reader/children's collection.

Sexton, Andrea W., and Alice L. Powers. *The Brooklyn Reader: 30 Writers Celebrate America's Favorite Borough.* New York: Harmony: Crown, 1994.

Whether it was their birthplace, their adopted hometown, or just another stop along the road, the borough of Brooklyn holds an influential place in the lives and work of many American writers. All the selections included here convey a strong sense of place, yet they also reflect the diversity of culture and style that is America as a whole. Two pieces of particular interest are Spike Lee's account of filming *Do the Right Thing* in Brooklyn and *The Poets in the Kitchen,* Paule Marshall's description of the West Indian women who gathered in her mother's kitchen and whose colorful and rhythmic conversations taught Marshall the art of storytelling.
Advanced new reader/adult collection.

Soto, Gary. *Lesser Evils: Ten Quartets.* Houston: Arte Publico Press, 1988.

Most frequently a young adult author, Soto wrote these autobiographical essays for an adult audience. Every aspect of life in this time and place—childhood and old age, love and sex, being a Mexican American in modern day California—becomes grist for Soto's writing mill. With a wry humor that he easily turns on himself, Soto's essays have a light touch, but the deeper questions are always lurking.
Intermediate new reader/adult collection.

———. *Living Up the Street.* New York: Dell Publishing, 1985.

Writing for young adults, Soto recalls his experiences growing up as a Mexican American in Fresno, California. Often left alone while his parents worked long hours, Soto and his brothers and sisters found their share of trouble as well as childhood fun. They also confronted doubts about self-worth as they learned to deal with the nasty taunts directed at their dark Mexican skin. As Soto tells his story, we recognize the pain, but we also feel the humor and joy that carry him through.
Advanced new reader/young adult collection.

———. *A Summer Life.* Hanover, NH: University Press of New England, 1990.

Soto mines his vivid memories of youth, telling stories about his adventures that readers will marvel at even as they hope their own children might never have such experiences. Soto's writing evokes the sights, sounds, and smells of a very particular time and place, but he also reveals feelings that any reader can identify with.
Advanced new reader/adult collection/young adult collection.

Staples, Brent. *Parallel Time: Growing Up in Black and White*. New York: Pantheon Books, 1994.

Staples was a young black male from a troubled neighborhood who succeeded, winning scholarships, getting a Ph.D. from the University of Chicago, and becoming an editor at *The New York Times*. Through all of his success, however, he was haunted by memories of his deteriorating Philadelphia neighborhood and his younger brother who couldn't escape its violent culture and was shot to death at the age of twenty-two. Staples's memoir is more intellectual in tone than Nathan McCall's *Makes Me Wanna Holler*. His narrative style is highly readable nonetheless, and would appeal to students able to read on their own and interested in the experience of someone who must contend with both the triumph and the pain of success.

Advanced new reader/adult collection.

Strickland, Dorothy S., ed. *Listen Children: An Anthology of Black Literature*. New York: Bantam, 1982.

An anthology of forms as well as authors, this collection includes poetry, speeches, folklore, excerpts from plays, and biography. The poems and some of the prose selections are very short and easy to read, and adults will enjoy them whether they read them for themselves or share them with children.

Beginning-intermediate new reader/children's collection.

Sullivan, Charles, ed. *Children of Promise: African-American Literature and Art for Young People*. New York: Harry N. Abrams, Inc., 1991.

In this collection, poetry, letters, speeches, essays, and folk songs are matched with paintings and photographs to tell the story of African Americans from the days of slavery to modern times. The thematic arrangement, featuring sections about slavery, emancipation, life in the South, the migration to northern cities, and the rise of Harlem as a cultural center, will add to the readers' knowledge of African American history. The beauty of the words and visual images will deepen understanding of the role that art in all its forms can play in the political and cultural life of a people and a nation.

Beginning-advanced new reader/children's collection.

————. *Here Is My Kingdom: Hispanic-American Literature and Art for Young People.* New York: Harry N. Abrams, 1994.

    Poetry, prose excerpts, paintings, and photographs present a rich and varied picture of Latino culture stretching from the classic Cervantes and Picasso to contemporary singer Gloria Estefan. The words and pictures are well matched, offering many windows into a world in which questions of home, identity, and crossing borders surface in everyday life.
Beginning-intermediate new reader/children's collection.

Terkel, Studs. *Race: How Blacks and Whites Think and Feel About the American Obession.* New York: Doubleday, 1992.

    Studs Terkel has built an extraordinary career talking to people about those aspects of life that really matter. From these interviews he has compiled several oral histories which provide a vivid and telling portrait of American life. In this book, Terkel opens a dialog on a vital but difficult topic: race. As in all his oral history books, excerpts from Terkel's interviews present a broad spectrum of background and opinion. Readers will find a few famous names along with the many ordinary folks encouraged to speak from their hearts. Terkel's other oral history titles include *Hard Times* (1970), a look back at the Great Depression, *Working* (1974), a discussion about how people work and how they feel about that work, *American Dreams: Lost and Found* (1980), stories of hope, failure, and survival, and *"The Good War"* (1984), collected memories of World War II.
Intermediate-advanced new reader/adult collection.

Thurber, James. *My Life and Hard Times.* New York: Harper & Row, 1933.

    Understanding the kind of subtle humor found in the writings of James Thurber requires readers to make inferences, see subtle connections, and generally apply critical thinking skills. These short and funny pieces provide a good introduction to the kind of writing that may appear on the classical literature section of the GED.
Advanced new reader/adult collection.

Turner, Faythe, ed. *Puerto Rican Writers at Home in the USA: An Anthology.* Seattle, WA: Open Hand Publishing, Inc, 1991.

    Divided loyalties—between island and mainland, between ancestral home and the place of present and future—is the theme that unites the poetry, essays, fiction, and newspaper columns in this fine collection. A stimulating

addition to any literacy classroom, as it will recall the search for a sense of place in a land to which we are all ultimately immigrants.
Intermediate-advanced new reader/adult collection.

VanderStaay, Steven, and Joseph Sorrentino. *Street Lives: An Oral History of Homeless Americans.* Philadephia: New Society Publishers, 1992.

VanderStaay interviewed hundreds of homeless people across America in shelters, halfway houses, and on the street. He mixes their narrative statements with his own brief and easy-to-read commentary on the particular individuals he met as well as the social conditions which create homelessness. The format of the book makes it easy to select excerpts for reading which can be followed by class discussions or writing assignments.
Intermediate new reader/adult collection.

Verhoeven, Rian, and Ruud van der Rol. *Anne Frank: Beyond the Diary: A Photographic Remembrance.* Introduction by Anna Quindlen. New York: Viking, 1993.

As Anna Quindlen says in her introduction, "We know Anne Frank the victim . . . this is Anne Frank the free, the living, the person who was able to write" the diary that moved the world. This newly-published companion to *The Diary of Anne Frank* introduces us to Anne and her family before they fled into hiding and provides additional information about the conditions of their life in the secret annex. Numerous family pictures, maps of the secret annex, excerpts from the diary, as well as accounts of life in Bergen-Belsen, the camp where Anne died, all serve to deepen our understanding of this young girl whose adolescent diary continues to remind us of the true realities of war.
Intermediate-advanced new reader/children's collection.

Wade-Gayles, Gloria. *Pushed Back to Strength: A Black Woman's Journey Home.* Boston: Beacon Press, 1993.

Now a professor of English at Spelman College, Wade-Gayles looks back to the rural Memphis environment she once longed to escape but now sees as the great source of her strength. It was from her mother, grandmother, and larger extended family and church community that she learned how to cope with her own personal triumphs and difficulties as well as confront a world vexed with racism and sexism. A poet as well as a teacher,

Wade-Gayles will draw even the inexperienced reader deeply into her inspiring story.
Intermediate new reader/adult collection.

Walker, Alice, ed. *I Love Myself When I Am Laughing . . . and Then Again When I Am Looking Mean and Impressive: A Zora Neale Hurston Reader.* New York: The Feminist Press at the City University of New York, 1979.

Virtually forgotten by the time of her death, Zora Neale Hurston has only recently been restored to an honored place among the writers of the Harlem Renaissance, and Alice Walker has been instrumental in righting this cultural wrong. This collection offers selected essays as well as excerpts from Hurston's longer works of fiction, autobiography, and folklore in which she vividly portrays the lives of black Americans in the early to middle twentieth century.
Advanced new reader/adult collection.

Washington, James Melvin. *Conversations with God: Two Centuries of Prayer by African Americans.* New York: HarperCollins, 1994.

Washington's definition of prayer as a "conversation with God" coupled with the depth of his knowledge of religious history have led him to include a fascinating range of material in this unusual collection of over 200 prayers, poems, hymns, and stories about the spiritual life. Although the introduction and notes make this a work of scholarly value, the prayers themselves are easily accessible to a wide range of readers. This book would be particularly useful to those literacy students who are initially motivated to learn to read by their desire to read the *Bible* and participate in other religious activities.
Beginning-intermediate new reader/adult collection.

Webb, Sheyann, and Rachel West Nelson. *Selma, Lord, Selma: Girlhood Memories of the Civil Rights Days.* As told to Frank Sikora. University, AL: University of Alabama Press, 1980.

As young girls, Webb and Nelson took part in the Civil Rights demonstrations in Selma, Alabama led by Dr. Martin Luther King. In this book, they look back on those days and tell of the fear and confusion they experienced, as well as the exhilaration that comes from participating in such a momentous event. Sikora interviews the women and presents their story

in their own words, adding background information only when necessary. With black and white photographs from the Selma of the 1960's, this is a stunning look back at a time of profound change in our society.
Intermediate new reader/adult collection.

White, Bailey. *Mama Makes Up Her Mind.* Reading, MA: Addison-Wesley Publishing Co., 1993.

Sometimes heard on National Public Radio, White charms us with folksy and funny details about her mother and various other characters living in their small Georgia town, revealing much about the nature of life in small towns all across America.
Intermediate new reader/adult collection.

Whitehead, Fred, ed. *Culture Wars.* Opposing Viewpoints Series. San Diego, CA: Greenhaven, 1994.

This book presents articles, newspaper columns, and book excerpts offering opposite opinions on issues such as the value of rap music and the relationship between government and the arts. Brief introductions to the topic and the writers precede each section and help the reader frame the issue under discussion. Intended for high school students, this book and others in the series would provide good source material for students learning to write the kind of opinion essays now required by the GED.
Advanced new reader/young adult collection.

Wideman, John Edgar. *Brothers and Keepers.* New York: Holt, Rinehart and Winston, 1984.

John Edgar Wideman overcame the difficulties of life in Homewood, a black section of Pittsburgh, to become a Rhodes Scholar, an English professor, and an accomplished novelist. From the same circumstances, his brother Robby, ten years his junior, grew into drugs, crime, and life imprisonment. In this memoir of two lives, Wideman weaves together family memories, his own story of struggle, doubt, and success, and the brutal facts of prison life recorded in Robby's vivid and poignant letters to create a compelling story of two brothers connected by blood and the searing questions of how their lives took such different tracks.
Advanced new reader/adult collection.

Wyse, Lois. *You Wouldn't Believe What My Grandchild Did . . .* Illustrated by Lilla Rogers. New York: Simon and Schuster, 1994.

Wyse writes a column for *Good Housekeeping* magazine in which she reports on the activities and charms of her own grandchildren and also shares stories sent to her by other grandparents. Any readers who enjoy being around children will be amused by these short, funny entries. They may also be inspired to tell some of their own tales. Similar collections published earlier include *Grandchildren are So Much Fun, I Should Have Had Them First* and *Funny, You Don't Look Like a Grandmother*.

Intermediate new reader/adult collection.

Yep, Laurence, ed. *American Dragons: Twenty-Five Asian American Voices*. New York: HarperCollins, 1993.

The universal search for "home" gives these stories, poems, and essays a poignancy that transcends any particular nationality. Collected for a middle and high school audience, these pieces recall childhood experiences, making them appealing to all who were once young.

Intermediate-advanced new reader/young adult collection.

Zall, P. M., ed. *Mark Twain Laughing: Humorous Anecdotes by and about Samuel Clemens*. Knoxville, TN: University of Tennessee Press, 1985.

Reading the stories and short quips of Mark Twain, whose wit not only makes us laugh but also pierces the polite facades of society, will help new readers learn to read beyond the surface to get to the deeper layers of meaning offered by good writing.

Intermediate-advanced new reader/adult collection.

Zamenova, Tatyana. *Teenage Refugees from Russia Speak Out*. In Their Own Voices series. New York: The Rosen Publishing Group, 1995.

Recent immigrants from Russia talk about the lives they left behind and the excitement and difficulty of adjusting to life in the United States. Their voices reveal an intriguing mix of the sophistication gained from their extraordinary circumstances and the innocence of the young looking to the future with optimism. This series includes books about teen refugees from China, Cambodia, and Nicaragua, among other places. They could lead to an interesting exchange of thoughts and experiences among students from various countries.

Intermediate-advanced new reader/children's collection.

Fiction

Alvarez, Julia. *How the Garcia Girls Lost Their Accents.* Chapel Hill, NC: Algonquin Books, 1991.
> Brief vignettes focus alternately on each of four sisters who flee with their family from the Trujillo regime in the Dominican Republic in the early 1960's. In contrast to their relatively privileged lives back home, the girls must learn to live in a cramped New York apartment and endure the suspicion and taunts directed at their accents and immigrant status. The lively narrative style and short chapters make this look at one immigrant family's story accessible to new readers.

Advanced new reader/adult collection.

———

Baldwin, James. *Go Tell It on the Mountain.* New York: Grosset & Dunlop, 1952.
> This classic work originally published in 1952 tells the story of three generations of a black family by painting a vivid picture of one Sunday among the congregation of a fundamentalist church in Harlem.

Intermediate-advanced new reader/adult collection/young adult collection.

———

———. *If Beale Street Could Talk.* New York: New American Library, 1974.
> Tish, nineteen and pregnant, and Fonny, twenty-two and in jail, discuss their problems and their dreams in this poignant love story. Poised on the brink of adulthood, these two must consider the consequences of the past and their many responsibilities to the future.

Advanced new reader/adult collection/young adult collection.

———

Berry, James. *Ajeemah and His Son.* New York: HarperCollins, 1992.
> Set in the slave trade of the nineteenth century, this book describes the circumstances that Ajeemah and his son Atu must endure after being kidnapped and sold as slaves in Jamaica. Separated from each other, they struggle to balance their desire to resist with their need to survive. This is a painful story, but a hopeful one as well.

Intermediate new reader/children's collection.

———

Cheuse, Alan, and Caroline Marshall. *Listening to Ourselves: More Stories from The Sound of Writing.* New York: Doubleday, 1994.

Called America's "short story magazine of the air," National Public Radio's program *The Sound of Writing* features contemporary short fiction read by actors. This collection of thirty-seven stories presents a diverse sampling of characters, experiences, and settings from the American landscape. Some stories are short enough to be read aloud within a class session; others would be appropriate for silent reading assignments. An earlier collection, *The Sound of Writing,* is also available.

Advanced new reader/adult collection.

Cisneros, Sandra. *The House on Mango Street.* New York: Random House, 1989.

In a series of brief, imagistic vignettes, the narrator tells the story of a young girl growing up in an Hispanic neighborhood in Chicago, facing the hard realities of life but maintaining an indomitable spirit. The chapters are brief, and each could stand alone as a story to be read aloud. The writing is evocative, lyrical, and poetic in its use of images and metaphors. Although such writing may present some difficulties to new readers, the literal meaning of these stories will be clear, and the power and beauty of Cisneros's language will challenge more able students.

Intermediate-advanced new reader/adult collection/young adult collection.

———. *Woman Hollering Creek.* New York: Random House, 1991.

Each of the brief stories in this collection creates a vivid picture of an individual or an event. Cisneros has an extraordinary ability to use a telling adjective or an apt metaphor to make her images crystal clear. While Cisneros's imagistic language and occasional use of unconventional sentence structure may make her stories difficult for some students to read on their own, a teacher reading them aloud can use phrasing and intonation to help students understand the meaning.

Advanced new reader/adult collection/young adult collection.

Collier, James Lincoln, and Christopher Collier. *My Brother Sam is Dead.* New York: Four Winds, 1974.

Set during the American Revolution, this novel tells the story of a family divided by differing loyalties. Like all good historical fiction, it helps readers

see the complexity and feel the human anguish of a war most of us know only as an impersonal event in our nation's history.
Advanced new reader/children's collection.

Dillon, Eilis. *Chidren of Bach*. New York: Charles Scribner's Sons, 1992.
All the characters, children and adults, are fully realized in their strengths and weaknesses in this gripping story of a group of refugees unsure of each other's company but bound together by their desperate need to escape the Nazis.
Advanced new reader/young adult collection.

Fleischman, Paul. *Bull Run*. New York: HarperCollins, 1993.
The format of this book is intriguing: eight voices from each side of this Civil War battle speak in alternating turns. Each chapter presents a different voice, and all are very brief. The interweaving of these stories creates a dramatic and intensely human picture of the excitement, impatience, and fear that precede the battle and the shock of its grisly effect. Students in a class might consider taking parts and reading the book as a play.
Intermediate-advanced new reader/children's collection/young adult collection.

Gaines, Ernest J. *The Autobiography of Miss Jane Pittman*. New York: The Dial Press, 1971.
Using the format of tape-recorded recollections, Gaines tells the story of Jane Pittman, a 110-year-old black woman, born into slavery and still living in the days of the 1960's Civil Rights movement. The basis for a popular video, this story of endurance and dignity personalizes history and would make an interesting companion to any factual accounts of the history of blacks in America.
Intermediate new reader/adult collection/young adult collection.

————. *A Lesson Before Dying*. New York: Alfred A. Knopf, 1993.
When Jefferson, a young black youth, is wrongly accused of murder, a court-appointed lawyer defends him by claiming he was too dumb to have planned such a crime. Sentenced to die despite his innocence and the lawyer's misguided defense, the youth is befriended by a teacher who sets out to prove the lawyer wrong. As he endures imprisonment and impend-

ing death, Jefferson gains a measure of dignity and self-esteem denied him in freedom. This is a powerful, though heart-rending, story.
Advanced new reader/adult collection/young adult collection.

Hamill, Pete. *The Gift*. New York: Random House, 1973.
The narrator recalls the Christmas twenty years earlier when he returned home to Brooklyn as a seventeen-year-old sailor. Amid Irish saloons, old songs, and the friends from his old gang, he loses his girl but finds his father. In an almost cinematic re-creation of a particular time and place, Hamill expresses the yearnings for identity, understanding, and love that we all feel throughout our lives.
Advanced new reader/adult collection.

————. *The Invisible City: A New York Sketchbook*. New York: Random House, 1980.
With a novelist's eye for the telling detail and a journalist's brevity, Hamill wrote these "sketches" to appear in his newspaper column. They offer glimpses of the lives of ordinary people who live in relative anonymity in cities like New York, but they also capture those moments that, though brief, can define a person or a relationship.
Intermediate-advanced new reader/adult collection.

Hamilton, Virginia, ed. *The People Could Fly: Black American Folk Tales*. Illustrated by Leo and Diane Dillon. New York: Alfred A. Knopf, 1985.
Noted children's author Hamilton has rewritten these African American folk tales for a new generation of readers. With a large layout and numerous illustrations, this book is perfect for adults to share with a child, but adults will enjoy reading it on their own as well.
Intermediate new reader/children's collection.

Harvey, Brett. *Immigrant Girl: Becky of Eldridge Street*. Illustrated by Deborah Kogan Ray. New York: Holiday House, 1987.
The time is 1910 and the setting the Lower East Side of New York where a young Jewish girl and her family have fled from the persecutions of Russia. The crowded living conditions, adjustment to a new language, taunts of other children, labor troubles, and dependence of the family on each

other are circumstances as common to present-day immigrants as they were to earlier generations.
Intermediate new reader/children's collection.

Hemingway, Ernest. *The Old Man and the Sea.* New York: Charles Scribner's Sons, 1952.
Hemingway's spare prose beautifully tells this now classic story of the lonely Cuban fisherman who struggles with a mighty fish.
Intermediate new reader/adult collection/young adult collection.

Hurston, Zora Neale. *Spunk: The Selected Short Stories of Zora Neale Hurston.* Berkeley, CA: Turtle Island Foundation, 1985.
Hurston's stories are rich in the cadences of the spoken word and create vivid pictures of the people and places she describes, whether they are based on her experiences growing up in the black town of Eatonville, Florida or mingling with the extraordinary talents that came together in the Harlem of the 1920's and 30's.
Advanced new reader/adult collection.

Johnson, Angela. *Toning the Sweep.* New York: Orchard Books, 1993.
"Toning the sweep" refers to an old folk custom of hitting a plow with a hammer to create a sound that will accompany the souls of the dead to their new life. In this story, Emily and her mother travel to the desert of California to help Emily's grandmother who is dying of cancer. Together, they must deal with the pain of impending loss and unresolved anger. In the process, they both learn a lesson in the art of dying as well as in the art of remembering.
Intermediate-advanced new reader/young adult collection.

Jones, Edward P. *Lost in the City.* New York: William Morrow & Co., 1992.
Washington, D.C. is the setting for these stories of life in urban America, but it is not the Washington that tourists see. It is the Washington of limits and losses, where residents face a daily struggle against the darker side of life. Jones tells their stories in an unaffected narrative style that will engage new readers.
Advanced new reader/adult collection.

Larsen, Nella. *The Intimation of Things Distant: The Collected Fiction of Nella Larsen*. New York: Doubleday, 1992.

In the 1920's, Larsen wrote two popular novels and several short stories, became the first black woman to win a Guggenheim fellowship, then abruptly stopped writing and worked as a nurse for the last thirty years of her life. This book revives the two novels and five stories. The stories are brief and good for reading aloud or recommending to students eager to read on their own. The longer novels are also accessible to advanced new readers. Larsen's main characters are black women who are poor but ambitious, struggling to balance their own strength against the burdens of race, gender, and class. The cultural details of the 1920's may differ from today's world, but the moral and personal dilemmas will be all too familiar.
Advanced new reader/adult collection.

Lester, Julius. *Long Journey Home: Stories from Black History*. New York: Dial Books, 1972.

The six stories collected in this book are based on the experiences of real people, all of whom were once slaves in the American South. They are suspenseful and moving, reminding us of the price some have paid for the sake of freedom. Lester has also written *This Strange New Feeling*, a collection of three stories adapted from slave narratives that describe daring escapes.
Advanced new reader/young adult collection.

Lipsyte, Robert. *The Contender*. New York: HarperCollins, 1967.

Frequently appearing on lists of best books for young adults and reluctant readers, this book tells the story of a seventeen-year-old high school drop-out who is faced with the reality of a bleak future: a dead-end job, no skills, and the awareness that many of his friends are tangled in the web of drugs and crime. At the local boxing club, he learns that it is the struggle—the effort to get back up when all seems lost—not the win, that makes the man.
Advanced new reader/young adult collection.

Lyons, Mary E. *Letters from a Slave Girl: The Story of Harriet Jacobs*. New York: Charles Scribner's Sons, 1992.

Harriet Jacobs was a slave who was taught to read and write by a kindly mistress, but when that mistress died Harriet fell victim to the cruelty and

sexual exploitation of other masters. She eventually fled north where, after several years in hiding from the fugitive slave law, an employer bought her freedom. The real Harriet Jacobs wrote an autobiography, one of the few such documents written by a woman. For this book, author Lyons has written a fictionalized account of Harriet's life in the form of letters that she might have written to dead and distant relatives. We see everything from Harriet's perspective, giving the reader a very personal view of the difficulties faced by this courageous woman.
Intermediate new reader/children's collection.

McKissack, Patricia C. *The Dark Thirty: Southern Tales of the Supernatural.* Illustrated by Brian Pinckney. New York: Alfred A. Knopf, 1992.

That half-hour before nightfall, when it is neither night nor day, was known in the author's family as "the dark thirty," a time when her grandmother would tell spine-chilling stories about people who had died but whose spirits still cast their influence over the events of the living. Black-and-white scratchboard illustrations add to the sense of mystery.
Intermediate new reader/children's collection.

Mazer, Anne, ed. *America Street: A Multicultural Anthology of Stories.* New York: Persea Books, 1993.

Writers from different backgrounds recall memories of growing up. Marketed for middle school level, the stories speak to kids because they are about childhood experiences, but they speak equally to adults because they remind us of our own memories of childhood. Called a "multicultural anthology," these stories convey the message that as different as our cultures and circumstances may be, we are all more alike than we are different. They succeed not simply because they are multicultural, but because they are good stories.
Advanced new reader/children's collection.

Meltzer, Milton. *Underground Man.* Scarsdale, NY: Bradbury Press, 1972.

Based on actual letters, court records, and newspaper accounts of the time that historian Meltzer had gathered for his nonfiction books about the days of slavery, this is a fictionalized account of a runaway slave who crosses back into slave territory to save others.
Advanced new reader/children's collection.

Myers, Walter Dean. *Somewhere in the Darkness*. New York: Scholastic, Inc., 1992.

A father who was imprisoned unexpectedly shows up at the house where his teenage son is living and takes him away with the promise of a new life. In their travels, the son must confront his own failures as well as his father's. The terse narrative style holds the reader's interest in this story of two generations struggling to reckon with the past in hopes of a better future. Myers has written many novels for young adults that will appeal to adult new readers. *Fallen Angels*, a story about Vietnam, is another good choice.

Intermediate-advanced new reader/young adult collection.

Naylor, Gloria. *The Women of Brewster Place*. New York: Viking, 1981.

The fictional Brewster Place could be many places in America: a poor neighborhood where people with few, if any, prospects end up. This book is really seven short stories linked by the common destiny of the seven different women who wind up in Brewster Place where they must face the realities of their lives that brought them there and the changes that are necessary to allow them to leave. The narrative style and format of seven individual stories make this book particularly appealing to adult new readers.

Intermediate-advanced new reader/adult collection.

Ortiz-Cofer, Judith. *An Island Like You*. New York: Orchard Books, 1995.

The main characters in these short stories are Puerto Rican teenagers who struggle to fit in—in the adult world that beckons them and in the mainland culture that tantalizes them. Rejecting the olds ways of their parents and "the island" they left behind, yet often rejected themselves by the mainstream world they seek to enter, these young people are alternately funny and irreverent, innocent and world-weary. Their stories will appeal to young adults facing similar dilemmas, but also to readers who still struggle to find their own place in a world that may be hostile or indifferent.

Advanced new reader/young adult collection.

Paulsen, Gary. *Nightjohn*. New York: Delacorte Press, 1993.

Nightjohn is a slave who had escaped to freedom, but returned to his former plantation in order to start a school to teach other slaves to read. Despite strict laws against such activity, the slaves still meet in the middle

of the night to have their lessons with Nightjohn. While the vivid descriptions of the cruel and humiliating punishment inflicted on the slaves may be hard for some readers to take, this brief, moving story reminds us all that learning leads to power and is a very political act.
Intermediate new reader/young adult collection.

Rylant, Cynthia. *I Had Seen Castles.* San Diego, CA: Harcourt Brace & Co., 1993.
As he nears seventy, a veteran of World War II recalls the year when he turned eighteen, fell passionately but briefly in love, and went off to war, consumed by the excitement of such a momentous event. Faced with the reality of fighting, he ponders many of the questions about the necessity of war that his girlfriend had raised. The events in this brief novel are those of the teenager, but the voice is that of the grown man, looking back with fondness and regret.
Intermediate-advanced new reader/young adult collection.

———. *A Kindness.* New York: Orchard Books, 1988.
A fifteen-year-old boy and his mother have been alone together for most of the boy's life, but their close relationship is threatened when the mother reveals that she is pregnant. Told alternately from the boy's and the mother's point of view, this is a story about love and the consequent responsibility that accompanies it.
Intermediate-advanced new reader/young adult collection.

Say, Allen. *The Inn-Keeper's Apprentice.* Boston: Houghton Mifflin Co., 1994.
Set in Tokyo in the days following World War II, this novel tells the story of a young boy who leaves home to apprentice himself to a master artist. Living on his own, he struggles to understand his parents' divorce, his own talents and interests, and the lure of the wider world. Based on the author's own experiences, this is a story of balancing the pain of leaving the past with the promise of new opportunities.
Advanced new reader/young adult collection.

Temple, Frances. *Grab Hands and Run.* New York: Orchard Books, 1993.
Before he disappeared amid the revolutionary turmoil of El Salvador, Jacinto tells his wife that if he doesn't come home one night, she is to gather

their two children, and "grab hands and run." This is the story of that flight, which takes the three to Canada. Although told in the voice of twelve-year-old Felipe, adult readers will respond to the fear, confusion, and courage of this family as they make their dangerous escape. This suspenseful story reads easily and offers much to spur discussion about the realities of revolution, repression, and the difficult choices some of us are forced to make.
Advanced new reader/young adult collection.

Walker, Alice. *The Color Purple.* New York: Harcourt Brace Jovanovich, 1982.
In this Pulitzer Prize-winning novel, young Celie, raped, abused, and married against her will, carries on an interior conversation through letters to her sister and to God. As she struggles to understand her place in the world around her, she finds spiritual peace in the bonds of love and friendship.
Advanced new reader/adult collection.

————. *To Hell with Dying.* Illustrated by Catherine Deeter. San Diego, CA: Harcourt, Brace, Jovanovich, 1988.
Recalling a story from her childhood, Walker tells of Mr. Sweet, an old man often on the verge of dying who could be revived by the attention she and her brother gave him. A powerful story of the passions, pain, and joy of life, it also reminds us of the gifts that the old can give the young, and what the young can give back in return. Beautiful illustrations, one per page, convey the story's emotional depth.
Intermediate new reader/children's collection.

Wolff, Virginia Euwer. *Make Lemonade.* New York: Scholastic, 1993.
The voice in this funny yet poignant novel is that of a fourteen-year-old girl who answers a babysitting ad so she can earn money for college, her ticket out of her deadend neighborhood, and finds herself working for a seventeen-year-old mother with two children, a shaky job, and no vision of a different future. As the two young women come to know and rely on each other, they also come to understand the world they live in and their own ability to cope with that world. Written in a kind of rollicking blank verse, this fast-reading novel will appeal to many adults who have felt powerless in the face of difficult circumstances.
Intermediate-advanced new reader/young adult collection.

Wright, Richard. *Rite of Passage.* New York: HarperCollins Publishers, 1994.
Though written in the 1940's, this book by the author of the classic novel *Native Son* was only recently discovered and published. It explores the psychological and sociological roots of violence in poverty and discrimination and in the process tells a gripping story in an easy-to-read style that will be accessible to new readers.
Intermediate new reader/adult collection.

Yep, Lawrence. *Hiroshima.* New York: Scholastic, 1995.
Fifty years after the United States dropped the atomic bomb on Hiroshima, controversy about this act of war continues. Yep describes the event and its aftermath through the story of a young girl on her way to school when the bomb is dropped. He also explains the physics of the bomb and the radiation it produces. Given the enormity of the subject, this slim volume with a particular point of view should not stand alone, but it can serve as a useful introduction that can be supplemented with other readings, both fiction and non-fiction, about the people and events of World War II.
Intermediate new reader/children's collection.

Chapter 4

A World of Information: Nonfiction Books to Help New Readers Learn What They Want and Need to Know

Hardly a day goes by without some reminder that we live in the Information Age, and that a mind-numbing cornucopia of facts and opportunities that could affect every aspect of our lives exists just beyond our fingertips. These are indeed exciting times, but they are somewhat daunting as well. We must keep up not only with what it is possible to know but also with the constantly changing technology that allows us access to all this information.

If an entire society, including the most educated among us, is challenged by the extraordinary quantity of information that is available as well as the fundamental and profound changes in the way we learn and receive it, where does this leave adult literacy students? They still lack mastery of the most basic information retrieval skill, the ability to read effectively. What is perhaps even more problematic, literacy students, because of their poor reading skills, missed much of the content that was presented to them through the printed word in history, social studies, science, civics, and other classes. As a result, they lack much of the background knowledge in which current information is rooted, as well as the habit of referring to and applying that knowledge to the problems and situations of their everyday lives. As a result, adult literacy students are among the most vulnerable citizens in this Information Age, surrounded by an ever-increasing flood of information, but increasingly limited in their ability to understand and apply it.

Information matters very much to literacy students. They are motivated to enter reading programs at least in part because they need information to improve their lives. They need to be able to read the directions on the asthma medication they must give to their child, or read the government pamphlet that explains how they can obtain the Social Security benefits they are eligible for. They want to be able to read the newspaper and discuss the issues of the day with their friends and coworkers.

In any public library, you will find books that can help adult literacy students become more skilled workers, wiser consumers, better parents, and more informed citizens. Some of these books will be in the adult section of the library, but many will come from the children's collection, which contains numerous nonfiction books appealing to adults, whether they are new or experienced readers. These books address their subjects in a direct, straightforward narrative intended to convey information accurately but simply. They make extensive and appealing use of photographs, illustrations, and graphic material. They are well-researched and written in a style that is not condescending and never identifies children as its target audience. Of course, these books will also be written at many different reading levels, but by using a variation of the language experience technique (discussed in Chapter 1) called the information reading technique, tutors can make any book that is of interest to students accessible, whatever their reading ability. This technique can be used with individual students or in a classroom setting. It can also be applied to any material—job orders, government pamphlets, product instructions, etc.—that students may bring to class. This is how it works:

The Information Reading Technique

1. Choose some material of interest to your students. It may be of personal importance, such as a job order or instructions for using a piece of kitchen equipment, or a subject of interest like gardening or places to take children when visiting a particular city.
2. Read the material to the students a paragraph or brief section at a time. At appropriate intervals, stop to discuss the information to make sure the students understand it.
3. As the students explain what's been read to that point, write their version of the information, using their words, but suggesting changes if necessary to ensure accuracy.
4. Read the rewritten version aloud, then ask a student to read it, with your assistance if necessary.
5. Once the students have mastered reading their own version of the information, use the words and phrases of that version to develop word recognition and critical thinking activities.

Consider also a few variations on this technique to help students develop further skills:

—Listening for details: Read a paragraph or two aloud to the students, then ask them to recall specific details you've read. This can help students improve their listening skills.

—Silent reading for information: Find books or other materials at students' reading levels that contain information important to them. Give them some questions, then ask them to skim the text on their own to find the answers to those questions or have them read first then ask questions based on the reading. Have them respond either orally or in writing.

—Reading charts, graphs, and diagrams: Give students information presented in graphic form such as bus routes and schedules, box scores from the daily paper, a weather map, or a map of the local mall, then ask them to find the answers to questions you pose.

Using the information reading technique, your and your students will generate reading material that teaches them something they want or need to know even as it teaches them to learn to read the words on the page. In the process of discussing the information with the students, you will help them understand, retain, and apply that information to their everyday lives.

A Sampling of Nonfiction Books

Once again, some of these books will be in the adult section of the library, but many of them will come from the children's collection. Let's look at a few examples of nonfiction books appropriate for literacy students. Library books can help students understand the events and issues that are topics of discussion in newspapers and on television news programs. For example, we have recently marked several fiftieth anniversaries of events related to World War II, one of the defining events of this century. There are numerous books in the children's section of the library that will help explain this period of history to adult new readers. Two examples are R. Conrad Stein's *The Manhattan Project*, part of the Cornerstones of Freedom series published by Childrens Press, which describes the secret project to build an atomic bomb, and Sylvia Whitman's *V is for Victory: The American Home Front During WWII*, which examines the various ways the war affected life in America.

The future of Social Security is another issue currently being discussed and shaped in Congress, newspapers, and public debates. It is an issue which will profoundly affect all of us but none more so than those citizens who must depend on a government retirement program because they have limited access to private ones. To help students understand this issue teachers could introduce articles from the daily newspaper in conjunction with a book such as Milton Meltzer's *Brother Can You Spare a Dime?* an account of the Great Depression, which gave rise to Social Security, as seen through the lives of the people who lived it. Meltzer makes extensive use of primary documents such as letters, journal entries, and newspaper accounts of the day to help modern readers understand this time from the perspective of those who lived and suffered through it.

Many of the nonfiction books in the children's collection are published in series intended to introduce readers at various skill levels to particular events and topics in history, science, the arts, and popular culture. Childrens Press, for example, publishes several series at different reading levels in the areas of history, biography, and science. The Cornerstones of Freedom series presents information about specific incidents or issues of American history. It is aimed at middle school children and will be appropriate for intermediate new readers. The *Picture-Story Biographies* series introduces younger readers or beginning new readers to contemporary and historical figures in sports, politics, and the arts. *Barbara Bush: First Lady of Literacy* is a representative title listed in the bibliography. Chelsea House Publishers produces several series of biographies that chronicle the lives and accomplishments of Black Americans of Achievement, Hispanic Americans of Achievement, and Women of Achievement. Their biography of photographer, film maker, and poet Gordon Parks is a good example of this series which is aimed at junior and senior high school students and delves more deeply into the experiences and influences that shaped the lives of their subjects. These books are perfect for adults at the advanced new reader level.

Some of the best nonfiction books are not in a series, but single titles written by gifted writers who combine their innate curiosity about people, places, or events with diligent research and a writer's sense of a good story to make their particular subjects come alive for young readers. Several of these authors appear more than once in this bibliography. Russell Freedman is one such author. His *Eleanor Roosevelt: A Life of Discovery* traces the fascinating story of the shy and awkward young girl who became known as "The First Lady of the World." James Haskins has written several books detailing specific aspects of the Civil Rights movement, and Milton Meltzer, mentioned above as the author of *Brother Can You Spare a Dime?* has also written about topics as diverse as the Civil War and the lure of gold.

Photo essays that explore particular events or places also appear in this bibliography, and two names deserve particular mention. Brent Ashabranner has produced several such books including *Still a Nation of Immigrants*, one of several titles he has produced about immigration, and *Always to Remember:*

The Story of the Vietnam Veterans Memorial, a beautiful account of the planning, building, and impact of what has become Washington's most-visited monument. Writer and photographer Raymond Bial's book *The Underground Railroad* is a moving evocation of the courage of slaves who risked everything to reach freedom and whites who helped to shelter and protect them on their perilous journey

The bibliography at the end of this chapter is divided into five categories. The **History, Biography, and Geography** section lists titles that will help new readers understand the events and people that gave birth to our modern world as well as take a closer look at issues that concern us today. **The Physical World** includes titles in health, science, and nature which address our questions about the world we live in. Titles in **Art and Music** introduce new readers to the lives and works of those who use their creative imagination to question and depict their view of our world. **Sports and Recreation** includes biographies of athletes as well as illustrated histories of sports and teams. Finally, **Cooking and Crafts** suggests titles that offer new readers a chance to read about a hobby or other activity in which they already have some skill or have always wanted to try. Books in this section also offer new readers the chance to develop the skill of reading information from charts, graphs, diagrams, and other graphic forms of information.

The books suggested in the bibliography are but a sample of the many titles that will teach adult literacy students things they want or need to know; books that can help them understand how past events affect their current lives; books that will help them improve their health and that of their families; books that will give them the knowledge they need to become active participants in the life of their communities; and books that will simply add to their enjoyment of life. Many more possibilities are waiting to be discovered at your local public library.

A Note to Librarians

Ask the children's librarians to look for nonfiction titles that will appeal to adults. If there are multiple copies available, add one to the new readers collection. Sensitize the children's librarians to consider use with adults when buying new titles, so they can purchase additional copies or share that information with adult librarians. In displays of books centered on a particular subject and intended to interest adults, add some titles from the children's collection. Identify "how-to" manuals in the adult collection that have particularly clear and uncluttered diagrams and a minimum of verbal explanation, then consider labelling them for new reader use or placing additional copies in the new readers collection. Sponsor lectures and discussions on issues important to your community and invite students and teachers from the literacy programs as well as the general public. Offer workshops on the new information technology to "new users." Make these sessions cooperative ventures with literacy programs to increase familiarity with and access to the new technology for literacy students. Consider seeking grant opportunities to fund equipment as well as training in the use of the equipment.

A Note to Literacy Teachers

Help students explore the issues being discussed in general society by displaying newspaper and magazine articles along with related library books in classrooms, tutoring rooms, and general reception areas. If you have a central building where tutors and students meet, purchase multiple subscriptions to newspapers and magazines so they are available for students and tutors to use on the spur of the moment and just for general browsing. Sponsor community information events, in cooperation with the library and other local agencies, at which speakers present information and respond to audience questions and opinions. Within a literacy program, sponsor debates on issues of importance to the community. Have students volunteer to take different sides of the issue and help them prepare by finding books and other resources in the library. Encourage students to write letters to the editor of their local newspaper about issues that affect them. Help them prepare those letters by conducting background research first. Whenever possible, connect the needs and interests of their lives, whether they be related to their jobs, families, community, or leisure time, with the habit of reading for further information as well as for enjoyment.

Bibliography

History, Biography, and Geography

Aaseng, Nathan. *Navajo Code Talkers.* New York: Walker & Co., 1992.
This book tells the fascinating but little-known story of the Navajo Indians who developed a code based on their native language that the United States Armed Forces used to great advantage during World War II. Neither the Germans nor the Japanese ever broke the code, and historians believe it was responsible for saving many lives and winning many battles. *Intermediate-advanced new reader/children's collection.*

Aikens, Maggie. *Kerry, a Teenage Mother.* Photographs by Rob Levine. Minneapolis, MN: Lerner Publications Co., 1994.

Although Kerry has a supportive family to help her, she still struggles to balance her roles as mother of a fifteen-month-old daughter and student trying to better her chances for a good job. A discussion of the social ramifications of teens caring for babies is interwoven with pictures and text describing a typical day for Kerry. This is a sobering account of the reality of teenage motherhood.

Intermediate new reader/children's collection.

Anderson, Joan. *Earth Keepers.* Photographs by George Ancona. San Diego, CA: Harcourt Brace & Co., 1993.

Three individuals whose lives are dedicated to environmental projects are profiled in this book. One works with the Clearwater project to restore the Hudson River, another creates beautiful gardens in desolate inner-city neighborhoods, and the third is a wildlife biologist studying the black bears of Minnesota. These inspiring stories about individuals who choose to make a difference in their community might spur students to investigate the environmental problems in their own neighborhood. Anderson and Ancona have also teamed up to produce *The American Family Farm,* a pictorial essay exploring a way of life that has helped shape the face of America.

Intermediate new reader/children's collection.

Archer, Jules. *They Had a Dream: The Civil Rights Struggle from Frederick Douglass to Marcus Garvey to Martin Luther King and Malcolm X.* New York: Viking, 1993.

In Archer's view, these four men were the major figures in the Civil Rights movement of the last 150 years, each leading a different phase of that movement. He begins the book with a brief historical overview and ends it with a discussion of present and future conditions. Each of the four leaders is profiled separately in this very readable collective biography.

Advanced new reader/children's collection.

Ashabranner, Brent. *Always to Remember: The Story of the Vietnam Veterans Memorial.* Photographs by Jennifer Ashabranner. New York: Dodd, Mead, & Co., 1988.

In the beginning, questions about the design and purpose of the Vietnam Veterans Memorial generated much controversy, just as the war itself had

done. This thoughtful book describes how the memorial came to be. It profiles the man whose idea it was to build the memorial and whose tenacious struggle in the face of controversy helped to see the project to completion, and the young Asian American architecture student whose design for the memorial was selected in a national competition. It also gives a brief history of the war itself and its divisive effect on the nation. Beautiful photographs and statements from some of the Memorial's thousands of visitors tell of its emotional impact. Ashabranner and his daughter Jennifer have also collaborated on a similar book, *A Memorial for Mr. Lincoln.*
Intermediate new reader/children's collection.

———. *Still a Nation of Immigrants.* Photographs by Jennifer Ashabranner. New York: Cobblehill Books/Dutton, 1993.

Immigration has been a major force in America's history, perhaps never more so than it is now. In this book, Ashabranner focuses on current trends in immigration from Latin America, Asia, and the Middle East, although he also reviews previous patterns and conditions of immigration as well. Chapters discuss important and sometimes controversial questions such as why immigrants come, how they view their new home, and whether or not they displace current citizens in the job market. Several personal profiles give a human face to this important social issue. This title updates Ashabranner's earlier book, *The New Americans: Changing Patterns in U.S. Immigration.*
Intermediate-advanced new reader/children's collection.

Atkin, S. Beth, ed. *Voices from the Fields: Children of Migrant Farm Workers Tell Their Stories.* Boston: Little, Brown/Joy Street, 1993.

Although these are the voices of children, there is a seriousness and maturity about them that makes this book appealing to adults. In revealing interviews, the children, ranging in age from eight to eighteen, describe their lives within migrant farm families. Sometimes the children themselves are the field workers, sometimes they are the observers, seeing the consequences of a life of hard labor on their parents. The strength of family members working together to improve their lives is a major theme that shines through all these interviews, as well as the parents' hope that through education their children will find a better life.
Intermediate new reader/children's collection.

Behrens, June. *Barbara Bush: First Lady of Literacy.* Picture-Story Biographies series. Chicago: Childrens Press, 1990.

This brief biography focuses on Barbara Bush's role in the White House where she served, in her own words, as "everybody's grandmother." A devoted wife, mother, and family advocate, Mrs. Bush is also portrayed as strong-minded and independent, choosing the issues on which she wanted to have a voice of her own. Her commitment to literacy is particularly highlighted. The Picture-Story Biographies series offers short books intended to introduce children to many of the famous names of our history and present culture. The writing style and good quality pictures make them appropriate for new readers as well. A few of the many other people covered in this series include Sandra Day O'Connor, Barbara Jordan, and Pope John Paul II.

Beginning-intermediate new reader/children's collection.

Berck, Judith. *No Place to Be: Voices of Homeless Children.* Foreword by Robert Coles. Boston: Houghton Mifflin Co., 1992.

Statements from children describing their experience of being homeless are interwoven with facts and the author's opinions about the problem of homelessness. Berck discusses how homelessness starts, what it does to families and individuals, and what it is like to live on the streets from day to day. The words of the children provide a compelling perspective on this social problem, and, as Robert Coles says in his foreword, they "give us [adults] pause. What kind of world are we content to let be? Or what kind of world . . . might we try to establish?" Many black-and-white photographs add to the somber message.

Intermediate new reader/children's collection.

Bernotas, Bob. *Spike Lee: Filmmaker.* People to Know series. Springfield, NJ: Enslow Publishers, Inc., 1993.

In his films, Spike Lee focuses on social issues that he wants his audiences to confront. Accordingly, this biography focuses not on Lee's personal life but on his films, how they were made and the controversy they aroused. As he says of his art, "I want to be remembered for honest, true portrayals of African Americans and for bringing our great richness to the screen."

Advanced new reader/children's collection.

Berry, Skip. *Gordon Parks*. Black Americans of Achievement series. New York: Chelsea House Publishers, 1991.

In his early years, Parks struggled to overcome poverty, racism, and his own deeply-rooted anger. He showed a knack for photography and was hired by the Farm Security Administration to document the ravages of the Great Depression on America's rural community. He became a photographer for *Life* magazine, a movie director, an acclaimed poet, and a distinguished American artist. His is a fascinating story of one man's triumph over adversity. The Black Americans of Achievement series from Chelsea House presents in-depth accounts of the lives of black artists, sports figures, and political leaders. Intended for middle and high school students, these books go beyond the basic facts of the subject's life and explore the complexities of the individual's motivation, influences, and life experiences.
Intermediate-advanced new reader/children's collection.

Bial, Raymond. *The Underground Railroad*. Boston: Houghton Mifflin Co., 1995.

Bial visited several sites along the routes that were once part of the Underground Railroad and photographed places where runaway slaves traveled by night and hid by day. There are crossing sites along the Ohio and other rivers, dense forest groves, safe houses in Ohio and Indiana with tunnels and attics, false-bottomed carts and hidden doorways. Bial also examined written records in an effort to imagine the loneliness, hardship, and danger that the runaways encountered on their journey to freedom. There are no faces in any of these photographs, and their absence underscores the sense of secrecy and mystery that surrounded the dangerous enterprise of escape. Reproductions of some of the handbills of the day advertising bounties for captured runaways remind us of the pervasive sense of danger and suspicion. This book is a beautiful example of how evocative pictures combined with a thoughtful, well-written text can teach a powerful history lesson. Bial has produced other photographic histories such as *Shaker Home* and *Amish Home*.
Intermediate new reader/children's collection.

Blake, Arthur. *The Scopes Trial: Defending the Right to Teach*. Spotlight on American History series. Brookfield, CT: Millbrook, 1994.

The debate between those who believed Darwin's theory of evolution and those who believed the Biblical account of creation was the basis for the famous Scopes Trial in Tennessee in 1925, and it remains a contested issue today. This engaging book explains the beliefs of both sides and introduces the two powerful legal minds that clashed in this historical trial: Clarence Darrow and William Jennings Bryan. It also brings the story into the present by outlining the current debate. Among the other titles in this series that highlights important events in American history are *Prohibition: America Makes Alcohol Illegal* and *The Dust Bowl: Disaster on the Plains*. *Intermediate-advanced new reader/children's collection.*

Brandenburg, Jim. *Sand and Fog: Adventures in Southern Africa*. New York: Walker & Co., 1994.

Brandenburg originally took these photographs while on assignment for *National Geographic* magazine in Namibia in southwest Africa. They show a land that is mostly desert and might seem barren to Western eyes. Seeing it through Brandenburg's camera, however, and reading his descriptions of the context in which he took his pictures, we sense the mystery and the majesty of this unusual landscape.
Intermediate new reader/children's collection.

Cocke, William. *A Historical Album of Virginia*. Historical Albums series. Brookfield, CT: The Millbrook Press, 1995.

In this series, the history and geography of each state are covered from the earliest known Native American communities through European explorations to current issues and events. The books are amply illustrated with photographs, archival documents, and maps, and they include a time line and reference guide to basic facts and statistics. So far, about twenty states have been profiled.
Intermediate-advanced new reader/children's collection.

Fisher, Leonard Everett. *Tracks Across America: The Story of the American Railroad 1825-1900*. New York: Holiday House, 1992.

The story of the building of the American railroad in the nineteenth century has always elicited romantic notions about the opening of a vast land to settlers and explorers. While readers will find evidence of that excitement here, they will also find a discussion of the darker side of the story: the resistance of the Indians, the greed of railroad tycoons, the exploitation of workers, and the danger of train robbery. To create this very browsable book, Fisher used primary sources such as quotes from railroad workers

and politicians of the time, letters, newspaper clippings, and numerous archival photographs.
Intermediate new reader/children's collection.

Ford, Barbara. *St. Louis.* A Downtown America Book series. Minneapolis, MN: Dillon Press, Inc., 1989.

Downtown America Books profile major American cities. They briefly review the city's history and describe those features which give the city its own particular character. Large color photographs and an attractive layout make the books in this series appealing to new readers. Maps, an index, and a list of places to visit, with addresses and phone numbers, make the books informative and good reading practice for new readers who must learn to read information in forms other than narrative text.
Beginning-intermediate new reader/children's collection.

Fradin, Dennis B. *Maryland.* From Sea to Shining Sea series. Chicago: Childrens Press, 1994.

This series offers books on every state in the Union. Each book includes an overview of the state's early history, a description of its geographical highlights, a discussion of current social conditions, facts about major cities, and brief statements about the state's famous citizens. Numerous color photographs and an attractive layout make this and other titles in the series highly suitable for new readers, even those at early levels. Books from this series may also introduce ESOL students to other parts of the country.
Beginning-intermediate new reader/children's collection.

Freedman, Russell. *Eleanor Roosevelt: A Life of Discovery.* New York: Clarion Books, 1993.

As a child, Eleanor Roosevelt was considered even by herself, to be an awkward and shy "ugly duckling," yet she became one of the most admired and influential women in American history. Biographer Freedman skillfully interweaves the threads of her story: her lonely childhood and marriage to her cousin Franklin; the difficulties of that marriage which caused Eleanor private pain but also enabled her to grow in confidence and independence as she became the eyes, ears, and legs of her charismatic but crippled husband; and the climactic events of the twentieth century that President Roosevelt had to address during his twelve years in office. With help from many photographs, this biography brings that time and the in-

dividuals who shaped it to life. Freedman has also written the Newbery award-winning *Lincoln: A Photobiography*.
Intermediate-advanced new reader/children's collection.

————. *An Indian Winter*. Illustrations by Karl Bodmer. New York: Holiday House, 1992.

In the 1830's, German Prince Maximilian, accompanied by the Swiss painter Karl Bodmer, traveled into what is now North Dakota and lived for some time among the Indians there. Travelling as curious observers without intent to conquer or convert the natives they befriended, Maximilian kept a journal of his experiences and Bodmer made many sketches and paintings. Author Freedman used Maximilian's journal to write the text of this account of the Indian life in winter, and the book is illustrated with Bodmer's paintings. It is an outsider's view, but one untainted by the complicated history of American white men settling already occupied territory. Freedman has written two other books about the American west that are suitable for new readers: *Buffalo Hunt*, a description of the relationship between the Great Plains Indians and the buffalo they hunted and worshipped, illustrated by the paintings of Bodmer and other artists who traveled west to record images of Indian life, and *Cowboys of the Wild West*, a depiction of the cowboy life, illustrated with archival photographs, maps, and drawings.
Intermediate new reader/children's collection.

————. *Kids at Work: Lewis Hine and the Crusade against Child Labor*. Photographs by Lewis Hine. New York: Clarion Books, 1994.

There are two storytellers at work in this biography of reform-minded photographer Lewis Hine. Freedman chronicles the life and work of Hine, who believed in the power of photography to bring about social change. The book is illustrated with Hine's documentary photographs which tell their own compelling story about young children deprived of the joys and protection of childhood and forced to work long hours in the mines and factories of industrial America. These photographs played a major role in bringing about laws that ended that practice. Together, words and pictures present a stirring example of how a committed individual can affect his society.
Intermediate new reader/children's collection.

Gold, Susan Dudley. *Roe v. Wade (1973): Abortion.* Supreme Court Decisions series. New York: Twenty-First Century Books, 1994.

Although the Supreme Court decision assuring a constitutional right to abortion is more than twenty years old, the issue remains controversial and deeply divisive. Gold traces the case from its origin in Texas to the written opinions of the Supreme Court Justices to the debate that still rages today. The Supreme Court Decisions series provides background information about decisions that have fundamentally changed American life. Decisions about book banning and school desegregation are two of the other topics covered in this series.

Intermediate-advanced new reader/children's collection.

Graff, Nancy Price. *The Strength of the Hills: A Portrait of a Family Farm.* Photographs by Richard Howard. Boston: Little, Brown & Co., 1989.

The hard work and uncertainty, as well as the laughter and the collective sense of accomplishment that this family feels are evident from the words and pictures in this evocative portrait of life on a small family farm in Vermont. This book also raises intriguing questions about a way of life in which children assume considerable responsibility for the family's success.

Intermediate new reader/children's collection.

———. *Where the River Runs: A Portrait of a Refugee Family.* Photographs by Richard Howard. Boston: Little, Brown & Co., 1993.

Graff profiles a Cambodian family living in Boston and gives us a personal view of the many dimensions of immigrant life as it affects three generations. The school-aged children learn English quickly, becoming the family's primary interpreters, but they also must learn to cope with stares and taunts when they leave their neighborhood. Their mother works and studies hard to improve at her job and become a citizen. The grandmother, who will not learn English because she remembers too many friends who were killed for knowing English in Cambodia, becomes the family cook and gardener as well as its link to a culture they want to remember even as they move ever more deeply into the American way of life.

Intermediate new reader/children's collection.

Hamilton, Virginia. *Many Thousand Gone: African Americans from Slavery to Freedom.* Illustrated by Leo and Diane Dillon. New York: Alfred A. Knopf, 1993.

In this unusual collection, Hamilton offers brief slave narratives, some from famous names like Frederick Douglass and Sojourner Truth, others from obscure men and women who were "running-aways." All speak with heartfelt eloquence about the powerful lure of freedom that enabled them to face the dangers of escape. The format is particularly appealing because each narrative is brief enough to read aloud in one class, and the moving stories will elicit much reaction.

Intermediate new reader/children's collection.

Harrison, Barbara, and Daniel Terris. *A Twilight Struggle: The Life of John Fitzgerald Kennedy.* New York: Lothrop, Lee & Shepard Books, 1992.

Taking a balanced, objective look at the life of John F. Kennedy, Harrison and Terris review the influence of his family life and school experiences and discuss his achievements as well as his disappointments. In this book, Kennedy is neither hero nor tabloid legend but a complex human being who lived an extraordinary life that continues to affect many of his "fellow Americans."

Advanced new reader/children's collection.

Haskins, James. *The Cotton Club: A Pictorial and Social History of the Most Famous Symbol of the Jazz Era.* New York: Random House, 1977.

In the years between the wars, Harlem was a place of thriving artistic creativity, and the Cotton Club was one of its most famous symbols as well as a showcase for the music of Duke Ellington and other bandleaders. Although most of its performers were black, the Cotton Club had, with few exceptions, a "whites only" policy for patrons. Historian Haskins, who has also written several history books for adults, presents a very readable account of a fascinating slice of American social history in the years before World War II. Many black-and-white photographs of the famous artists and their equally famous patrons make this book an attractive social history for new readers.

Intermediate new reader/adult collection.

———. *I Have a Dream: The Life and Words of Martin Luther King, Jr.* Introduction by Rosa Parks. Brookfield, CT: The Millbrook Press, 1992.

Numerous photographs and excerpts from King's writings and speeches are interwoven with Haskins's clear, well-researched text. The book focuses on King's work as pastor in Alabama and Georgia that propelled him to a leadership position in the Civil Rights movement. The layout and format of this biography make it particularly suitable for adult new readers. *Intermediate new reader/children's collection.*

———. *The March on Washington.* New York: HarperCollins, 1993.

A march on Washington to demonstrate for civil rights was first proposed by black leader A. Philip Randolph in 1941 but was not carried out for fear of disrupting the Roosevelt Administration's efforts to secure changes in the laws affecting race relations. Randolph never gave up his idea, however, and he was one of the major architects of the 1963 march in which 250,000 people heard Martin Luther King deliver his "I Have a Dream" speech. In this book, Haskins reviews the history that led to the 1963 event and profiles some of the leaders who organized it. Amply illustrated with black-and-white photographs, this is a very readable account of one of the defining events of twentieth century American history. Haskins has written several other histories for children and young adults which are suitable for adult new readers. *Get on Board: The Story of the Underground Railroad* (1993) and *Freedom Rides: Journeys for Justice* (1995) are two outstanding examples. *Intermediate-advanced new reader/children's collection.*

Henry, Christopher. *Henry Cisneros.* Hispanics of Achievement series. New York: Chelsea House, 1994.

This book presents a portrait of a dynamic political leader. Born into the Mexican American community in San Antonio, Texas Cisneros grew up immersed in two cultures: the heritage that his family and neighbors carried with them across the border and the American dream played out in the growing prosperity and power of the United States in the 1950's and 60's. A successful student and athlete, Cisneros went on to serve several terms as Mayor of San Antonio before joining the Clinton Administration as Secretary of Housing and Urban Development. For those who might be interested, this book also offers a substantial review of Mexican American history. The Hispanics of Achievement series presents a thoughtful and detailed look into the lives of Hispanics in the arts, sports, and politics. A few of the other persons profiled include singer Gloria Estefan, actor Anthony Quinn, labor leader Cesar Chavez, and baseball star Roberto Clemente.

Intermediate-advanced new reader/children's collection.

Hoobler, Dorothy, and Thomas Hoobler. *Vietnam: Why We Fought.* New York: Alfred A. Knopf, 1990.

Beginning with a clear and understandable account of the occupation of Vietnam by the Chinese, the Japanese, and then the French prior to America's involvement, this book tells the story of America's most unpopular war from many perspectives. Numerous photographs add to the book's appeal and accessibility.

Intermediate-advanced new reader/adult collection/children's collection.

Hoyt-Goldsmith, Diane. *Celebrating Kwanzaa.* Photographs by Lawrence Migdale. New York: Holiday House, 1993.

By following the activities of one Chicago family, this book explains the principles and practices of the seven-day African American festival of Kwanzaa. Started in the United States in 1966, the holiday is based on traditional African celebrations of the harvest or "first fruits." In America, it is also a time to celebrate the strength of family and community. With bright colorful photographs and an African print motif forming the border of each page, this is a visually appealing as well as informative book. A glossary of terms and map of Africa are also helpful.

Beginning-intermediate new reader/children's collection.

Huber, Peter. *Sandra Day O'Connor.* American Women of Achievement series. New York: Chelsea House Publishers, 1990.

From the early days of her career, O'Connor has been a trailblazer. She was a lawyer and working mother with three sons in the 1960's, following a path that would eventually lead to her appointment as the first woman on the United States Supreme Court. This biography reviews the facts of her life as well as some of the important legal cases which she has considered. The American Women of Achievement series provides an in-depth look at women whose lives have had a significant affect on American culture. Intended for middle and high school students, they are written in a style that allows for exploration of the background and influences of the subject, making them very appealing to an adult audience as well.

Among the other women profiled are Gloria Steinem and Marian Anderson.

Intermediate-advanced new reader/children's collection.

Jacobs, William Jay. *Ellis Island: New Hope in a New Land.* New York: Charles Scribner's Sons, 1990.

Focusing on the year 1907, Jacobs describes the experiences of immigrants from many different countries arriving at Ellis Island. Black-and-white photographs emphasize the human drama of this fascinating aspect of American history that touches all of us in some way. It would be interesting for students to compare this book to any one of the books by Brent Ashabranner which discusses immigration in the last two decades.

Intermediate new reader/children's collection.

Kotlowitz, Alex. *There Are No Children Here: The Story of Two Boys Growing Up in the Other America.* New York: Doubleday, 1991.

Kotlowitz follows the lives of two boys living in a Chicago inner-city housing project. Their story is a grim tale of violence, poverty, and neglect, but it is not without a sense of hope that things can change. When Kotlowitz first proposed this project to the boys' mother, she readily agreed, hoping that the book "would make us all stop and listen."

Advanced new reader/adult collection.

Lerner, Gerda, ed. *Black Women in White America: A Documentary History.* New York: Vintage Books, 1992.

Originally published in 1972, this collection of letters, speeches, diaries, newspaper accounts, and personal memoirs tells the history of black women in their own words. These primary sources give voice to women from the days of slavery to the early 70's who speak with courage, conviction, and originality about their struggles and joys. Brief but informative introductions open sections which are thematically-arranged by topics such as slavery, the fate of women, education, work, social and political organizations, and civil rights. Most of the pieces are short, inviting browsing as well as reading aloud.

Intermediate-advanced new reader/adult collection.

Lester, Julius. *To Be a Slave*. Illustrated by Tom Feelings. New York: Dial Books for Young Readers, 1968.

During the time of slavery, abolitionists collected narratives from runaways and freed slaves in order to document the injustices of slavery and to support their contention that it should be abolished. Years later, writers working for the Federal Writers Project interviewed former slaves to preserve a record for subsequent generations. Lester used both of these sources to create a history of slavery as seen through the experiences of those who suffered its humiliation. Slave narratives are interspersed with brief commentary from Lester. A Newbery Honor Book in 1969, *To Be a Slave* remains a very personal and compelling history told by the people who lived it.
Intermediate new reader/children's collection.

Levinson, Nancy Smiler. *Turn of the Century: Our Nation One Hundred Years Ago*. New York: Lodestar Books/Dutton, 1994.

The major issues which shaped turn-of-the-century America are presented in this book, including immigration, the developing cities, and the rise of the labor unions, but it is the personal accounts of real individuals affected by those issues that make this book stand out from other nostalgic looks at the past. Coupled with numerous black-and-white photographs, these personal stories will appeal to a wide range of readers. It might be an interesting project for students in a class or within a literacy program to review this book than create one of their own chronicling life in late twentieth century America as we look to the turn of the century and of the millennium.
Intermediate new reader/children's collection.

McKissack, Patricia, and Fredrick McKissack. *A Long Hard Journey: The Story of the Pullman Porter*. New York: Walker & Co., 1989.

The Pullman Porters were originally freed slaves, grateful for the freedom to work and to travel the growing network of railroads. Over the years, they developed a reputation for courtesy, friendliness, and efficiency, but behind the smiles lurked a growing resentment of the low pay and unjust working conditions. This book tells the story of these black workers and their long struggle to form a union, the Brotherhood of Sleeping Car Porters. The McKissacks have taken this small chapter from American history and written a compelling David and Goliath story with the immensely

wealthy railroad owners pitted against the black workers and their inspired, tenacious leader, A. Philip Randolph.
Intermediate-advanced new reader/children's collection.

Meltzer, Milton. *Brother, Can You Spare a Dime?: The Great Depression 1929–1933.* The Library of American History series. New York: Facts on File, 1991.
As with other titles in this series, first-hand accounts of ordinary Americans living through the Depression are interwoven with Meltzer's fluid narrative, presenting a vivid picture of this pivotal time in American history. Song lyrics, newspaper headlines, and photographs add to the sense of living history.
Advanced new reader/children's collection.

————. *Thomas Jefferson: The Revolutionary Aristocrat.* Milton Meltzer Biographies series. Chicago: Franklin Watts, 1991.
Meltzer traces Jefferson's evolution from shy, scholarly young man into complex and sometimes contradictory world leader. Portraits, maps, and other documents from the period personalize the story. Other notable figures whom Meltzer has profiled are George Washington, Mark Twain, and Theodore Roosevelt.
Advanced new reader/children's collection.

Meltzer, Milton, ed. *The Black Americans: A History in Their Own Words.* Revised edition. New York: Thomas Y. Crowell, 1984.
Using letters, speeches, diaries, interviews, and other primary sources, this book tells the story of blacks in America from the first days of slavery through the Civil War and a continuing quest for freedom and equality. A brief introduction to each piece sets the historical time and place and introduces the writers, some of whom are famous, some unknown. By focusing on the particulars of individual lives, the book makes a powerful statement about the struggle for equality that has been at the core of American history. Using a similar format, Historian Meltzer has also written *Voices from the Civil War: A Documentary History of the Great American Conflict.*
Advanced new reader/children's collection.

Mettger, Zak. *Till Victory is Won: Black Soldiers in the Civil War.* New York: Lodestar Books/Dutton, 1994.

Only recently has the story of the black soldiers who fought in the Civil War been examined in any depth for the general reader. Initially rejected by the Union Army, these soldiers had to fight discrimination within their own ranks even as they faced the Confederate Army. This book explores the ambivalence some black soldiers felt, their determination to prove their worth as soldiers as well as human beings, and the effect of the war on black families. Vintage photographs and prints enhance this very readable history.

Intermediate-advanced new reader/children's collection.

Moss, Nathaniel. *Ron Kovic: Antiwar Activist.* Great Achievers: Lives of the Physically Challenged series. New York: Chelsea House, 1994.

Kovic was in many ways a typical American boy in the 1960's. He grew up in suburban Long Island and, as our involvement in Vietnam accelerated, eagerly enlisted in the Marines to do his patriotic duty. His experience in Vietnam changed him profoundly. Severely wounded, paralyzed, and confined to a wheelchair, he became embittered and suicidal, but managed to channel his anger into passionate political activism. By the early 70's he was an outspoken opponent of the war and wrote an autobiography, *Born on the Fourth of July,* which became the basis for a popular film. Kovic continues to work for alternatives to war and has come to see his injuries as "a blessing in disguise." This series of in-depth biographies from Chelsea House concentrates on the lives of individuals who were born or became disabled in some way. A few of the other persons profiled are Roy Campanella, Franklin Delano Roosevelt, and Stevie Wonder.

Advanced new reader/children's collection.

Myers, Walter Dean. *Malcolm X: By Any Means Necessary.* New York: Scholastic Inc., 1993.

With flowing, readable prose Myers follows the transformation of Malcolm X from street hustler to devout Muslim to fiery orator to conciliatory leader.

Advanced new reader/adult collection/young adult collection.

Nichelason, Margery G. *Homeless or Hopeless.* Pro/Con Series. Minneapolis, MN: Lerner Publications Co., 1994.

> Should the government help the homeless, or are they "homeless by choice"? That is the basic question behind this discussion of the roots and statistical facts of homelessness in America. Many photographs, plus a focus on the plight of homeless families, give a human face to this social issue. All the titles in the Pro/Con series discuss current social issues. Some other topics addressed include abortion, capital punishment, and gun control. These books would be particularly useful for students preparing to write essays for the GED writing test.

Intermediate-advanced new reader/children's collection.

Parks, Rosa, and James Haskins. *Rosa Parks: My Story.* New York: Dial Books, 1992.

> Parks recalls her early life and experiences leading up to the day she refused to give up her seat on the Montgomery, Alabama bus. In the aftermath of that event and her subsequent celebrity, Parks left Montgomery for the sake of her family's privacy, but she continued to be an active participant and model for the continuing Civil Rights movement. Many books have been written about Rosa Parks; this is her own story, told with the help of Jim Haskins, who has also written several books about the Civil Rights movement. Numerous photographs enhance the text.

Intermediate-advanced new reader/adult collection/children's collection.

Sattler, Helen Roney. *The Earliest Americans.* Illustrated by Jean Day Zallinger. New York: Clarion Books, 1993.

> Tracing evidence from 15,000 years before Columbus, Sattler follows the migration of the early settlers who apparently crossed the land bridge that is now the Bering Sea and moved throughout what we know as North and South America. Numerous illustrations of artifacts such as teeth, tools, and jewelry help us imagine the human lives of these ancestors, and the maps and timelines help us grasp the enormous stretch of time and distance these civilizations covered.

Advanced new reader/children's collection.

Schemenauer, Elma. *Canada.* A New True Book series. Chicago: Childrens Press, 1994.

> Childrens Press publishes many titles in the New True Book series. They

include books about geography, history, science, and nature. This title discusses the various regions of Canada, its geography and major industries, early history, and facts about popular culture and entertainment. All the New True Books contain color pictures on each page, large print, and clean layout with ample white space, making them appropriate for early readers. A glossary and index provide helpful assistance as well as a chance for beginning to intermediate new readers to learn to use these tools.
Beginning-intermediate new reader/children's collection.

Stanley, Jerry. *I Am an American: A True Story of Japanese Internment.* New York: Crown Publishers, Inc., 1994.
Weaving the personal story of one young man, a high school student at the beginning of World War II, with an historical account of the internment of Japanese Americans (many of whom were American citizens and relatives of American servicemen) Stanley tells a compelling tale. Interviews from other internees, along with numerous photographs, personalize this controversial chapter in American history. Using a similar format, Stanley has also written *Children of the Dustbowl.*
Intermediate-advanced new reader/children's collection.

Stein, R. Conrad. *The Manhattan Project.* Cornerstones of Freedom series. Chicago: Childrens Press, 1993.
This book tells the story of the Manhattan Project and America's efforts to build an atomic bomb during World War II. It gives some background on the threats to peace and stability that existed at the time, profiles the scientists who worked on the project, and briefly discusses the controversy that arose over America's use of the bomb at the end of the war. Each title in the Cornerstones of Freedom series focuses on a particular story within American history, giving sufficient background to place the story in a larger historical context. Numerous photographs and other illustrations add to their appeal and accessibility. Some of the more than fifty titles are *The Saigon Airlift, Watergate, The Cuban Missile Crisis, The Boston Tea Party,* and *The Pony Express.*
Intermediate new reader/children's collection.

————. *West Virginia.* America the Beautiful series. Chicago: Childrens Press, 1991.
Books in this series about the states contain more detailed information

than those in the series titled From Sea to Shining Sea (see entry under Fradin, above), but the type of information and overall format are similar.
Intermediate - advanced new reader/children's collection.

Steins, Richard. *The Postwar Years: The Cold War and the Atomic Age (1950-59).* First Person America series. New York: Twenty-First Century Books, 1993.

The books in this series personalize history by presenting letters, songs, speeches, poems, and other writings to complement the factual discussion of a particular time. In this title, events such as the rise and fall of Senator Joseph McCarthy, the Supreme Court decision ending racial segregation in schools, the growing popularity of television, and American teenagers' embrace of Elvis Presley and the cult of rock and roll are examined in the context of a country enjoying unparalleled power and prosperity. Other titles in the series include *The Nation Divides: The Civil War (1820-1880)* and *The Allies Against the Axis: World War II (1940-1950).*
Intermediate-advanced new reader/children's collection.

Wexler, Sanford. *The Civil Rights Movement.* An Eyewitness History. New York: Facts on File, 1993.

This book tells the story of the Civil Rights movement through primary sources including letters, speeches, posters, photographs, and other documents connected by an easy-to-read narrative. Several helpful appendices include maps, a list of acronyms, and biographies of major personalities. Other titles in this series include *The Civil War and Reconstruction, Westward Expansion* and *Women's Suffrage in America.*
Intermediate-advanced new reader/adult collection.

Whitman, Sylvia. *V is for Victory: The American Home Front During WWII.* Minneapolis, MN: Lerner Publications, 1993.

Other than the attack on Pearl Harbor, the United States was not invaded by any army during World War II, but life in America was profoundly changed by our involvement in the war. This lively and well-written book documents those changes: children involved in recycling campaigns, women going to work to support the war effort who were then abruptly sent home to make room for the returning GIs, the post-war prosperity that engendered the growth of the suburbs. Whitman also discusses the

controversial internment of Japanese Americans. Numerous photographs, including many of posters and advertisements promoting patriotic activities, add to the book's information as well as its appeal.
Intermediate new reader/children's collection.

Wormser, Richard. *Hoboes: Wandering in America, 1870-1940.* New York: Walker & Co., 1994.

Hoboes were men who travelled in search of work, as opposed to tramps who travelled but did not work. This book chronicles a group of people who existed in their own well-defined society outside the American mainstream and have established their place in the romantic legends of America. Large black-and-white photographs of hoboes clinging to the tops and bottoms of railroad cars, gathering around an open fire, and working to support their next journey will undoubtedly generate comparison with images of the homeless of today who live in most American cities and towns.
Intermediate new reader/children's collection.

Zeinert, Karen. *Those Incredible Women of World War II.* Brookfield, CT: Millbrook Press, 1994.

Looking back on the important role women played during World War II, we see the seeds of the modern women's movement. This book profiles a few individuals and discusses the roles that women played as pilots, nurses, and factory workers, as well as the difficulties and obstacles they faced. Archival photographs and magazine advertisements illustrate this very informative and attractive history.
Intermediate-advanced new reader/children's collection.

The Physical World

Ballard, Robert D. *Exploring the Titanic.* Illustrated by Ken Marschall. Toronto: Madison Press Books, 1988.

Ballard is a marine geologist who discovered the wreck of the *Titanic* in 1985. In the first half of the book he tells how the *Titanic* was built and then sank on its maiden voyage. The second half tells how it was found. This informative and fascinating book includes a glossary and chronology.
Intermediate new reader/children's collection.

Beshore, George. *Sickle Cell Anemia.* Venture—Health and the Human Body series. Chicago: Franklin Watts, 1994.

This book describes what happens within the body afflicted by sickle cell anemia, discusses treatment for young children, suggests ways that older patients can cope with the disease, and examines the research currently underway to discover a cure. Many diseases and physical conditions are explored in this series, including asthma, the common cold, obesity, and stress.

Advanced new reader/children's collection.

Carlisle, Norman, and Madelyn Carlisle. *Bridges.* A New True Book series. Chicago: Childrens Press, 1982.

The Carlisles explain the history of bridges and describe many different types. All the books in this series are written at a basic level with large print, spacious layout, and color photographs, with informative and appealing text. Among the many science topics covered in the series are animals and plant life, satellites, and weather.

Beginning new reader/children's collection.

Kramer, Stephen. *Lightning.* Nature-in-Action Series. Minneapolis, MN: Carolrhoda Books, 1992.

Stunning photographs capture the beauty as well as the terrifying power of thunderstorms while the clear, concise text helps us understand why they happen. A review of safety measures is included. Kramer has also written *Tornado* for this series.

Beginning-intermediate new reader/children's collection.

Landau, Elaine. *Diabetes.* Understanding Illness series. New York: Twenty-First Century, 1994.

Each title in this series begins with the story of a person, usually of high school age, who has the disease or condition that is the focus of the book. The information provided about the causes, treatments, and effects of the disease, however, is straightforward and substantive and will appeal to adult readers as well as young adults. Other subjects covered in the series include cancer, blindness, and epilepsy.

Intermediate-advanced new reader/children's collection.

Lauber, Patricia. *Journey to the Planets.* 4th ed. New York: Crown Publishers, Inc., 1993.

With beautiful color photographs taken from space, Lauber explores the planets in our universe. Her simple but fluid text provides much information, even as it encourages us to imagine what it might be like to visit these other planets. Lauber has written several wonderful books on scientific subjects for children which are highly appropriate for adults. *Volcano: The Eruption and Healing of Mt. St. Helens* is one such title.
Intermediate-advanced new reader/children's collection.

Macaulay, David. *The Way Things Work.* Boston: Houghton Mifflin Co., 1988.

With incredible visual clarity and humor, David Macaulay explains how the many machines which shape our lives actually work. From levers to lasers and cars to computers, his drawings and diagrams dissect the machines and present them to readers from the inside out. Macaulay also explains the underlying principles that connect even the most disparate of tools. Did you know, for example, that the principle behind the zipper also governed the building of the pyramids? Intended for readers of all ages and especially "those who find technology intimidating," this book will amuse and instruct the casual browser as well as the more determined reader.
Intermediate-advanced new reader/adult collection/children's collection.

————. *Underground.* Boston: Houghton Mifflin Co., 1976.

Under an imaginary intersection of a large city, Macaulay exposes the foundations that support the tall buildings and the water, electrical, telephone, gas, and sewer systems that make modern life possible. This is a fascinating and creative look at an unknown but vital part of any city. Equally imaginative descriptions can be found in two other titles, *Pyramid* and *Cathedral.*
Advanced new reader/children's collection.

Meltzer, Milton. *Gold: The True Story of Why People Search for It, Mine It, Trade It, Steal It, Mint It, Hoard It, Shape It, Wear It, Fight and Kill for It.* New York: HarperCollins, 1993.

The title says it all. With his usual thoroughness as well as a real sense of the fun of the subject, Meltzer travels across the years and into several different cultures in search of an understanding of the ageless lure of gold.
Intermediate new reader/children's collection.

Ride, Sally. *To Space and Back*. With Susan Okie. New York: Lothrop, Lee & Shepard Books, 1986.

Ride, the first American woman astronaut, talks about her experiences aboard the space shuttle. Photographs of crew members at work and play are informative and amusing, while photographs of Earth from space are awe-inspiring. The tone is factual yet clearly touched by the wonder Ride felt on such an extraordinary journey.
Intermediate new reader/children's collection.

Robbins, Ken. *Bridges*. New York: Dial Books, 1991.

In contrast to the informational style of Norman Carlisle's *Bridges*, listed above, Robbins's hand-tinted photographs gives the reader a sense of the beauty of form and its relationship to function and of the bridge as an integral part of its environment. To compare the two is to consider the many styles and functions of a book.
Intermediate new reader/children's collection.

———. *Building a House*. New York: Four Winds Press, 1984.

With black-and-white photographs and simple, explanatory text, Robbins describes the process of building a house from drawing the design to moving in.
Intermediate new reader/children's collection.

Rotter, Charles. *Hurricanes*. Images series. Mankato, MN: Creative Education, 1994.

This book will inspire creative writing about the mysteries of the natural world as well as aid understanding the how and why of hurricanes. While the text gives us a brief but clear explanation of the causes and effects of hurricanes, the artistic photographs speak of their awesome power and majesty.
Intermediate new reader/children's collection.

Silverstein, Dr. Alvin. *The Circulatory System*. Human Body Systems series. New York: Twenty-First Century Books, 1994.

Good writing, a spacious layout, and clear and colorful diagrams all combine to make the books in this series highly readable introductions to the

various systems of the human body. This title examines all parts of the circulatory system, explains how the heart and blood work with other body organs, discusses circulatory diseases, and recommends ways to keep the heart and its circulatory pathways healthy.
Intermediate new reader/children's collection.

Simon, Seymour. *Autumn Across America.* New York: Hyperion Books for Children, 1993.

With large, beautiful color photographs and clear text, this book follows autumn as it takes hold in various sections of the United States. While the words explain such basic facts as where the brilliant reds of New England's trees come from and what happens to the snow geese, the pictures elicit those wistful feelings of nostalgia, regret, and promise that make autumn "the season of memory and change." Seymour has produced similar books on the other three seasons as well.
Intermediate new reader/children's collection.

————. *Earthquakes.* New York: Morrow Junior Books, 1991.

With striking color photographs and clear text, Simon explains why earthquakes happen and discusses a few of the most famous ones. Simon has written numerous science books for children that will also appeal to adults. *Volcanoes* and *Storms* are two particularly good titles.
Intermediate new reader/children's collection.

The Visual Dictionary of the Earth. Eyewitness Visual Dictionary series. London and New York: Dorling Kindersley, 1993.

Volcanoes, rocks, lakes and rivers, and weather are among the topics presented in this informative and visually appealing book. Dorling Kindersley books are masterpieces of the visual presentation of information. All the titles in this series feature brief introductions to the overall topic, accompanied by several drawings and diagrams which present most of the factual information in a distinctive and easy-to-follow visual format. Information charts, a glossary, and an index appear at the end. Some other subjects covered in the series are the human body, cars, and flight.
Intermediate new reader/children's collection.

Yancey, Diane. *The Hunt for Hidden Killers: Ten Cases of Medical Mysteries.* Brookfield, CT: The Millbrook Press, 1994.

Each of the ten cases presented here reads like a mystery: an unknown "assailant" has either killed or seriously harmed a victim, and doctors and scientists work feverishly to find the culprit. Legionnaires' disease, Lyme disease, and a rare case of human rabies are among the cases discussed. Good for silent or oral reading, these stories will entertain as well as teach readers about the world of medicine.
Advanced new reader/children's collection.

Art and Music

Ancona, George. *Cutters, Carvers and the Cathedral.* New York: Lothrop, Lee & Shepard Books, 1995.

The massive Cathedral of St. John the Divine in New York City is an extraordinary work of art that is still under construction, even after one hundred years. With wonderful photographs and a clear text, author and photographer Ancona chronicles the complex and unique task of building a medieval-style cathedral in the middle of a crowded and poor city neighborhood. In Indiana he photographs the limestone as it is quarried from the earth, then hauled by truck to New York. Back at the cathedral, he interviews the master stone carvers and other artisans from Europe as well as the neighborhood youths they are training in the art of stone sculpture. Photographs show the cornices, gargoyles, and other figures that will adorn the cathedral in various stages of production. Although the building remains unfinished, the work of the church goes on as the cathedral holds regular worship services, sponsors community festivals, and helps to feed the poor and homeless who live in its enormous shadow.
Intermediate new reader/children's collection.

Collier, James Lincoln. *Duke Ellington.* New York: Macmillan Publishing Co., 1991.

A noted jazz critic and prolific author of books for children, Collier has adapted his adult biography of Duke Ellington for a middle and high school audience. He reviews Ellington's career, paying particular attention to some of his most famous compositions. Although lacking photographs, the text gives a clear and engaging profile of one of America's best known

composers, as well as an intriguing glimpse into the vibrant world of jazz, America's most celebrated and original form of music.
Advanced new reader/children's collection.

Gonzalez, Fernando. *Gloria Estafan: Cuban-American Singing Star.* Hispanic Heritage series. Brookfield, CT: The Millbrook Press, 1993.

The books in this series of biographies look beyond the particulars of fame to give readers a more personal view of the lives of the celebrities profiled. This title focuses on Gloria Estafan's family, the early days of her career as a singer, and her remarkable recovery from the 1990 bus accident in which she suffered a broken back. Other subjects in this series include political figures such as Henry Cisneros and Jose Marti, and sports stars such as Roberto Clemente.
Intermediate new reader/children's collection.

Haskins, James. *Black Music in America: A History Through Its People.* New York: Thomas Y. Crowell, 1987.

This book surveys the music of black Americans from early slave songs through jazz, the blues, and soul. Profiles of major figures personalize the story.
Advanced new reader/children's collection.

Hautzig, David. *DJs, Ratings, and Hook Tapes: Pop Music Broadcasting.* New York: Macmillan Publishing Co., 1993.

Through visits to two radio stations in New York City, Hautzig explains the process behind the music we hear on the radio. He talks about how producers and DJs choose music and then prepare it for the air, discusses the working day of the DJ, both on and off the air, and explores the business and engineering aspects of radio production. This behind-the-scenes look at a medium that pervades and influences our culture will appeal to anyone who spends time listening to the radio, whatever their choice of music or format might be.
Intermediate new reader/children's collection.

Heslewood, Juliet. *Introducing Picasso.* Introducing . . . series. Boston: Little, Brown & Co., 1993.

Picasso's name is widely known and several of his paintings have become familiar images, yet much of his work remains an intriguing mystery to many viewers. This book helps explain the development of his art from representational paintings to cubism and other modern techniques. A sampling of his paintings illustrates the text.
Intermediate new reader/children's collection.

Isaacson, Philip M. *A Short Walk Around the Pyramids and Through the World of Art.* New York: Alfred A. Knopf, 1993.

Beginning with the pyramids, Isaacson explores the basic principles of art: color, form, and the marriage of materials, subject, and style. His discussion of various kinds of art from ancient sculpture to photography helps us see how the creative spirit connects us across cultures separated by time and space. An earlier work, *Round Buildings, Square Buildings, and Buildings that Wiggle Like a Fish,* is a fascinating exploration of architecture that is also very suitable for new readers.
Intermediate new reader/children's collection.

Jones, Hettie. *Big Star Fallin' Mama.* Revised edition. New York: Viking, 1995.

First published in 1974, this book profiles Ma Rainey, Bessie Smith, Mahalia Jackson, Billie Holiday, and Aretha Franklin, women who lived as well as sang the blues. This well-written book documents their lives and careers in the context of the social conditions of their time. The revised edition updates the career of Aretha Franklin.
Advanced new reader/children's collection.

Jones, K. Maurice. *Say It Loud! The Story of Rap Music.* Brookfield, CT: The Millbrook Press, 1994.

Jones traces the strong connection between rap music and a long tradition of black artistry with language that includes the storytelling techniques of the West African griots, the hidden messages of slave songs and folktales, the call and response of the black church, the pain and rhythmic patterns of the blues, and the jive talk of the jazz musicians. Photographs, reproductions of paintings, and excerpts from poetry and other writing showcase the beauty and vitality of this artistic heritage.
Intermediate-advanced new reader/children's collection.

Kiracofe, Roderick. *Cloth & Comfort: Pieces of Women's Lives from Their Quilts and Diaries.* Photographs by Sharon Risedorph. New York: Clarkson Potter/Publishers, 1994.

Piecing together photographs of detailed quilt designs with fragments from the diaries and letters of the women who created them, Kiracofe offers a unique picture of the social history of women in the nineteenth and early twentieth centuries. In many ways, these quilts were the voices of women who held families together in good times and bad, and this small book pays tribute to their dedication, resourcefulness, and artistry.

Beginning new reader/adult collection.

Lyons, Mary E. *Starting Home: The Story of Horace Pippin, Painter.* African American Artists and Artisans series. New York: Charles Scribner's Sons, 1993.

This biography focuses on the events of Pippin's life which affected his painting, and many of his works illustrate the volume. Despite severe wounds that crippled his right arm in World War I, he continued to paint and express his vision of racial injustice, the horror of war, and the strength of family. Considered a folk artist because he received no formal training, his paintings are, nevertheless, beautiful and compelling, all the more so when one realizes the difficult conditions under which he labored. Teachers might consider reading from this biography while having a collection of his work on hand. Two such collections, *Horace Pippin* and *I Tell My Heart: The Art of Horace Pippin,* are listed in the bibliography of Chapter 1.

Intermediate new reader/children's collection.

———. *Stitching Stars: The Story Quilts of Harriet Powers.* African American Artists and Artisans series. New York: Charles Scribner's Sons, 1993.

Powers learned to quilt while still a slave. After Emancipation, she made two story quilts based on Bible stories and folklore which now hang in the Smithsonian and the Boston Museum of Fine Arts. They are beautifully reproduced here, both in full and small sections that highlight their intricate detail, as Lyons explains what various panels mean. Extraordinary works of art, these quilts are also vivid reminders of the creative ways slaves, who were forbidden to learn to read, communicated with each other and with us. Lyons has written two other books in the African American Artists and Artisans series, *Deep Blues: Bill Traylor, Self-Taught Artist,* and *Master of Mahogany: Tom Day, Free Black Cabinetmaker.*

Intermediate new reader/children's collection.

Meryman, Richard. *Andrew Wyeth.* An Abrams First Impressions Book series. New York: Harry N. Abrams, Inc., 1991.

Wyeth depicted the ordinary: an open window, a blowing curtain, an old man's craggy face. The exquisite detail of these simple elements draws the viewer into the painting to imagine the story behind the scene. In this biography, Meryman explains the paintings reproduced here and also discusses how Wyeth's life has influenced his work. Adapted from a more comprehensive biography which Meryman wrote for an adult audience, this clearly-written book marketed for children will also appeal to many adult readers. Other titles in the Abrams First Impressions series follow a similar format and have the same clear and informative writing. They profile artists such as Mary Cassatt and Leonardo da Vinci.

Intermediate new reader/adult collection/children's collection.

Monceaux, Morgan. *Jazz: My Music, My People.* Foreword by Wynton Marsalis. New York: Alfred A. Knopf, 1994.

In this unique and intriguing book, Monceaux, who is both a singer and a painter, gives us brief profiles of the most famous names in jazz from Buddy Bolden, the first jazz musician, up through more contemporary figures such as Miles Davis, Dizzy Gillespie, and Sarah Vaughn, illustrated by his own music-inspired portraits of these legendary musicians.

Intermediate new reader/children's collection.

Munthe, Nelly. *Meet Matisse.* Boston: Little, Brown & Co., 1983.

With clear explanations of his techniques, photographs of the artist at work, and color plates of several works, Munthe introduces readers to the playful but compelling paper cutouts of Matisse's later years.

Intermediate new reader/children's collection.

Powell, Richard J. *Homecoming: The Art and Life of William H. Johnson.* New York: Rizzoli, 1991.

Unlike Horace Pippin (discussed above in *Starting Home* by Mary E. Lyons), Johnson was highly trained as an artist, but his pictures have a folk-like quality that invites even the casual viewer into these deceptively simple paintings that explore many issues about life for blacks in urban America. This book weaves back and forth between a discussion of his work and a review of the life experiences that influenced it.

Intermediate-advanced new reader/children's collection.

Sills, Leslie. *Visions: Stories About Women Artists.* Morton Grove, IL: Albert Whitman & Co., 1993.

Biographical facts are interwoven with a very readable and informative discussion of the art of four women artists: Mary Cassatt, Leonora Carrington, Betye Saar, and Mary Frank. Photographs and reproductions of their works appear on most pages, making this a very attractive introduction to the women and the art they make. Sills has also produced a similar work entitled *Inspirations: Stories About Women Artists*, profiling Georgia O'Keeffe, Frida Kahlo, Alice Neel, and Faith Ringgold.
Intermediate new reader/children's collection.

Turner, Robyn Montana. *Faith Ringgold.* Portraits of Women Artists for Children series. Boston: Little, Brown & Co., 1993.

Artist Faith Ringgold is best known for quilts which are embellished with paintings and a written story. Some of the stories, including *Tar Beach*, have been made into children's books illustrated by the pictures on the quilts. This biography describes Ringgold's early life and the influence of her seamstress mother on the development of her fascinating and highly original art. Other artists profiled in this series include Mexican painter Frida Kahlo and Dorothea Lange, a photographer famous for her pictures of people during the Great Depression.
Intermediate new reader/children's collection.

Wahlman, Marie Southwell. *Signs and Symbols: African Images in African American Quilts.* New York: Studio Books in association with the Museum of American Folk Art, 1993.

This book introduces us to several African American quilters and their work as it explains various signs and symbols that appear in quilts and other fabric art from Africa, the needlework of slaves, and the quilts and fiber art of contemporary artisans. As the book jacket says, African American quilts are "the visual equivalent of blues, jazz, or gospel, rich with color and symbolism," and the numerous color photographs with brief descriptive captions amply illustrate that point.
Intermediate-adult new reader/adult collection.

Walker, Lou Ann. *Roy Lichtenstein: The Artist at Work*. Photographs by Michael Abramson. New York: Lodestar Books, 1994.

Pop artist Roy Lichtenstein is best known for paintings with comic-book style dots. In this visit to his studio, the reader encounters Lichtenstein discussing his techniques and works in progress. Excellent photographs capture the vibrant and sometimes playful effect of his work.
Intermediate new reader/children's collection.

Westray, Kathleen. *A Color Sampler*. New York: Ticknor & Fields, 1993.

Color is such a part of our world that we take it for granted until something causes us to look at it with different eyes, and this simple but stunning book does just that. Using the geometric shapes of classic patchwork quilt designs, Westray explains primary, secondary, intermediate, and complementary colors then demonstrates how the interactions of color alter our perception of it. Introducing this book along with an actual quilt or other colorful object could spark interesting discussions and writing activities based on an exploration of the effects of color and design.
Beginning new reader/children's collection.

Wolf, Sylvia. *Focus: Five Women Photographers*. Morton Grove, IL: Albert Whitman & Co., 1994.

In her introduction, Wolf says that anyone can take a picture but to create art, that is, "to make images that capture beauty, that tell us about the world we live in, or that make us feel deep emotions—is a different thing entirely." The five women profiled are photojournalists Margaret Bourke-White and Julia Margaret Cameron who documented the people and events of their time and contemporary photographers Flor Garduno, Sandy Skoglund, and Lorna Simpson who use photography to express their unique perspective on the world they live in.
Intermediate new reader/children's collection.

Sports and Recreation

Bjarkman, Peter C. *Roberto Clemente*. Baseball Legends series. New York: Chelsea House Publishers, 1991.

Focusing on players who have left an indelible mark on the game, this biography series from Chelsea House features clear writing and a well-documented presentation of an interesting life. The books focus on the interplay between the ordinary events we all recognize and the extraordinary circumstances of outstanding athletic achievement. Among the other players featured in this series are Lou Gehrig, Bob Feller, Willie Mays, and Hank Aaron.

Intermediate new reader/children's collection.

Cooper, Michael L. *Playing America's Game: The Story of Negro League Baseball.* New York: Dutton/Lodestar, 1993.

The story of the Negro Leagues, which were formed because blacks were unofficially but effectively barred from major league baseball, is the story of American segregation in microcosm. This book's informative text reads like a good story, enhanced by spacious layout and numerous photographs. Other recommended titles in the children's collection are *Black Diamond: The Story of the Negro Baseball Leagues* by Patricia and Frederick McKissack, written at a slightly higher reading level and tracing the roots of baseball back to colonial times; *Leagues Apart: The Men and Times of the Negro Baseball Leagues* by Lawrence Ritter, which focuses on particular players; and *Shadow Ball: The History of the Negro Leagues*, by Geoffrey C. Ward and Ken Burns, which is derived from their epic series *Baseball: An Illustrated History*. For a title in the adult collection, see the entry under David Craft.

Intermediate-advanced new reader/children's collection.

Craft, David. *The Negro Leagues: 40 Years of Black Professional Baseball in Words and Pictures.* New York: Crescent Books, 1993.

This book balances reports on the history of black baseball with a discussion of its place in the larger context of American culture. It features pictures from the time of the Civil War up through the 1962 induction of Jackie Robinson into the Baseball Hall of Fame. An uncluttered layout with photographs on every page and captions clearly separated from other text makes this an appealing book for new readers. Beginners can browse through the pictures, reading captions if they are able, while more advanced students can read selected sections of the text.

Beginning-advanced new reader/adult collection.

Galt, Margot Fortunato. *Up to the Plate: The All American Girls Professional Baseball League.* Minneapolis, MN: Lerner Publications Co., 1995.

This is fascinating social history as well as a good sports story. When many of the big-name baseball players went off to war in 1942, baseball owners

looked for ways to keep fans coming to the ballpark, and a girls' league was one of the ideas that succeeded beyond anyone's expectations. Dressed in skirts to maintain their feminine image, these women played a rough and ready brand of baseball that delighted the fans and gave the players a chance to live what they had thought was an impossible dream.
Advanced new reader/children's collection.

Gutman, Bill. *Michael Jordan: Basketball to Baseball and Back*. Millbrook Sports World series. The Millbrook Press: Brooklield, CT, 1995.

The story of Michael Jordan's rise to fame as a basketball player, the tragedy of his father's murder, his decision to leave basketball and try to work his way up to the major leagues in baseball, and his subsequent move back to the game he still dominated even in his absence makes a fascinating human interest story which is well presented in this book. A few of the other titles in this series are *Magic Johnson: Hero On and Off the Court* and *Ken Griffey, Sr. and Ken Griffey Jr.: Father and Son Teammates.*
Intermediate new reader/children's collection.

Hammond, Tim. *Sports*. Eyewitness Books series. New York: Alfred A. Knopf, 1988.

Visually striking, books in this series present a pictorial introduction to a variety of subjects. In this case, the subject is sports, ranging from the familiar football and basketball to the less well-known sports of fencing, shooting, and racquetball. For each sport, pictures and diagrams show equipment needed, explain how the game is played, and give brief histories of the sport's development and popularity. Intended for children, the visual arrangement and quality of information make the books in this series appropriate for adults, and many libraries have copies in both the children's and adult collections. Other subjects covered by the series include arms and armor, rocks and minerals, and money.
Beginning-intermediate new reader/adult collection/children's collection.

Honig, Donald. *The American League: An Illustrated History*. Revised edition. New York: Crown Publishers, 1987.

Photographs dominate this very browsable book, arranged and introduced by Honig, who supplies many informative and amusing anecdotes about the players as well as statistical reviews of their careers. There are numerous illustrated histories of sports teams and the sports themselves, and

Honig, one of the most respected sports writers working today, wrote several of them including the companion to this volume, *The National League.* *Beginning-intermediate new reader/adult collection.*

Isaacs, Neil D., and Dick Motta. *Sports Illustrated Basketball: The Keys to Excellence.* Winner's Circle Books series. New York: Time, Inc., 1988.
Sportswriter Isaacs and former basketball coach Motta team up to present the basics of basketball for those who want to play, coach, or simply understand the game. Numerous photographs from actual professional and college games illustrate the various plays and strategies they discuss. Clear writing and an attractive layout make this book accessible to advanced students reading on their own; by reading sections aloud, teachers can also make it accessible to beginning and intermediate level students. This series also includes books on other team sports such as football and hockey as well as individual sports such as bowling and tennis.
Advanced new reader/adult collection.

Jacobs, William Jay. *They Shaped the Game: Ty Cobb, Babe Ruth, Jackie Robinson.* New York: Charles Scribner's Sons, 1994.
Citing Shakespeare's dictum, "Some are born great, some achieve greatness, and some have greatness thrust upon them," noted children's author Jacobs profiles three of baseball greatest players. Ruth is the one born great, a man with prodigious talents who made it all seem easy; Cobb struggled all his life to achieve as much as he possibly could; and Robinson was chosen to be the man to break the color line and endure the pain so others could follow. This is an interesting perspective on these three legendary sports figures in which character plays as much a role as athletic talent.
Intermediate-advanced new reader/children's collection.

Lipsyte, Robert. *Joe Louis: A Champ for All America.* Superstar Lineup series. New York: HarperCollins Publishers, 1994.
Lipsyte is the author of numerous nonfiction and fiction titles for young adults, including *The Contender,* written in 1967 and still on many young adult reading lists (See listing in Chapter 3). His life of boxer Joe Louis is an outstanding example of a sports biography written for young adults but appropriate for adult new readers as well. In telling the story of Joe Louis, Lipsyte chronicles the life of an extraordinary athlete who became a hero to all Americans when he beat the German fighter Max Schmeling

in the days preceding World War II. Lipsyte has written three other biographies in this series, *Arnold Schwarzenegger: Hercules in America, Michael Jordan: A Life Above the Rim,* and *Jim Thorpe: 20th-Century Jock.*
Intermediate-advanced new reader/children's collection.

Littlefield, Bill. *Champions: Stories of Ten Remarkable Athletes.* Illustrated by Bernie Fuchs. Boston: Little, Brown & Co., 1993.

The ten athletes profiled here are remarkable not only for their accomplishments on the playing field, but because of their determination in the face of adversity. Littlefield tells the stories of Satchel Paige, arguably the best baseball pitcher ever, who didn't make it to the major leagues until the color line was broken and he was already in his forties; Diane Golden, a champion skier with one leg; and Susan Butcher, the only woman to win the Iditarod sled dog race, as well as seven other inspiring athletes. Given that the focus is on character as much as on athletic skill, these stories will appeal to a range of readers, even those who are not sports fans.
Intermediate-advanced new reader/children's collection.

Margolies, Jacob. *Kareem Abdul-Jabbar.* First Books—Biographies series. Chicago: Franklin Watts, 1992.

By virtue of size and achievement, Kareem Abdul-Jabbar dominated the game of basketball for much of his career. This book examines his athletic record as well as his personal struggles and accomplishments. The books in this First Books—Biographies series present the lives of famous people in many fields. Among other sports celebrities featured are Jackie Robinson and Hank Aaron.
Intermediate new reader/children's collection.

Rivers, Glenn, and Bruce Brooks. *Those Who Love the Game: Glenn "Doc" Rivers on Life in the NBA and Elsewhere.* New York: Henry Holt and Co., 1993.

With the assistance of young adult writer Brooks, basketball star Rivers talks about life in the NBA. Brief chapters discuss matters of family, the game, individual players, and lessons from basketball and from life. The voice is clearly that of Rivers himself, and he offers a revealing and highly readable look behind the scenes into the world of professional sports.
Advanced new reader/children's collection.

Ward, Geoffrey C., and Ken Burns. *25 Great Moments*. Baseball: The American Epic series. New York: Alfred A. Knopf, 1994.

This series is intended to introduce children to particular chapters of the baseball story presented in the larger volume, *Baseball: An Illustrated History*, which is the companion book to the PBS television series. Using illustrations from the parent volume, this book captures twenty-five of the most memorable moments in the game's history: Jackie Robinson stealing home and Joe Carter hitting a home run to win the 1993 World Series are just two examples. Other titles in this series include *Shadow Ball: The History of the Negro Leagues* and *Who Invented the Game?*
Intermediate new reader/children's collection.

———. *Baseball: An Illustrated History*. New York: Alfred A. Knopf, 1994.
A companion volume to the documentary film *Baseball*, produced by Ken Burns, this book contains over 500 photographs, essays from a variety of commentators, and an historical review of baseball that traces its earliest roots in colonial America, connects it to the Civil War, and follows its growth and development from the nineteenth century to the 1990's. There is social history here too: baseball struggling through the Depression, players on leave to fight in World War II and Korea, and the unwritten agreement among owners to exclude black players. The game's most enduring faces, numbers, and stories are presented in this very browsable book which will accommodate readers at all levels. Beginners will enjoy the many pictures with brief captions; more advanced students will be able to read the text. Students can also coordinate their reading of the book with viewing the video which will be available in many libraries.
Beginning-advanced new reader/adult collection.

Wissel, Hal. *Basketball: Steps to Success*. Steps to Success Activity Series. Champaign, IL: Human Kinetics, 1994.
Professional coach Wissel writes for anyone interested in mastering the skills of basketball, whether they are aspiring young players, adults learning to play for fun, or coaches working with players of all levels and ages. He emphasizes the basics: exercises for good conditioning and numerous skill drills to perfect the routine moves. He also explains potential play situations. Compared to Isaacs and Motta's book, described above, this book is more detailed and uses diagrams rather than photographs. These diagrams, as well as the writing style and the overall layout, are very clear

and attractive, offering literacy students ample opportunity to learn to read information presented in chart form.

Intermediate-advanced new reader/adult collection/children's collection.

Cooking and Crafts

Beaton, Clare. *The Felt Book: Easy-to-Make Projects for All Ages.* New York: Sterling Publishing Co., 1994.

Many useful, fun, and relatively easy projects, including some for holidays, are suggested in this book which will appeal to a wide range of readers, especially those interested in making crafts with children. There is a wealth of material here, but good visual design makes the templates, diagrams, stitching techniques, and other information attractive and easy to follow.

Beginning-intermediate new reader/adult collection.

Crocker, Betty. *Betty Crocker's Kitchen Secrets.* New York: Random House, 1983.

This is not a recipe book but a guide to cooking all kinds of food. Information is organized according to food category, such as pastry, vegetables, etc. Each section is presented in question-and-answer format. The questions are basic ones all cooks ask; the answers are easy to read and understand. Charts present information on cooking equipment, measurements, and equivalencies.

Intermediate-advanced new reader/adult collection.

————. *Betty Crocker's Quick Dinners.* New York: Prentice Hall Press, 1992.

Color photographs and a spacious, easy-to-follow layout make this collection of recipes for busy cooks very attractive. Using a similar format, Prentice Hall has produced other Betty Crocker cookbooks that will appeal to new readers including *Betty Crocker's Great Chicken Recipes* and *Betty Crocker's Mexican Made Easy.*

Beginning-intermediate new reader/adult collection.

Dietrich, Mimi, et al. *The Quilters' Companion: Everything You Need to Know to Make Beautiful Quilts.* Bothell, WA: That Patchwork Place, 1994.

The chapters in this book cover cutting techniques, advice on matching pieces, a description of various stitches, and other basic information for

producing a finished quilt. Clear diagrams as well as color photographs of finished work make this book informative and easy to follow.
Intermediate-advanced new reader/adult collection.

Eliot, Rose. *The Classic Vegetarian Cookbook*. London and New York: Dorling Kindersley, 1994.

This publisher has produced a series of cookbooks for adults that feature the same stunning visual design found in many of its books for children, such as the popular *Visual Dictionary* series. Pictures of the food, utensils, and preparation accompany clear directions for assembling each recipe.
Intermediate-advanced new reader/adult collection.

King, Elizabeth. *Chile Fever: A Celebration of Peppers*. New York: Dutton, 1995.

As colorful and appealing as the many varieties of peppers it features, this book explores the history of peppers, explains their growth cycle, and discusses the peppers' importance in many cultures in the Southwest. Adults will enjoy this intriguing look at a small but potent ingredient in many popular foods.
Intermediate new reader/children's collection.

Owen, Peter. *Knots*. Philadelphia: Courage Books, 1993.

This is an excellent example of a book which uses visual display to explain how to do a task: in this case, the very useful art of tying secure knots appropriate to particular situations. Photographs as well as clear diagrams accompany brief text explaining a bit of the history of each knot, if known, as well as a description of its best uses.
Beginning-intermediate new reader/adult collection/children's collection.

Patent, Dorothy Hinshaw. *Nutrition: What's in the Food We Eat*. Photographs by William Munoz. New York: Holiday House, 1992.

This book explains the importance of eating healthful foods and describes the specific contributions of carbohydrates, proteins, vitamins, and minerals. A matter-of-fact discussion of the reasons to limit fat, sugar, and junk food will help adults explain their restrictions of these foods to children. A glossary defines all the biological vocabulary used in the book.
Intermediate new reader/children's collection.

Vegetarian Cooking Around the World. Easy Menu Ethnic Cookbooks series. Minneapolis, MN: Lerner Publications Co., 1991.

All of the cookbooks in this series follow a similar format: an introduction to the country or culture that is featured in the book, a review of terms for utensils and special ingredients, and recipes suitable for breakfast, lunch, dinner, and dessert. The recipes are nicely spaced and clearly written. Pictures accompany most recipes. There are more than twenty books in this series, including recipes from Africa, Russia, South America, and Vietnam, to name a few, and a book of holiday recipes. In a classroom or program setting where several different books from the series are available, each student could choose a recipe to prepare and share with the class.

Intermediate new reader/children's collection.

Wilkes, Angela, and Carol Garbera. *Knitting.* Usborne Guides series. London: Usborne Publishing Ltd., 1991.

Designed to convince readers that knitting is not as hard as it may seem, this book clearly explains basic techniques and equipment, and suggests several patterns for the beginning knitter, including options to encourage personal variations. Brightly illustrated with color drawings and diagrams, this is one of the many Usborne Guides that is easy to follow.

Intermediate new reader/children's collection.

Willan, Anne. *Creative Casseroles.* Anne Willan's Look and Cook Book series. London: Dorling Kindersley, 1993.

As is customary in a Dorling Kindersley book, every stage of the process, from the preparation of the ingredients to the cooking to the final presentation is beautifully photographed, as is all the equipment needed. Other titles in this series include *Perfect Pasta, Superb Salads,* and *Perfect Pies and Tarts.*

Beginning-intermediate new reader/adult collection.

Chapter 5

You Could Look It Up: Information-Seeking Skills and Reference Materials for Adult New Readers

These days, anyone who goes to a library for information has to contend not just with a multitude of books that may hold the necessary information, but also with an array of media that can be used to find the information: books and reference sources in print, electronic versions of encyclopedias, atlases, and other texts, electronic databases that provide access to periodical literature, and full text journal articles in electronic format. Even some experienced library users feel intimidated by the variety of choices.

The focus of this chapter is twofold: to suggest some of the basic information-seeking skills that literacy students should develop and to suggest various information sources, both print and electronic, that teachers can introduce to literacy students to help them find the information they need. The format of this chapter differs from preceding ones. Instead of listing a number of potentially useful books, it offers sample exercises designed to help students practice information-seeking skills, using particular reference sources from the library as examples. These examples will come from both print and electronic sources, although the emphasis will be on print sources for two reasons. First, print sources are more familiar and readily available. In some cases, they are also faster and easier to use. But there is another, equally important reason. Using print indexes, abstracts, tables of contents, dictionaries, and statistical charts gives users a visual image of the way in which information is arranged. Having this visual image of how information is stored makes it easier to understand how that information can be retrieved. When students eventually use an electronic resource to obtain information, a visual image of how information is organized, along with the knowledge that the same principles of organization apply in the electronic form, makes that machine-based source less intimidating.

Alphabetical and Subject Indexes

Alphabetical indexes are perhaps the most basic method used to organize information. Many students will be familiar with indexes, although they might not use that term, because they are among the common items we use in our everyday lives. Phone books and building directories, for example, are alphabetical indexes, as are indexes to nonfiction books. Students should also become familiar with subject indexes, and the local Yellow Pages is one good resource to introduce them to this concept.

Sample Exercises Using Alphabetical and Subject Indexes

1. Ask your students to create a list of family members and friends. Using the local phone book, have them look up each person's name, then copy down the address and phone number. Have them create a similar list of out-of-town relatives as well, then go to the library to find phone books for other cities. In addition to providing practice in using indexes, this activity will remind students that telephone books from cities across the nation are among the resources found at most public libraries.

2. Prepare a list of five services or commodities for which students must find a local merchant: for example, an auto repair shop, a store that sells sporting goods, a movie theater, a bookstore, and a dentist.

3. Ask students to find out how many different denominations of churches are listed in their local phone book.

4. Choose a multi-volume encyclopedia that students would be interested in using. *The World Book Encyclopedia of People and Places,* published by World Book of Chicago, is one example of an encyclopedia that is marketed for children but will be appealing to adults. It is a geographical encyclopedia that provides information about countries and cultures around the world. Ask them to choose a country, look that country up in the index volume, then find all the references to that country in the content volumes.

5. In the library, have the students choose two newspapers, each from a different city. Have them look in the index to each paper to find a particular section, the weather maps, for example, or the television listings. Then have them compare the information available in each newspaper.

Library Catalogues

A library's catalogue is also an index. Many public libraries now have computerized catalogues that are user-friendly and menu-driven; that is, the computer asks the user a number of questions, and the answers to those questions lead the user through a series of steps to find the books or information needed. Learning to use a computerized library catalogue offers new readers a chance to learn a particular computer application as well as some basic skills that can be applied to other computer systems. If tutors are unfamiliar with the computerized version of the library catalogue, they can learn to use them right along with their students.

Students need to learn that in a library's catalogue, books and other materials are indexed by title, author, and subject. They need to be able to read and understand the information that appears on the screen, such as the call number and location of the book. Reading the subject headings under which a title is indexed is also helpful for finding other books about the same subject. Students should know, too, that with a call number for one or two books, they can browse the shelves in that area and find numerous other titles about their subject.

Sample Exercises with Library Catalogues
1. With a copy of a familiar book in hand, have students find its catalogue record. Then have them check to find other books by the same author.
2. Have students make a list of favorite movies, then help them check the title index of the catalogue to see if those movies are available in video format in the library's collection.
3. Ask them to name a few celebrities they like then use the subject index of the catalogue to find any biographies of those celebrities in the library.
4. If students are planning to go on a trip, have them use a subject index to find books about the cities they will be travelling to.
5. Prepare a list of five or six books that students are familiar with or possibly interested in. Have the students find call numbers for each title, then, using a map of the library, find the books.

Basic Reference Books

Library reference collections include expected resources such as atlases, encyclopedias, and dictionaries. Browsing the reference collection reveals a surprising variety in the subjects and formats of these basic sources. For example, there are general knowledge encyclopedias such as *The Academic American Encyclopedia*, published by the Grolier Education Corporation and aimed at the high school and college market, and *World Book,* published by World Book Inc. for middle and junior high students. There are also many specialized encyclopedias such as *The Grolier Wellness Encyclopedia,* published by the Dushkin Publishing Group for the middle and junior high school market, which includes several brief volumes, each covering a particular aspect of health. The single volume *Baseball Encyclopedia* published by Collier Macmillan includes just about everything anyone could ask about baseball, and *The Ultimate Encyclopedia of Rock* presents the singers, songs, and trends of rock & roll.

Among dictionaries too there is a variety of choices, ranging from the *American Heritage Dictionary,* a general dictionary published by Houghton Mifflin which is noted for its clear definitions and quotations to illustrate word usage, to an array of dictionaries of slang, colloquial expressions, rhyming words, and abbreviations to specialized subject dictionaries that define words in particular fields such as law or medicine.

Sample Exercises Using Reference Books
Some of the exercises suggested below are based on particular books but can be applied to any number of similar titles. All of the books mentioned will be accessible to advanced new readers and some to intermediate new readers as well.

1. Using *The Ultimate Encyclopedia of Rock,* published by Harper-Perennial, ask students to name two popular songs from 1955, explain Chuck Berry's place in the evolution of rock and roll, and describe the origin of "the twist."

2. Some dictionaries present their information in a highly visual format, relying more on the skillful arrangement of descriptive pictures than verbal explanations. These dictionaries can be particularly useful for intermediate level and even beginning level new readers. One example is the *Visual Dictionary of Plants,* a part of the *Eyewitness Visual Dictionaries* series produced by Dorling Kindersley. Ask students to use the index to find out, for example, what moss is, what kinds of seaweed are commonly found on beaches, and what happens in the process of photosynthesis. Another visual dictionary series, called *Eyewitness,* is produced by Knopf. Using the volume *Crystal and Gem,* for example, have students answer such questions as how crystals are cut, what is amethyst, and where do diamonds come from.

3. Several publishers produce multivolume reference works for elementary, junior, and senior high school students that cover the span of American history. One such series is *The American Heritage Illustrated History of the United States* published by Silver Burdett. Each volume in this series covers a particular aspect or era of American history, such as *Colonial America, The Roosevelt Era,* and *The Vietnam Era.* In the latter volume, students could find answers to such questions as who was Spiro Agnew, what was the Tet Offensive, and when did the Vietnam War end.

4. Some reference works are sources of in-depth information about one particular topic. *The Biographical Dictionary of Black Americans,* edited by Rachel Kranz and published by Facts on File, is one example. It is an alphabetical listing of black Americans who have made contributions in the areas of politics, science, education, the arts, and entertainment. With this book, students could find biographical information on Ma Rainey, A. Philip Randolph, and other black leaders.

5. Even more specific is the two-volume comprehensive study *Black Women in America,* edited by Darlene C. Hine and published by Carlson Publishing of Brooklyn, New York. This major encyclopedia contains 804 entries on historical and contemporary figures, issues, and movements that have affected black women. Sitting in the library, students might browse this book, looking at the photographs, identifying names they recognize, and choosing an entry at random to read. Although encyclopedias are most often thought of as tools to answer specific questions, they are also good for browsing, especially if, as in this case, they are attractively laid out with well spaced text, good illustrations, and an engaging subject.

6. Another reference work that will inspire browsing is the *Smithsonian Timelines of the Ancient World: A Visual Chronology from the Origins of Life to AD 1500,* published by Dorling Kindersley. The chapters of this visually striking book are arranged around time charts that highlight important developments and social changes, making it possible to see in a graphic way, for example, when the Islamic religion began and what other religious, social, and political conditions existed at that time. Just browsing in a book such as this reminds readers of the enormous changes that have occurred in our physical, social, cultural, and human worlds.

7. Geographic data is also available in many sources in the library. The *World Encyclopedia of Cities,* published by ABC-CLIO of Santa Barbara, has two volumes covering North America in which 136 cities in

the United States and Canada are profiled. The information in each entry is attractively and clearly presented, with some statistical information presented in distinctly boxed sections that are easy to read. This would be a good reference to practice reading and comparing information in chart form. Teachers could ask students to choose two cities of interest to them and compare them according to size, population, weather patterns, job opportunities, etc.

8. Road atlases are among the most used reference sources in any public library. Using the latest edition of the *Rand McNally Road Atlas of the United States,* students could map out a planned or imaginary trip from home to another city. Ask them to compare possible routes for distance, quality of the roads, and interesting places to pass along the way. Ask them also to identify geographical features such as rivers, lakes, forests, or mountains.

9. Dictionaries are another basic reference source that libraries have in abundant number and variety. Consider for example the *Acronyms, Initialisms, and Abbreviations Dictionary* published annually by Gale Research. Students could look up abbreviations found on food products and other everyday items such as **g.**, **kg.**, **lbs.**, and **bht**. They could find out the full names of organizations mentioned frequently in the news such as EPA, NRA, and UAW and learn the origin of commonly-used words that are actually acronyms such as SCUBA, RADAR, LASER, and ASAP.

10. Another interesting type of dictionary lists slang terms, their origins, and their meanings. The easy-to-use *Oxford Dictionary of Modern Slang* defines colloquial phrases such as "in the catbird seat" and "to raise cain," as well as currently popular terms such as "kidvid" and "hotshot."

11. Once students are comfortable using encyclopedias and dictionaries in print format, find out if your library has electronic versions of some of these resources. Introduce your student (and perhaps yourself) to the resource. Approach it with a playful attitude. Name people, places, or words you'd like to look up, then try it and see what happens. Having a relaxed, exploratory attitude and no particular destination is a non-threatening way to become familiar with computer-based resources.

Periodical Indexes

Periodical indexes lead users to articles covering every subject of interest imaginable in popular magazines and scholarly journals. While their use might be more frequently associated with school research papers, they are in fact extremely useful resources for the general reader interested in anything from buying a new car to becoming a volunteer at the local zoo.

Periodical indexes are produced in print and electronic formats, but the increasing ease and power of the electronic formats make them more attractive, even to users who are not skilled in using computers. Most libraries now offer computer access to systems such as *Infotrac,* a product of Information Access Company, which provides access to many periodical indexes as well as full text articles from some magazines and newspapers.

Sample Exercises Using Periodical Indexes
Note: These exercises can be used on any computer-based index to periodical literature.

1. *Newspaper Abstracts* is a database that indexes articles from twenty-seven newspapers across the United States. It includes major mainstream papers such as *The New York Times* and *The Los Angeles Times* as well as papers serving specific communities such as *The Call and Post* which is addressed primarily to the black community. The database offers a list of the newspapers it indexes as well as hints for searching. It is a menu-driven system that takes users through the processes necessary to find the information they are looking for step-by-step. Students could find references to articles about topics in the news, recent sports events, movies and concerts they are interested in, and weather conditions across the country. Most of the entries have abstracts which, in some cases, give enough information to satisfy the user's need. If the full article is needed, many libraries have the newspapers available in print or on microfilm.

2. *Periodical Abstracts*, another electronic index, is similar to the print index *Reader's Guide to Periodical Literature,* but much more useful. In addition to indexing magazine articles on a wide range of topics, it also provides abstracts, giving users an idea of whether or not they want to retrieve the actual article. It also enables users to find articles by using key words rather than knowing what specific subject headings to look under. With a tutor's help, students can use this resource to find information on topics related to their work, their children, their city, or their hobbies.

3. *Health Reference Center,* another Information Access Company product, is a subject-oriented database. It offers access to health-related materials that are geared toward consumers, not medical professionals. A student whose daughter has been diagnosed with diabetes, for example, can turn to *Health Reference Center* and find clear definitions of diabetes and related terms, references to magazine articles about juvenile diabetes, and the full text of pamphlets that have been produced by such groups as the Juvenile Diabetes Foundation. *The Encyclopedia of Associations,* available in any public library reference department, can supply the addresses and phone numbers of the Foundation and other organizations that share information about this disease.

A Note to Librarians

Consider offering workshops to teach literacy students and their tutors how to use the many resources in the reference department that contain information that is important or interesting to them. Include computer-based resources as well as those in print. Create displays which feature a frequently asked question—or just a fun question—along with the answer and the source used to find it. Highlight reference books in your collection that are unusual or that cover 'hot' topics such as rock and roll and other kinds of popular music, television shows, movies, and celebrities. In every way possible, remind literacy students that the library is often their best source for information and that librarians are there to help them find that information.

A Note to Literacy Teachers

Model the use of books and the library as information sources. Make a point of looking things up with students when they raise questions. Have some basic reference materials on hand in the tutoring center. Look for some of these materials at local library book sales. Even older editions of encyclopedias, atlases, and dictionaries will contain relevant information, and they are also a record of the way things once were, an interesting subject in itself. Tell your students about information needs that you have and the ways you satisfy them. If you are unfamiliar with computer-based information sources, share that with your students and explore these systems together. At every opportunity, help your students develop the skills and, more importantly, the attitude that they will need to function in a society increasingly based on the ability to find and use information.

Chapter 6

Not for Children Only:
Picture Books for All Ages

Those of us lucky enough to have personal or professional reasons to explore children's literature know that it is a treasure trove of entertaining stories, beautiful art work, and clearly-written information on every imaginable subject and that adults not familiar with these books are missing out on a good thing. Consider these examples. Jacob Lawrence is best known for his series of paintings which tell stories from African American history. His "Migration Series" has recently been exhibited in several American museums, including the Museum of Modern Art in New York City. These sixty beautiful drawings, each accompanied by one or two sentences explaining the scene, are a powerful depiction of the migration of blacks from the rural South to the industrial North during the years between the wars. Reproductions of these paintings are now available in a children's book, *The Great Migration: An American Story*. It contains all sixty panels and Lawrence's original captions and nothing else, but it teaches an unforgettable lesson of American history and of the power of art to tell stories, convey a message, and profoundly move us.

Faith Ringgold's picture book *Tar Beach* also features original artwork. Ringgold is best known for her story quilts, beautiful fabric creations that contain a narrative. In this example, the author recalls her childhood, when she and her family would escape the heat of their Harlem apartment by spending the evening socializing with neighbors on the roof, which they called "tar beach." The original quilt hangs in the Guggenheim Museum in New York City, but a reproduction is available to anyone who picks up *Tar Beach*, which is illustrated with pictures from the quilt.

Reading reviews of children's books, or just browsing through them in the library or book store, one cannot help but notice the increasingly frequent appearance of the designation "for all ages." Many books for children now address issues which are also of interest to adults and frequently contain high quality art. George Ella Lyon's book *Mama is a Miner*, for example, presents a simple story of a mother who works all day in the dark and dangerous coal mine but spends the evenings cooking, mending, and helping her children with schoolwork. A heartwarming story for children, it also suggests many issues that adults will notice and want to discuss, such as the need for women to work to support their families, the difficulty of being a woman in a "man's" profession, and the conflict many women feel between their obligations and ambitions in the workplace and their responsibilities at home.

Looking back on childhood is a frequent theme in children's books that appeal to adults. Acclaimed poet Donald Hall has written several titles which vividly recall his youth spent on his grandparents' New Hampshire farm. In *The Farm Summer of 1942*, illustrated by Barry Moser, a young boy, whose father is away in the war, flies from San Francisco to Boston, then takes a train to New Hampshire. He is met by a horse and buggy. Children will share the boy's sense of discovery of a totally different world. They may also be inspired to write stories of their own childhoods.

Another format found in children's literature is the single poem accompanied by illustrations. Most of the poems were originally written for adults but are simple enough for children to read and understand, which is part of their appeal to adult new readers, too. In addition, the beauty of the artwork and the clarity of the images help to explain and extend the meaning of the poem, especially to those who are not familiar with poetry and its metaphorical and imagistic language. Reading simple poems will help prepare readers, whether they are children or adults, for written works they will later encounter that make use of metaphor and visual images. Some particularly fine examples of this kind of book are Nikki Giovanni's *Knoxville, Tennessee*, illustrated by Larry Johnson; Robert Frost's *Stopping by Woods on a Snowy Evening*, illustrated by Susan Jeffers; and William Blake's *The Tyger*, illustrated by Neil Waldman.

Picture books can also tell true stories, and some introduce difficult subjects to children with a sensitivity that adults will appreciate. Jeanne Moutoussamy-Ashe's book *Daddy and Me* is a photographic chronicle of her daughter's relationship with her husband Arthur Ashe, who was stricken with AIDS. Chana Byers Abells's book *The Children We Remember* photographically records the experiences of children whose lives were devastated and, in some cases, ended by the Holocaust.

The books just mentioned and several others are listed in the first part of this chapter's bibliography, **Picture Books for All Ages**. The second part of the bibliography lists children's books that are appropriate for family literacy programs in which adults learn to read books they can then share with children. Any book written for children could become part of a family literacy program, but some are particularly suitable because they have themes of family interest. *The Wall*, for example, written by Eve Bunting and illustrated by Ronald Himler, tells of a father who takes his young son to the Vietnam Veterans Memorial in Washington, D.C. to find his grandfather's name inscribed on the wall. In Valerie Flournoy's *The Patchwork Quilt*, a grandmother teaches her granddaughter how to quilt, and together they finish the grandmother's "masterpiece." James Stevenson's trilogy, ending with *July*, is a witty but poignant evocation of the lives of two children in the 1930's.

Other books may help adults teach a particular concept to a child. Alphabet books and counting books have an important place in a family literacy collection, and one rather unusual example is Jane Bayer's *A My Name is Alice* which goes through the alphabet with a four-line rhyme for each letter that is the basis for a bouncing ball game that children play. Adults and children can read the book, then play the game. Cooking is another activity that children like to participate in, and Helen Drew's *My First Baking Book* offers clear, and very tempting, illustrations and instructions for several recipes. Many children's books tell religious stories, sometimes illustrating the words from the standard Bible version, sometimes retelling the stories in simpler language. Warwick Hutton has illustrated *Adam and Eve: The Bible Story* and *Moses in the Bulrushes*. Religious festivals are recalled in George Ancona's *Pablo Remembers: The Fiesta of The Day of the Dead*, a photo essay about the Mexican festival that celebrates the yearly visit from the spirits of ancestors, and in Andrea Davis Pinkney's *Seven Candles for Kwanzaa*, illustrated by J. Brian Pinkney, which examines the origins and practices of this African American holiday.

One of the great benefits of reading to a child, beyond helping them learn to love books and reading, is the simple experience of sharing time, ideas, and a view of the world. Adults and children who read the same books have common knowledge of characters to refer to when they meet a real person who reminds them of someone in a story. They may have a model to refer to when they encounter a situation in real life that is similar to one they have read about in a book. Reading books together offers adults and children shared references that can help them discuss people, behavior, and events that affect the way they live their lives.

A Note to Librarians

Mount a display of "Picture Books for All Ages" and place it in an area of the library to attract all readers, not just literacy students. Many libraries already have multiple copies of these titles, so consider placing one in the new readers collection. Sponsor "read-aloud" workshops in which librarians offer adults of all reading abilities tips on choosing books and reading aloud to children. Invite authors and illustrators to the library and include literacy students among the audience. Ask patrons to name their favorite picture books and have a display of the results. Whenever you have displays for adults centered around a particular theme, include some picture books from the children's collection. Whenever an opportunity arises, remind readers of all ages and reading abilities that picture books are not just for children.

A Note to Literacy Tutors

When introducing children's books to adult new readers, be forthright in explaining your reasons for doing so and sensitive to the reactions of the students. If they seem willing, read some of your favorites to them, pointing out the things you particularly like about a book, whether it is the illustrations, the clever rhymes, or the memories it conjures up. In conjunction with the local library, sponsor workshops to help adults learn to share books and stories with children. Have staff and tutors mount a display of their favorite children's books, whether they are new ones or books from their childhood. Remember the children's collection whenever you are looking for books that address issues of interest like mothers who work, homelessness, or learning to cook. Take every opportunity to mine the treasure trove of children's literature for aids in advancing the skills and reading pleasure of adult literacy students.

Bibliography

Picture Books for All Ages

Abells, Chana Byers. *The Children We Remember*. New York: Greenwillow Books, 1986.
> The many photographs of German Jewish children in school and at play before the rise of the Nazis and then the very few photographs of children taken after the war all serve to underscore the horrible reality of what happened to many of those children. This powerful book will open up a dialogue on the Holocaust, a potent issue even fifty years after the last camps were liberated.

Beginning new reader.

Angelou, Maya. *Life Doesn't Frighten Me*. Illustrated by Jean-Michel Basquiat. New York: Stewart, Tabori & Chang, 1993.

Facing fear is the subject of this collaboration of two extraordinary artists. The words to the book-length poem are simple but boldly defiant in confronting the darker elements of life. Basquiat's illustrations echo that boldness, at times appearing streetwise, at times expressing a childlike bravado in the face of danger. Brief biographies of both poet and painter capture the uniqueness of each artist's approach to life and art.

Beginning new reader.

————. *Now Sheba Sings the Song*. Illustrated by Tom Feelings. New York: E.P. Dutton/Dial Books, 1987.

Feelings first sketched the sepia-toned drawings of black women contained in this book during his travels to Africa and throughout the United States over a period of several years. He then asked Angelou to create a poem that would express the beauty and strength he found in these women. She "lived" with the pictures for six months, then wrote this intensely sensuous poem that gives words to the powerful spirit inherent within the drawings and the women themselves.

Intermediate new reader.

Bates, Katharine Lee. *America the Beautiful*. Illustrated by Neil Waldman. New York: Atheneum, 1993.

The text of this book is the first verse of the patriotic song of the title. The illustrations were inspired by real places across the United States, including Niagara Falls, the Statue of Liberty, the Grand Tetons, and the ancient cliff dwellings of Mesa Verde. Dabs of color of varying gradations give the illustrations a vibrancy that is almost palpable and create a sense that we are flying low over the country's most beautiful scenery. Full text of all the verses along with the musical notation appear on the end pages.

Beginning new reader.

Baylor, Byrd. *The Way to Start a Day*. Illustrated by Peter Parnall. New York: Charles Scribner's Sons, 1978.

With poetic text and vivid but reverent illustrations, author and illustrator collaborate to describe how people from different cultures celebrate the sunrise. All the rituals reflect the belief that humans live in rhythm with nature's cycles.

Beginning new reader.

————. *When Clay Sings.* Illustrated by Tom Bahti. New York: Charles Scribner's Sons, 1972.

> Baylor writes that Indians "say that every piece of clay is a piece of someone's life." In this unusual book, Baylor tells the story of American Indian children who find pieces of pottery from generations past and imagine the lives of the people who made and used them. The colors, designs, and motifs used throughout the book are common to the art of southwestern peoples. The text suggests a belief in the interdependence of people and nature.

Beginning new reader.

Baynes, Pauline. *Noah and the Ark.* Text from Revised Standard Version of the *Bible.* New York: Henry Holt & Co., 1988.

> Many adult new readers are familiar with the *Bible*; some even know stories and verses by heart. Books such as this provide the opportunity for new readers to encounter words they have known and loved for years in print. Baynes's lovely illustrations accompany the standard Biblical text. Middle-level students can read the text on their own, or tutors can read the text to beginning students interested in Biblical stories.

Beginning-intermediate new reader.

————. *Thanks Be to God: Prayers from Around the World.* New York: Macmillan Publishing Co., 1990.

> This simple collection includes a range of heartwarming prayers from many countries and religious points of view. The words and pictures show diversity in forms of expression, yet all the prayers address our basic human need to recognize some power beyond our understanding or control.

Beginning new reader.

Blake, William. *The Tyger.* Illustrated by Neil Waldman. San Diego, CA: Harcourt Brace & Co., 1993.

> "Tyger, Tyger, burning bright, in the forests of the night . . . " So begins Blake's famous poem envisioning the magical force that created a beast such as the tiger. The text of the book is the complete poem, and the bold illustrations heighten the sense of mystery and majesty that the poem has expressed for almost two hundred years. The language of this poem is not easy, and students will best appreciate it if it is read aloud. Even if the meaning is not obvious, the pounding beat and deeply physical images

will give students a lesson in the power of language to reach deep into the soul.
Intermediate new reader.

Brother Eagle, Sister Sky: A Message from Chief Seattle. Illustrated by Susan Jeffers. New York: Dial Books, 1991.

The words of this book have been attributed to Chief Seattle, speaking as he signed a treaty granting rights to the northwest lands of his people to the U.S. Government. He tells of our place in the balance of nature and our responsibility to care for the earth we have been given. Jeffers's soft, crayon-like coloring suffuses the drawings with a gentle spirit.
Beginning-intermediate new reader.

Bryan, Ashley. *Sing to the Sun.* New York: HarperCollins, 1992.

Bryan joins his own poems with illustrations that look like woodcuts brightly colored with African hues and motifs. Celebrating the ordinary and the creative, the poems are simple; the illustrations make them sing.
Beginning new reader.

Bryan, Ashley, ed. *Walk Together, Children.* New York: Atheneum, 1982.

Accompanied by lovely woodcuts and musical notation, this collection of black spirituals will appeal to all students who know and love these soul-stirring songs that are a uniquely American art form. A second volume, *I'm Going to Sing,* is also available.
Beginning-intermediate new reader.

Bunting, Eve. *Smoky Night.* Illustrated by David Diaz. San Diego: Harcourt Brace & Co., 1994.

Reflecting upon the distressing events of recent riots in Los Angeles, Bunting wrote this story of one family's reaction to the chaos outside their window. The illustrations are truly extraordinary. Vivid, darkly-colored paintings are set against collages made of an odd but arresting assortment of the stuff of everday life.
Beginning new reader.

Cohn, Amy L., ed. *From Sea to Shining Sea: A Treasury of American Folklore and Folk Songs.* New York: Scholastic, 1993.

This anthology of folk songs and folk tales is illustrated by eleven award-winning children's book illustrators. Words and music from many familiar songs are here, as well as stories from various regions and historical movements in America. This is a good collection to share favorite songs and stories with children.

Beginning-advanced new reader.

Coles, Robert. *The Story of Ruby Bridges.* Illustrated by George Ford. New York: Scholastic, Inc., 1995.

Psychiatrist Coles has written several award-winning books for adults about children in crisis and the moral and spiritual development of children. In this picture book, he tells the true story of Ruby Bridges, a six-year-old girl who for several months walked past angry white mobs to integrate a New Orleans public school. Coles tells the story simply and quietly, allowing the power of the events to make their own statement about moral courage and perseverance in the face of fear.

Beginning new reader.

Everett, Gwen. *John Brown: One Man Against Slavery.* Paintings by Jacob Lawrence. New York: Rizzoli, 1993.

Everett tells the story of the abolitionist John Brown through the eyes of his daughter Annie. We see John Brown the father and husband as well as John Brown the zealous fighter against slavery, and we appreciate more deeply the sacrifice that some make in the name of a cause they truly believe in. The illustrations are from Jacob Lawrence's series of paintings about John Brown (see the listing under Lawrence in Chapter 1). This picture book is a beautiful work of art as well as a lesson in history and in the power of an idea.

Beginning-intermediate new reader.

————. *Li'l Sis and Uncle Willie: A Story Based on the Life and Paintings of William H. Johnson.* Illustrated with the paintings of William H. Johnson. New York: Rizzoli, 1991.

This picture book is a good companion piece to Richard J. Powell's book, *Homecoming: The Art and Life of William H. Johnson,* listed in the **Art and**

Music section of Chapter 4. Based on actual events, it tells the story of Johnson's summer visit to his small hometown in South Carolina, where a six-year-old girl is fascinated by his paintings and stories about life in Europe and New York City.
Beginning-intermediate new reader.

Farber, Norma. *How Does It Feel To Be Old?* Illustrated by Trina Schart Hyman. New York: E.P. Dutton, 1979.

A grandmother's response to this simple question is honest and realistic, with a sprinkling of humor and irony that makes it particularly appealing to adults.
Beginning-intermediate new reader.

Fisher, Leonard Everett. *The Wailing Wall.* New York: Macmillan Publishing Co., 1989.

The Wailing Wall, which stands in Jerusalem, is all that remains of the first and second temples of the Jewish people. Today it is a reminder to Jews of many sad episodes in their history and of their determination to maintain their cultural identity. With terse prose and paintings in tones of black, white, and gray, Fisher reviews the long history of the Jewish people and their roots in the city of Jerusalem.
Intermediate new reader.

Frost, Robert. *Stopping by Woods on a Snowy Evening.* Illustrated by Susan Jeffers. New York: E.P. Dutton, 1973.

The ending of this poem, "And miles to go before I sleep," is among the best known lines of American poetry. In this illustrated version of Frost's poem, soft black-and-white drawings with a touch of warm crayon-like color echo the soft, rhythmic language that describes a solitary man stopping for a moment's contemplation of newly fallen snow.
Beginning new reader.

Giovanni, Nikki. *Knoxville, Tennessee.* Illustrated by Larry Johnson. New York: Scholastic, 1994.

The text of this picture book is a single poem which appears in many poetry anthologies. It recalls a young girl's fond memories of childhood: eat-

ing fresh corn and homemade ice cream, listening to the sounds of gospel music, and feeling safe and loved within her grandparents' world. The illustrations nicely match the dream-like sentiment.
Beginning new reader.

Greenfield, Eloise. *Daydreamers.* Illustrated by Tom Feelings. New York: Dial Press, 1981.

The daydreamers in this book-length poem are children caught in a still moment of solitude and reverie. Feelings's muted drawings convey the mood of contemplation and childlike hope perfectly. Children may well enjoy this book, but only adults can truly appreciate the mingling of art and language that captures that innocent yearning of the young that we recognize and remember.
Beginning new reader.

Hall, Donald. *The Farm Summer of 1942.* Illustrated by Barry Moser. New York: Dial Books, 1994.

In this book, a nine-year old boy whose naval officer father is fighting in the South Pacific flies from his San Francisco home to spend a summer at his grandparents' New Hampshire farm. He is met there by a horse and buggy. In the course of the summer he learns to hay, collect eggs, and listen to his grandfather's stories. Adult readers will recognize the tension between the lure of the modern and the warmth and contentment of a life spent in concert with nature's cycles. Another beautiful book about New England farm life, this time in the nineteenth century, is Hall's *The Ox-Cart Man.*
Beginning-intermediate new reader.

———. *I Am the Dog, I Am the Cat.* Illustrated by Barry Moser. New York: Dial Books, 1994.

Adults who are cat and/or dog owners will delight in the humor of this simple book. In alternating statements, the dog and cat muse about a life spent in human company: eating, sleeping, dealing with the children, and so on. The subtle distinctions in their animal personalities are cleverly expressed in Hall's simple but poetically concise prose. The rich paintings mirror and extend the words perfectly.
Beginning new reader.

————. *Lucy's Christmas.* Illustrated by Michael McCurdy. San Diego, CA: Harcourt Brace & Co., 1994.

A fond look back at a Christmas celebration in rural New England in the early 1900's, this book is based on stories the author's mother told about her girlhood. The details of the life of those times, when the arrival of a new stove was a memorable event and most Christmas presents were made by hand from whatever materials were available, will appeal to adults for its own sweet nostalgia.

Beginning new reader.

Horwitz, Joshua. *Night Markets: Bringing Food to a City.* New York: Thomas Y. Crowell, 1984.

The phrase "New York night life" brings images of theatres, fancy restaurants, and glitter, but this book chronicles a less familiar, though essential, aspect of night life in the big city: the markets and workers that supply fresh food to stores and restaurants every day. Descriptive and appealing black-and-white photographs accompany a clearly-written text set in large, easy-to-read type.

Beginning-intermediate new reader.

Hughes, Langston. *Black Misery.* Illustrated by Arouni. New York: Oxford Press, 1994.

Originally published in 1969, this small volume was reissued by the Opie Library of Children's Literature. While it looks like a children's picture book, its content and tone are much more suited to adults. Hughes's talent for wry wit and understated irony is evident in his catalogue of things that make blacks miserable. Although some of the references are now dated, the use of verbal skill as a weapon against racism and stereotyping makes this book as timely as ever.

Beginning new reader.

Isadora, Rachel. *Ben's Trumpet.* New York: Greenwillow Books, Inc., 1979.

With striking black-and-white illustrations reminiscent of the art deco period, Isadora tells the story of a young black boy who dreams of being a jazz trumpeter like the men he sees in the club in his neighborhood.

Beginning new reader.

Jesus of Nazareth: A Life of Christ Through Pictures. Illustrated with Paintings from the National Gallery of Art, Washington, D.C. New York: Simon and Schuster, 1994.

Pivotal stories from the life of Jesus are told with excerpts from the King James Version of the *Bible*. The illustrations are paintings of European masters that hang in the National Gallery. The reverence of the art and the elegance of the language make a lovely match.

Intermediate new reader.

Johnson, James Weldon. *The Creation.* Illustrations by Carla Golembe. Boston: Little, Brown & Co., 1993.

This book features one sermon in verse taken from Johnson's collection *God's Trombones* (see entry in Chapter 2). It is a vivid, rhythmic retelling of the creation story that virtually begs to be read aloud. Golembe's boldly-colored illustrations match the imagery and mystery of the story. Another version of this same sermon in verse was published by Holiday House in 1993; also titled *The Creation*, it is illustrated by James E. Ransome. The words are the same, but the softer and more realistic illustrations create a different, yet equally appropriate, feeling. Comparing the two might make an interesting exercise.

Beginning new reader.

———. *Lift Every Voice and Sing.* Illustrated by Elizabeth Catlett. New York: Walker & Co., 1992.

The linocuts which illustrate this volume, originally published in the 1940's, are a dramatic accompaniment to the words of this triumphant song, which is known as the black national anthem. Sheet music is included at the back.

Beginning new reader.

Langstaff, John, ed. *Climbing Jacob's Ladder: Heroes of the Bible in African American Spirituals.* Illustrated by Ashley Bryan. New York: Margaret K. McElderry Books, 1991.

Brief stories of nine great figures of the Bible, including Abraham, Jacob, Daniel, and Noah, are illustrated by Bryan and matched with a black spiritual. Musical notation is included. This book is similar in style and potential use to *What a Morning*, listed below.

Beginning new reader.

————. *What a Morning! The Christmas Story in Black Spirituals.* Illustrated by Ashley Bryan. New York: Margaret K. McElderry Books, 1987.

Five Biblical quotations declaring the birth of Jesus are matched with five black spirituals. Brilliantly-colored paintings illustrate each entry, which includes the musical notation for the spirituals. This is a simple, lovely book. Anyone who knows the stories of the Bible or enjoys black spirituals will recognize the words in the limited text.

Beginning new reader.

Lawrence, Jacob. *The Great Migration: An American Story.* New York: Harper-Collins, 1993.

Jacob Lawrence is known for his series paintings, several panels of which tell a story from his African American heritage (see listing in Chapter 1). His Migration Series, which tells the story of the migration of blacks from the agrarian South to northern industrial cities in the years between the wars, is perhaps his most famous work, and all sixty panels were recently exhibited at the Museum of Modern Art in New York City. Accompanied by a brief statement written by Lawrence, those same sixty panels are presented in this picture book that will delight and inspire readers of all ages. An earlier picture book, *Harriet and the Promised Land,* based on Lawrence's series paintings about Harriet Tubman, has recently been reissued.

Beginning new reader.

Lessac, Frane. *Caribbean Canvas.* New York: J.B. Lippincott, 1987.

This beautiful book is a collection of paintings by the Caribbean artist Frane Lessac, each accompanied by a poem from a Caribbean writer. With bright tropical colors and an almost folk-like style, the paintings portray various aspects of life in the islands. Many of the poems are simple and easy to read, while others are written in dialect.

Beginning-intermediate new reader.

Locker, Thomas. *Family Farm.* New York: Dial Press, 1988.

Locker tells the story of one farm family which finds a creative way to stay solvent for at least one more year. The luminous, museum-quality oil paintings that illustrate this very contemporary story remind us that the struggle to work the land is an old and noble one. Part of the proceeds of the book go to Farm Aid.

Intermediate new reader.

————. *Snow Toward Evening: A Year in a River Valley.* Poems selected by Josette Frank. New York: Dial Books, 1990.

There are thirteen poems by various writers in this collection, one for each month of the year plus one to sum up the year in the river valley. All the poems are simple, although they were originally written for adults. Locker's lush oil paintings provide a rich and sensitive perspective on one landscape as it moves through a year's growth and change. The combination of words and pictures offers ample opportunities for students to reflect on the ways in which our natural environment, whatever it may be, as well as the passage of time, affects the way we live our lives.

Beginning new reader.

Longfellow, Henry Wadsworth. *Paul Revere's Ride.* Illustrated by Ted Rand. New York: Dutton Children's Books, 1990.

"One if by land, two if by sea." This is perhaps the most famous phrase from Longfellow's poem describing Paul Revere's ride to alert the New England colonists to the British attack. The complete poem is presented here, with descriptive illustrations that help explain some of the more difficult passages. Standards from American literature often appear on the GED, so a book such as this one becomes a beautiful as well as helpful way to introduce new readers to some of these classic pieces of writing.

Intermediate new reader.

Lyon, George Ella. *Mama is a Miner.* Illustrated by Peter Catalanotto. New York: Orchard Books, 1994.

"Wherever she is, Mama means light." In the depth of the coal mine, the light comes from Mama's headlamp that pierces the forbidding darkness under the mountain where Mama and her colleagues face danger and physically demanding work. At home, it is Mama's smile and dedication to her family that lightens the burden of hard times. On alternating pages, the rich illustrations contrast Mama in the darkness of the mine with Mama in the warmth of her simple home which work in the mine makes possible.

Beginning new reader.

McKissack, Patricia C., and Fredrick L. McKissack. *Christmas in the Big House, Christmas in the Quarters.* Illustrated by John Thompson. New York: Scholastic, Inc., 1994.

On a plantation in Virginia in the fall of 1859, a family and their slaves begin to prepare for Christmas. Both owners and slaves share in the excitement of the coming holiday, but the contrast between the stately plantation mansion, with its elegant decorations and sumptuous meals, and the one-room cabins with dirt floors is stark. Hints of the coming revolution are in the air, as the plantation owners talk of secession and war, and the slaves sing their songs of freedom in the midst of rumors that their day is coming nearer.

Intermediate new reader.

Mochizuki, Ken. *Baseball Saved Us.* Illustrated by Dom Lee. New York: Lee & Low Books, Inc., 1993.

There are many stories about how success in one sport or another wins acceptance for a child considered an outsider by other children. This particular version has an unusual and historic twist. When a Japanese American family is forced to live in an internment camp during World War II, the father decides the children need a diversion, so he organizes the adults to build a baseball diamond. His young son learns the game and becomes a good player, skills he then uses to win a place in the world he returns to once the war is over. Issues of racial intolerance and prejudice are treated sensitively, and the sepia-toned illustrations have a documentary quality that complements the historical context nicely.

Intermediate new reader.

Morimoto, Junko. *My Hiroshima.* New York: Viking Penguin, 1987.

In this true story, Morimoto recalls the events of August 6, 1945, when an atomic bomb fell on her city of Hiroshima. Illustrated by her own drawings as well as photographs of Hiroshima before and after the bomb, this account of a still-controversial event, told from the viewpoint of one survivor, makes compelling reading.

Beginning new reader.

Moutoussamy-Ashe, Jeanne. *Daddy and Me.* New York: Knopf, 1993.

This book take a matter-of-fact approach to the reality of children helping to care for a family member who is dying of AIDS. Children will be

intrigued by the story of a little girl who helps take care of her Daddy, but adults who remember her father, Arthur Ashe, as a star tennis player and champion of equality in the world of sports will find this book moving and sad. It is joyful too, for as Moutoussamy-Ashe, Ashe's wife and the author and photographer for this book, says, "The power of love is everlasting." Her words and photographs are testimony to that belief.
Beginning new reader.

Patterson, Francine. *Koko's Kitten.* Photographs by Ronald H. Cohn. New York: Scholastic, Inc., 1985.
Patterson tells the true and intriguing story of a gorilla who learned to communicate with her keeper through sign language. The gorilla developed a deep attachment to a little kitten, and when the kitten was killed, the gorilla used sign language to express her grief and sadness.
Beginning-intermediate new reader.

Pienkowski, Jan. *Easter.* Text from the King James Version of the Bible. New York: Alfred A. Knopf, 1989.
The illustrations in this book are silhouette figures on watercolor wash backgrounds set within gilded borders, creating an effect that is dramatic and opulent. The text from the Bible, with no additions, will be familiar to many students. Pienkowski has also created a companion volume, *Christmas.*
Beginning-intermediate new reader.

Polacco, Patricia. *Pink and Say.* New York: Philomel Books, 1994.
Polacco shares a family story, passed down from her great-great-grandfather, a white Union soldier in the Civil War. He was injured and left for dead on a battlefield, but a black soldier found him and carried him home where his mother nursed the Union man back to health, knowing all the while the dire consequences for blacks found harboring Yankees in their southern town. These two soldiers became close friends, but that friendship was shattered when they were found by the Confederate Army. The white soldier survived his imprisonment; the black soldier was killed almost immediately after capture. Throughout the rest of his long life, that white soldier told this story, ensuring that the tale of his black friend's kindness and horrible fate survived, even though he did not. This beautiful story of friendship is made all the more powerful because it has been pre-

served these long years by a family determined to keep the lessons of history alive for their own children, and now for everyone.
Intermediate new reader.

Radin, Ruth Yafee. *A Winter Place.* Illustrated by Mattie Lou O'Kelley. Boston: Little, Brown & Co., 1982.
It is the paintings by folk artist O'Kelley (see listing under her name in Chapter 1) that tell this story of a rural family heading out to the frozen pond in the mountains to skate on a winter's afternoon then home again to warmth and comfort. This is a book which will inspire discussions and writing about favorite memories.
Beginning-intermediate new reader.

Ringgold, Faith. *Dinner at Aunt Connie's House.* New York: Hyperion Books for Children, 1993.
Following the success of her first book for children, *Tar Beach* (listed below), Ringgold created another book based on a painted story quilt, a unique art form which tells a story in words and pictures painted and quilted on fabric. The twelve dinner guests at Aunt Connie's house are African American women including Marian Anderson, Rosa Parks, and others who have made significant contributions to American history and culture. These twelve come magically alive as they tell their stories to the two black children who come to Aunt Connie's special dinner.
Beginning-intermediate new reader.

———. *Tar Beach.* New York: Crown Publishers, 1991.
The story quilt upon which this picture book is based now hangs in the Guggenheim Museum in New York City. It tells the story of a young girl and her family who seek relief from the summer heat on the roof of their Harlem apartment. Up on the roof, with the lights of the George Washington Bridge beckoning in the distance, the girl dreams of flying, freedom, and righting life's wrongs.
Beginning-intermediate new reader.

Rylant, Cynthia. *Appalachia: The Voices of Sleeping Birds.* Illustrated by Barry Moser. San Diego, CA: Harcourt Brace Jovanovich, 1991.
Both writer and illustrator grew up in Appalachia, and their deep feelings

for that place are obvious. Rylant describes the people whose lives are defined by the seasons and the surrounding mountains which protect, isolate, and inspire them. Moser's illustrations are transparent watercolors originally produced on handmade paper. Many were inspired by actual photographs from family and friends as well as famous photographs by professional photographers such as Ben Shahn and Walker Evans. This book is a beautiful collaboration of writer and artist.
Beginning-intermediate new reader.

———. *Waiting to Waltz: A Childhood.* Drawings by Stephen Gammell. Scarsdale, NY: Bradbury Press, 1984.
The voice of these poems is that of an adult looking back on the people and places she knew in the Appalachian village where she grew up. The pencil drawings add a quiet tone to this reminiscent journey.
Beginning-intermediate new reader.

Sara. *Across Town.* New York: Orchard Books, 1990.
With illustrations that at first seem gloomy and disturbing, this wordless book tells the story of a man alone in a city at night until he meets a welcome friend. The format and starkly black-and-white illustrations will surely evoke responses and lead to discussions and reading and writing activities.
Beginning new reader.

Say, Allen. *Grandfather's Journey.* Boston: Houghton Mifflin, 1993.
Grandfather's journey is that of every immigrant and immigrant's child, whether from one country to another or just from one kind of life to another. For the immigrants and their children, there will always be a longing for both places. As the grandson in the story, who is Allen Say himself, says, "The moment I am in one country, I am homesick for the other." Immigration and the search for home are dominant themes in American life, and this book of simple words and exquisite paintings captures the essence of the immigrant's fate.
Beginning new reader.

Schroeder, Alan. *Ragtime Tumpie*. Illustrated by Bernie Fuchs: Boston, Little, Brown & Co.

> This fictional story is based on the real life adventures of Josephine Baker, who grew up in the midst of poverty in St. Louis but ultimately became a star, especially in Europe, in the world of ragtime and jazz. The text and illustrations ring with the warmth and rhythm of their subject.
> *Intermediate new reader.*

Sendak, Maurice. *We Are All in the Dumps With Jack and Guy*. New York: HarperCollins Publishers, 1993.

> Unique and controversial, this book will engage a wide-ranging audience who will respond with a wide range of opinions. Sendak has taken two traditional, though not very familiar, Mother Goose rhymes and joined them to tell a modern story about the life of an abandoned child living among homeless people. There are many social references within the pictures that adults will see more readily than children.
> *Beginning new reader.*

Siebert, Diane. *Heartland*. Illustrated by Wendell Minor. New York: Thomas Y. Crowell, 1989.

> In one rhythmic celebratory poem, Siebert sings of the beauty, simplicity, and power of nature as seen in the farming heartland of America. Minor's bright, realistic paintings convey the clarity and cyclical nature of farming life. This is an exquisite collaboration between writer and artist, who also produced *Mojave*, celebrating the vast California desert.
> *Intermediate new reader.*

Volavkova, Hana. *I Never Saw Another Butterfly . . . : Children's Drawings and Poems from Terezin Concentration Camp 1942–1944*. 2nd expanded ed. New York: Schocken Books, in association with the United States Holocaust Museum, 1993.

> Although the poems and drawings in this collection come from children, the extraordinary circumstances under which they were created give them wisdom and understanding beyond their years. Adults will marvel at the ability of human beings, whatever their age, to adapt and survive, despite unimaginable suffering. Pain and yearning for freedom are obvious but so are hope and courage.
> *Beginning-intermediate new reader.*

Whitman, Walt. *I Hear America Singing.* Illustrated by Robert Sabuda. New York: Philomel Books,

Whitman's hymn is as straightforward as it is celebratory. Though some readers may not share his rosy outlook, they will appreciate his exaltation of workers. Whatever their reaction, this book will generate much discussion about the nature and meaning of work. Whitman is another classic American writer whose work may appear on GED tests, so this picture book offers a good introduction to his writing for new readers. See also *Voyages: Poems by Walt Whitman,* an anthology listed in Chapter 2.

Beginning new reader.

Family Literacy

Aardema, Verna. *Misoso: Once Upon a Time Tales from Africa.* Illustrated by Reynold Ruffins. New York: Alfred A. Knopf/Apple Soup, 1994.

The word "misoso" comes from a tribe in Angola and describes stories told for entertainment which always begin, "Let me tell you a story about . . . " For this collection, storyteller Aardema has gathered twelve tales that involve justice and revenge, greed and generosity, trickery and silliness. All are particularly well-suited for reading aloud. An afterword following each story explains its origins. The brightly-colored illustrations have a contemporary look even as they conjure up a fantasy world.

Beginning-intermediate new reader.

Ahlberg, Janet, and Alan Ahlberg. *The Baby's Catalogue.* Boston: Little, Brown & Co., 1982.

With very few words, this book introduces the idea of categorization by grouping illustrations of items and situations familiar to babies and their older siblings. It is a good book to help children learn to name their world.

Beginning new reader.

———. *The Jolly Postman.* Boston: Little, Brown & Co., 1986.

Real little letters arrive in real little envelopes for real little fingers to open. This is a delightful example of a "participation" book, that is, a book which encourages children to participate in some kind of language-related activity. *Each Peach Pear Plum* and *Peek-a-Boo* are two other titles by these same authors which engage adults and children in fun language activities.

Beginning new reader.

Ancona, George. *Pablo Remembers: The Fiesta of the Day of the Dead.* New York: Lothrop, Lee & Shepard Books, 1993.

Focusing on one Mexican family's celebration, this book examines the festival known as *El Dia de Los Muertos*, or the Day of the Dead. Bright color photographs of the market place, the flowers, the family all dressed up, and especially the *calaveras de dulce*, or sugar skulls, showcase the festive nature of this day on which Mexicans remember the spirits of their loved ones and welcome them home. A similar book, *Days of the Dead*, by Kathryn Lasky has also been recently published. Ancona has produced many other photo essays, including *Powwow*, which chronicles an American Indian Powwow in Montana.

Beginning-intermediate new reader.

Bayer, Jane. *A My Name is Alice.* Illustrated by Steven Kellogg. New York: Dial Books for Young Readers, 1984.

A rhyme for every letter fits the pattern of "A My Name is Alice," a four-line verse that identifies the wife, husband, country they live in, and item they sell, all of which must begin with the correct letter. The rollicking rhymes and slightly wacky illustrations make this book fun for adults and children to share, and making up new rhymes together will add to the fun and be instructive as well. Directions for playing this ball bouncing game are included at the end.

Beginning new reader.

Blizzard, Gladys S. *Come Look With Me: Enjoying Art with Children.* Come Look With Me series. Charlottesville, VA: Thomasson-Grant, 1990.

This book was specifically designed for adults and children to share together. The left hand page of each two-page spread offers one of twelve masterworks of art of various styles. On the opposite page are some open-ended questions to spur study and discussion, as well as a brief commentary about the art to help the adult understand the picture and discuss it with the child.

Beginning-intermediate new reader.

Bolten, Linda. *Hidden Pictures.* New York: Dial Books for Young Readers, 1993.

Each illustration in this clever book contains hidden images. Bolten provides clues for finding them, as well as a mirrored sheet of paper that comes with the book. This is one of those situations in which children, with open minds and more flexible eye muscles, might perform better than adults. *Intermediate new reader.*

Bunting, Eve. *A Day's Work.* Illustrated by Ronald Himler. New York: Clarion Books, 1994.

A young Mexican American boy tells a lie in order to get a job for his abuelo, or grandfather, who has just arrived in California and doesn't speak English. When the lie is discovered, the grandfather teaches the boy a lesson in maintaining the honor of one's word.
Beginning new reader.

————. *The Wall.* Illustrated by Ronald Himler. New York: Clarion Books, 1990.

At the Vietnam Veterans Memorial, a little boy helps his father find his grandfather's name on the granite wall. This is a simple story, but it speaks poignantly about strong family connections and the deep and lasting losses that war inevitably brings.
Beginning new reader.

Chapman, Cheryl. *Snow on Snow on Snow.* Illustrated by Synthia Saint James. New York: Dial Books for Young Readers, 1994.

The rhythmic repetition of phrases, bright acrylic illustrations that have the look of cutouts, and timeless appeal of a boy, his dog, and snow make this book an easy and thoroughly delightful reading experience.
Beginning new reader.

Cisneros, Sandra. *Hairs = Pelitos.* Illustrated by Terry Ybanez; Translated by Liliana Valenzuela. New York: Knopf/Apple Soup, 1994.

The text of this book is actually one of the vignettes from Cisneros's novel *The House on Mango Street,* listed in Chapter 3. Cisneros is a Latina writer, although her book was originally published in English. Here, the words appear in English at the top of the page, and in Spanish at the bottom. A young girl characterizes the hair of each member of her family and in the process reveals something of their personality as well. The brightly-colored illustrations reflect an appropriately child-like view of the world. Each picture is framed within the page, with sketches of objects connected to that

family member embedded in the frame. The pictures will give adults and children as much to talk about as the simple but very poetic text.
Beginning new reader.

Cooper, Floyd. *Coming Home: From the Life of Langston Hughes*. New York: Putnam/Philomel Books, 1994.

Cooper has illustrated many children's books; this is the first he has written. It is a brief sketch of the life of poet Langston Hughes which focuses on his lonely childhood away from his parents and lifelong search for a secure home. Ultimately, says Cooper, Hughes found that home within himself where all the people and places he had known came to life through his writing. With its focus on the young Langston and the meaning of family, this book is particularly suitable for family literacy programs. A collection of Hughes poetry, *The Dream Keeper*, listed in Chapter 2, contains several poems easy enough for beginning and intermediate new readers.
Intermediate new reader.

---

dePaola, Tomie. *The Miracles of Jesus*. New York: Holiday House, 1987.

dePaola is a prolific and award-winning illustrator of children's books. In this book, he has adapted the text of the New Testament slightly and illustrated twelve miracles of Jesus, including the Wedding at Cana, the Loaves and the Fishes, and the Raising of Lazarus. dePaola has also done a companion book, *The Parables of Jesus*.
Beginning-intermediate new reader.

Desimini, Lisa. *My House*. New York: Henry Holt and Co., 1994.

Using a fascinating patchwork of painting, collage, and her own photographs, Desimini presents a humorous, child-like, and very imaginative view of home in various seasons and times of day. This is a bedtime story book to delight the eye and the imagination, even as it offers the comfort and security of home.
Beginning new reader.

Drew, Helen. *My First Baking Book*. New York: Alfred A. Knopf, 1991.

Baking cookies, pies, cupcakes, and holiday treats together appeals to most adults and children, and this book is the perfect ingredient for such an activity. Every item you will need is individually pictured, down to the

smallest drop of food coloring. The step-by-step instructions are clearly explained in words and photographs, and the artfully-pictured final products will send anyone who examines this book into the kitchen, whether there happens to be a child handy or not.
Beginning new reader.

Fleischman, Paul. *Rondo in C.* Illustrated by Janet Wentworth. New York: Harper & Row, 1988.
As a young piano student plays Beethoven's "Rondo in C," each member of the audience is stirred by a different and personal memory. This book might inspire parents and grandparents to share some of their special memories.
Beginning new reader.

Flournoy, Valerie. *The Patchwork Quilt.* Illustrated by Jerry Pinckney. New York: Dial Books for Young Readers, 1985.
A grandmother takes the time to teach her granddaughter how to quilt. When the grandmother becomes ill, the young girl tries to finish her grandmother's "masterpiece."
Beginning-intermediate new reader.

Greenfield, Eloise. *Nathaniel Talking.* Illustrated by Jan Spivey Gilchrist. New York: Black Butterfly Children's Books, 1988.
In the format of a rap song, nine-year-old Nathaniel talks about his "philosophy," as he works at making sense of parents, loss, and his world. He raises lots of questions, but there is a lot of love to help him find answers.
Beginning-intermediate new reader.

———. *Night on Neighborhood Street.* Illustrated by Jan Spivey Gilchrist. New York: Dial Books for Young Readers, 1991.
Individual poems describe life for the children in an urban neighborhood. For the most part, it is a warm and nurturing world with family, friends, and neighbors, but there are fear and uncertainty lurking in the presence of the drug-seller and the times when Daddy is out of work. The illustrations are warm and tender and reflect the strength and security that comes from feeling connected.
Beginning new reader.

Grifalconi, Ann. *The Village of Round and Square Houses.* Boston: Little, Brown & Co., 1986.

In words and pictures, Grifalconi tells the true story of a remote village in Central Africa where the men live in square houses and the women in round ones.

Intermediate new reader.

Grossman, Patricia. *Saturday Market.* Illustrated by Enrique O. Sanchez. New York: Lothrop, Lee & Shepard Books, 1994.

A busy and lively day at the Saturday market in Oaxaca, Mexico is described in words and pictures. We meet women selling huaraches (sandals), and other crafts, families selling their fruits and vegetables, and children reluctantly selling the animals they have raised. Spanish words are sprinkled throughout the text. While their meaning is not immediately explained, the story and pictures give many contextual clues. Figuring them out could be a good exercise for both adults and children who do not speak Spanish, and a glossary at the back gives the phonetic pronunciation as well as the English meaning.

Beginning-intermediate new reader.

Gryski, Camilla. *Friendship Bracelets.* New York: Morrow Junior Books, 1993.

Here is a book to help adults and children work together on a project, in this case making the popular friendship bracelets that children like to wear and exchange. All that is needed are some embroidery thread, scissors, a safety pin, and something like a small pillow to form a work surface. The directions are well-written and clearly illustrated, and they range from the simplest styles to difficult ones that encourage creativity. Craft books such as this offer new readers two advantages. First, they give practice in reading information from diagrams. Secondly, for adults who are knowledgeable about the particular task involved, they permit application of knowledge of a certain skill to the task of reading the words on a page. Gryski has also written two books about children's string games, *Cat's Cradle, Owl's Eyes: A Book of String Games* and *Super String Games.*

Intermediate new reader.

Hendershot, Judith. *In Coal Country.* Illustrated by Thomas B. Allen. New York: Alfred A. Knopf, 1987.

Hendershot recalls her memories of growing up in an Appalachian coal-mining town where life was hard, but children found fun in whatever was available. Physical labor and soot, as well as love and family loyalty, prevail in the story and in the gritty illustrations, which convey a certain dogged optimism.

Beginning-intermediate new reader.

Hoban, Tana. *I Walk and Read.* New York: Greenwillow Books, 1984.

Award-winning photographer Hoban has produced shelves full of books that are likely to be found in any public library. Her immensely appealing and imaginative photographs illustrate just about everything in a child's world. In this title, she presents various street signs that will be familiar to any child growing up in an urban or suburban environment. There is no additional text. Many of Hoban's titles are also useful for vocabulary and language discussions among ESOL students. Two particularly good ones are *More Than One*, which presents photographs to explain various words for groups such as pile, crowd, team, etc., and *Push Pull Empty Full,* which imaginatively depicts words that are opposites.

Beginning new reader.

Hoberman, Mary Ann. *My Song is Beautiful: Poems and Pictures in Many Voices.* Boston: Little, Brown & Co., 1994.

The child's search for an understanding of self in the midst of family, school, and ever-widening world is the theme that unites this diverse collection of poems, each written by a different poet and illustrated by a different children's book illustrator. This unique collaboration is a colorful, humorous, and deeply thoughtful book that may help children frame some of the questions they inevitably have but often cannot articulate.

Beginning new reader.

Houston, Gloria. *The Year of the Perfect Christmas Tree: An Appalachian Story.* Illustrated by Barbara Cooney. New York: Dial Books for Young Readers, 1988.

It is Ruth's family's turn to choose the Christmas tree for the village church. In spring, she and her father go to mark the perfect one, but as Christmas approaches and her father has not yet returned from duty in World

War I, the town begins to wonder if it will get its tree. Ruth and her mother save the day and create a mountain legend in the process.
Beginning-intermediate new reader.

Hudson, Wade, ed. *Pass It On: African American Poetry for Children.* Illustrated by Floyd Cooper. New York: Scholastic, 1993.
Poems from African American writers are illustrated with warm, oil-wash paintings that reflect their energy and emotional content. All of the poems included are good for reading aloud.
Beginning-intermediate new reader.

Hutton, Warwick. *Adam and Eve: The Bible Story.* Text from the King James Version of the *Bible.* New York: Margaret K. McElderry Books, 1987.
Soft watercolors illustrate this presentation of the Biblical story of Adam and Eve. Hutton has illustrated other *Bible* stories, including *Jonah and the Great Fish* and *Moses in the Bulrushes.*
Beginning new reader.

Isadora, Rachel. *At the Crossroads.* New York: Greenwillow Books, 1991.
At first glance, this story of children joyous at the prospect of seeing their fathers come home from work seems simple and heartwarming; then you see the underside of the story: the fathers have been away at work for ten months, the children live in corrugated shacks, they make their toys from the scraps on the garbage pile, and they sit by the roadside until the early morning hours when the truck carrying their fathers finally arrives. In the understatement and simplicity of this selective incident, Isadora has painted a searing image of life in South Africa under apartheid.
Beginning new reader.

Lessac, Frane. *Caribbean Alphabet.* New York: William Morrow/Tambourine Books, 1989.
In this alphabet book, words beginning with each letter and richly colored pictures all depict life on a Caribbean island. The delightfully primitive illustrations and simple text make this a good choice for early readers unsure of their skills.
Beginning new reader.

Lester, Julius. *John Henry.* Illustrated by Jerry Pinckney. New York: Dial Books for Young Readers, 1994.

> Lester has written many wonderful books for children and young adults, and some of his best are recreations of folk tales. In this rendition of the popular tall tale about the contest between John Henry and the steam drill, both words and illustrations reflect the rhythmic labor of the work and the nobility of the working man.

Beginning-intermediate new reader.

Lindbergh, Reeve. *Grandfather's Lovesong.* Illustrated by Rachel Isadora. New York: Viking, 1993.

> Metaphors of nature in its changing seasons describe a grandfather's love for his grandson in this single rhythmic poem. The accompanying illustrations reflect the moods and colors of the seasons.

Beginning new reader.

Livingston, Myra Cohn. *Sky Songs.* Illustrated by Leonard Everett Fisher. New York: Holiday House, 1984.

> This is a collection of poems that address the beauty and mystery of what we see in the sky: the sun, moon, stars, planets, and storms. Fisher's paintings echo that mystery. This author/illustrator team has produced several other illustrated collections of poetry, including *Earth Songs* and *Sea Songs.*

Beginning-intermediate new reader.

Locker, Thomas. *Where the River Begins.* New York: Dial Books, 1984.

> With beautiful paintings reminiscent of the landscapes of the Hudson River School, this book tells the story of an old man and his two grandsons who set off on a camping trip to find the source of the river that runs by their house. It is also a story of death and enduring love, as the adults who read this book to children will understand.

Beginning-intermediate new reader.

McGuire, Kevin. *Woodworking for Kids: 40 Fabulous, Fun and Useful Things for Kids to Make.* New York: Sterling Publishing Co., 1993.

> This book opens with a brief but informative chapter about wood, where it comes from and how it behaves once it is cut into lumber. Another chapter pictures and explains the basic tools needed. The rest of the book gives

step-by-step instructions for making projects, most of them attractive as well as useful to children: a balance beam, a tic-tac-toe game, a bicycle rack, and a simple display shelf, to name a few. A well-spaced layout, appealing and descriptive photographs, and clearly written instructions make this a book for adults skilled in woodworking to share with the children in their lives.
Intermediate-advanced new reader.

Micklethwait, Lucy. *A Child's Book of Art: Great Pictures First Words.* London and New York: Dorling Kindersley, 1993.
The masterworks of art reproduced here are organized according to subjects that children relate to such as play, opposites, numbers, etc. Each picture is accompanied by a single word or phrase, meant to start a conversation between adult and child about the art and anything the art inspires.
Beginning new reader.

————. *I Spy Two Eyes: Numbers in Art.* New York: Greenwillow Books, 1993.
For each number 1–20, Micklethwait presents a masterwork of art that contains that number of something. Adult and child count the items together, but in the process of hunting, they discover much more within these richly-detailed paintings that range in style from the medieval to the modern. In fact, talking about these works of art involves many of the pre-literacy skills important for children—and for adult new readers—such as building vocabulary, seeing details, describing what you see, and explaining your reaction. This is an instructive as well as highly imaginative book. Micklethwait has also produced *I Spy: An Alphabet in Art.*
Beginning new reader.

Miller, Margaret. *Where's Jenna.* New York: Simon & Schuster, 1994.
Wonderful color photographs tell the story of a little girl playing a game of hide-and-seek with her mother in an effort to delay the inevitable bath. In the process, the story emphasizes all the prepositions that describe where Jenna is: under, behind, between, etc. This simple, fun book will appeal to young children, but the language lessons make it useful with ESOL students as well.
Beginning new reader.

Pinkney, Andrea Davis. *Seven Candles for Kwanzaa.* Illustrated by J. Brian Pinkney. New York: Dial Books for Young Readers, 1993.

Kwanzaa is an African American holiday begun in the United States in 1966 and based on traditional harvest festivals in Africa. Lighting one candle each day over a seven day period from Dec. 26 to Jan. 1, African American families celebrate the seven principles of Kwanzaa which honor strong family and community ties. This lovely book features a typical family preparing for and celebrating the holiday. See also *Celebrating Kwanzaa* by Diane Hoyt-Goldsmith, listed in Chapter 4.

Beginning new reader.

Pinkwater, Daniel. *Guys from Space.* New York: Macmillan Publishing Co., 1989.

This is a wry, funny book about visitors from space who appear in a backyard and take a little boy on a fantastic voyage then bring him back in time for dinner. The language is particularly helpful to adult new readers because many words and phrases are repeated, although in humorous and enjoyable ways.

Beginning new reader.

Pomerantz, Charlotte. *The Chalk Doll.* Illustrated by Frane Lessac. New York: J.B. Lippincott, 1989.

A mother tells her daughter stories about growing up on the island of Jamaica. She was too poor to own a "chalk doll," that is, one bought from the store, so she made her own rag dolls. After listening to her mother's stories, the little girl decides that she is lucky to have so many "chalk dolls," but she would also like to have a rag doll. Wonderful illustrations by Caribbean artist Lessac match the tenderness of the story.

Intermediate new reader.

Raschka, Chris. *Yo! Yes?* New York: Orchard Books, 1993.

Raschka has turned a simple and commonplace encounter into a funny, innovative, and thoroughly delightful picture book. With only thirty-four words and exuberant drawings, he tells the story of two young boys, one outgoing and one shy, exploring the possibility of friendship. Another title by this author/illustrator which new readers and children will enjoy is *Charlie Parker Played Be Bop.*

Beginning new reader.

Rylant, Cynthia. *When I Was Young in the Mountains.* Illustrated by Diane Goode. New York: E.P. Dutton, 1982.

Introducing each memory with the rhythmic title phrase, Rylant recalls the days of her youth spent with her grandmother in Appalachian West Virginia. It is a lyrical portrait of that life as seen through the eyes of a child and spoken through the experienced heart of an adult.

Beginning new reader.

Say, Allen. *Tree of Cranes.* Boston: Houghton Mifflin, 1991.

Two cultures meet for a little Japanese boy when his American-born mother tells him stories of Christmas in California and makes origami cranes to decorate a tree in their garden. The holiday spirit of family, goodwill, and peace pervade the words as well as the beautiful drawings.

Beginning new reader.

Silverstein, Shel. *The Giving Tree.* New York: Harper & Row, 1964.

Now a classic modern fable, this simple story illustrated by line drawings presents a boy, a tree, and an important lesson about the gift of giving.

Beginning new reader.

———. *A Light in the Attic.* New York: Harper & Row, 1981.

Silverstein understands the fears, silliness, and disarming truthfulness of children. Young readers are instinctively drawn to his poems and sketches because they recognize that he speaks to them as well as for them. Adults who follow the child's lead will be glad they did. *Where the Sidewalk Ends* is another collection of Silverstein's poetry that will appeal to adults and children alike.

Beginning-intermediate new reader.

Stevenson, James. *July.* New York: Greenwillow Books, 1990.

In this third installment of a series of reminiscences of childhood summers in the 1930's, soft, almost child-like pastel drawings complement a story of children eager to grow beyond the constraints of their elders. Two earlier titles are *When I Was Nine* and *Higher on the Door.*

Beginning-intermediate new reader.

Thomas, Jane Resh. *Lights on the River*. Illustrated by Michael Dooling. New York: Hyperion Books for Children, 1994.

This story portrays a Mexican American family of migrant farm workers, as seen through the eyes of their young daughter. While she babysits for younger children or helps her parents with other chores, she observes the hard work and often humiliating living conditions the families must endure. Throughout their ordeal, adults and children are sustained by their faith and their strong family bonds.

Beginning-intermediate new reader.

Thomas, Joyce Carol. *Brown Honey in Broomwheat Tea*. Illustrated by Floyd Cooper. New York: HarperCollins Publishers, 1993.

Thomas offers a dozen simple poems that celebrate home, family, a growing sense of self, and pride in one's heritage. Cooper's golden paintings echo the warmth of this tribute to family strength.

Beginning new reader.

Tucker, Jean S. *Come Look with Me: Discovering Photographs with Children*. Come Look With Me series. Charlottesville, VA: Thomasson-Grant, 1994.

Intended for a slightly older audience than Blizzard's *Come Look with Me: Enjoying Art with Children*, from the same series and listed above, this title presents photographs for adults and children to look at and talk about together. Most are black-and-white, although they have a contemporary feel, and all picture children. As with other titles in this series, a brief commentary is offered to help the adult understand the work and open-ended questions are provided to spark discussion.

Beginning-intermediate new reader.

Whipple, Laura, ed. *Celebrating America: A Collection of Poems and Images of the American Spirit*. Art provided by the Art Institute of Chicago. New York: Putnam/Philomel, 1994.

Whipple calls this collection "a visual and verbal patchwork" of the unique and varied American spirit. Poems that will appeal to adults and children are matched with reproductions of works of art that echo and extend the feel and meaning of the words. The layout is spacious and the selections are deep and rich. A very similar and equally lovely book is titled *Celebrate America: In Poetry and Art* (edited by Nora Panzer and published by Hyperion).

Beginning-intermediate new reader.

Wildsmith, Brian. *The Easter Story.* New York: Alfred A. Knopf, 1993.

For this book, Wildsmith has taken the Gospel text of the Easter story, which he considers "the world's greatest story, burning with history, passion, and tragedy," and retold it in simpler language intended for children. To illustrate this epic, he says he decided to "treat it like grand opera, to create the sets and place the characters within them, capturing the symbolism of the Crucifixion and Resurrection in color, shape, and form." The resulting work is both reverent and celebratory. Wildsmith has also created a companion volume, *A Christmas Story.*

Beginning new reader.

Wilkes, Angela. *The Children's Step-by-Step Cook Book.* London and New York: Dorling Kindersley, 1995.

As noted in other entries in this bibliography, Dorling Kindersley produces masterpieces of visual information. Here the subject is cooking, a perfect activity for adults and children to do together. With bright and distinct photographs that picture everything required, down to the garlic clove and $1/4$ teaspoon measuring spoon, each recipe gives the step-by-step instructions needed to prepare the dish. The recipes will appeal to the varied tastes of adults and to the delight children take in the look of food that is artfully and amusingly decorated and arranged.

Beginning new reader.

Yenawine, Philip. *Colors.* New York: The Museum of Modern Art and Delacorte Press, 1991.

Using paintings and photographs from the collection of the Museum of Modern Art, Yenawine explains how artists use color. The book is simply and spaciously laid out, with one artistic principle explained on each page and accompanied by an illustrative work of art. The works of art are so rich and varied, they will lead to discussion among adults and children, not only about art, but about the life that art reflects. Yenawine has also produced *Shapes, Stories, People,* and *Places.*

Beginning new reader.

Young, Ed. *Lon Po Po: A Red-Riding Hood Story from China*. New York: Putnam/Philomel, 1989.

Children the world over are instinctively drawn to fairy tales which address some of their deepest fears, so the many variations of these stories are good for adults and children to share. It will be intriguing to adults that such similar stories arise in such diverse cultures. This ancient Chinese tale bears much resemblance to our familiar *Little Red Riding Hood*. Young presents his richly-colored watercolors in the manner of Chinese panel drawings, adding to the dramatic effect of the story.

Beginning new reader.

Chapter 7

Finding Books Suitable for New Readers

The key to finding books suitable for adult new readers in the general library collection is collaboration between librarians who know the books and teachers who know the students. Just as school librarians suggest books to sustain and enrich the lessons of the classroom teacher, public librarians can suggest books from their collections that will support and extend the reading instruction that students receive from their tutors. Here are some suggestions to help librarians and teachers support each other in their efforts to build a community of active readers.

A Note to Librarians

Keep the categories and examples listed in this bibliography in mind as you select books for your particular area, whether that be adult services, young adult services, or children's services. *Booklist*, published by the American Library Association, has several features that are useful in identifying books for literacy students. In its adult reviews, for example, it marks certain titles as also being appropriate for young adults. This YA designation indicates that the reading level of the book, though not necessarily easy, is not overly complex; the book may be consequently accessible to adults reading at the advanced new reader stage. The YA designation also suggests that the subject matter is one that teens and young adults might enjoy, as well as the adults the books were originally marketed to. *Booklist* also separates reviews of children's books into those for young readers, middle readers, and older readers and then into fiction and nonfiction categories. The nonfiction books reviewed for middle and older readers often include titles that are good crossover books for adult new readers. The *Journal of Adolescent and Adult Literacy*, formerly titled the *Journal of Reading* and published by the International Reading Association, is another source of books for adolescents that might appeal to adult new readers. Their monthly column "Books for Adolescents" suggests both fiction and nonfiction titles. The reviews are more descriptive than evaluative, but still helpful in identifying potentially useful books. Check other bibliographies which list titles of interest to reluctant readers or to young adult readers, since many will also appeal to adult literacy students, and share them with literacy teachers. Sponsor staff training workshops in which librarians from the adult, children's, and young adult departments share information about books suitable for new readers as well as ideas for promoting those books in the literacy community. Recognize that while you and your collection are valuable assets that all literacy programs need, you may have to take some initiative in marketing yourself to literacy teachers. Many do not realize the wealth of materials in the library that are in fact accessible and potentially useful to their students. They will welcome your knowledge about books as well as the support and involvement of a highly visible and respected organization within their community.

A Note to Teachers

Establish a collaborative relationship with the librarians in your local public library, including adult librarians, young adult librarians, and children's librarians. Acquaint them with the needs and interests of your students as well as the instructional methods you use, especially those that depend on library books and outside sources as reading materials. With your help, librarians can look at titles already in their collections, as well as new ones they are considering for purchase, with an understanding of the needs and interests of adult new readers. Consult the booklists mentioned in the bibliography at the end of the chapter and ask your librarian to identify others. Browse the shelves which contain books in the categories described in the bibliographies of this book, especially the art and photography sections and the nonfiction sections of the children's department. Serendipity can be a very useful tool in finding books: you may go to the shelves, call number in hand to find a particular title, and find another, and possibly better, choice right next to it. Browsing the shelves of the local public library reminds us of the depth and richness of the library's offerings and is a wonderful habit to pass along to new readers, as they learn that the library is a place where they are welcomed and where they will find the books they need to improve their reading and to become lifelong readers.

Several books that have been particularly helpful in preparing the booklists for *Choosing and Using Books With Adult New Readers* are listed in the bibliography that follows. The books listed under **Resources for Teaching Adult Literacy Students** discuss teaching methods that are particularly adaptable to a literacy program that emphasizes reading from a wide range of sources.

Those listed under **Resources for Library Literacy Programs** discuss how libraries and literacy programs can work together to promote literacy in their communities. Books that specifically examine family literacy programs are listed under **Resources for Family Literacy Programs**. **Additional Book Lists** contains annotated bibliographies that suggest books for other groups of students such as junior and senior high school students and reluctant readers that may be helpful in identifying titles for the adult new reader population.

Bibliography

Resources for Teaching Adult Literacy Students

Barasovska, Joan. *Getting Started with Experience Stories.* Syracuse, NY: New Readers Press, 1988.
    By using actual language experience stories, the author suggests how tutors can integrate the language experience technique into their reading lessons.

Brookfield, Stephen D. *Developing Critical Thinkers.* San Francisco, CA: Jossey-Bass, 1987.
    This book reviews the nature and importance of critical thinking and offers practical suggestions for classroom exercises that will help students improve their thinking skills. Though not focused on literacy students, the discussion and exercises have many applications for this population of learners.

Collum, Jack. *Moving Windows: Evaluating the Poetry Children Write.* New York: Teachers and Writers Collaborative, 1985.
    Drawing on his many years of experience teaching poetry to children, Collum offers numerous examples of children's poetry along with comments about what makes particular poems work. From these comments, we can learn more about poetry than textbooks alone can explain. Although Collum works with children, his insight into the teaching of poetry applies to adult students as well.

Hazen, Edith P. *The Columbia Granger's Index to Poetry.* 9th ed. New York: Columbia University Press, 1990.
    Teachers and students will find poems for any topic or occasion in this basic reference. Many of the poems are collected in anthologies available in most public libraries.

Hopkins, Lee Bennett. *Pass the Poetry, Please.* Rev. ed. New York: Harper & Row, 1987.

Bennett, who has compiled many poetry anthologies, offers suggestions for bringing poetry to children that can be readily adapted to adults.

Jones, Edward V. *Reading Instruction for the Adult Illiterate.* Chicago: American Library Association, 1981.

Jones begins the book with a comprehensive overview of the scope of adult illiteracy and a profile of the adult illiterate in society and as a learner. In Part II, he offers a detailed, well-presented, and sound program of reading instruction for adults, emphasizing methods that incorporate familiar language and meaningful contexts.

Kaminsky, Marc. *What's Inside You It Shines Out of You.* New York: Horizon Press, 1974.

Kaminsky writes of his experience teaching poetry to senior citizens, many of whom were immigrants and lacked formal education. Kaminsky believed that reading poetry to these students would help them express their ideas and feelings more clearly. His enthusiasm for poetry and for reading books of all kinds is inspiring, and his practical suggestions of activities to help students appreciate and create poetry will be very useful to adult literacy teachers.

Koch, Kenneth. *I Never Told Anybody: Teaching Poetry in a Nursing Home.* New York: Random House, 1977.

Himself a renowned poet, Koch describes how he taught poetry to nursing home residents. His faith in the power of poetry was affirmed by the moving and heartfelt poems many of his students wrote. As is the case in the two titles mentioned below, Koch offer numerous insights into the meaning and beauty of particular poems as he describes his methods for teaching students not accustomed to reading, let alone writing, poetry.

————. *Rose, Where Did You Get That Red? Teaching Great Poetry to Children.* New York: Random House, 1973.

Believing that teaching children only simple, childish poems means giving them "nothing to understand they have not already understood," Koch set out to stretch his young students' minds by introducing them to great poetry, mostly written for adults. The power and complexity of the poetry generated by the students in response affirmed his belief. Many of the techniques described can be used with adult new readers.

————. *Wishes, Lies, and Dreams: Teaching Children to Write Poetry.* New York: Random House, 1970.

Koch outlines his methods for teaching children to write poetry. The comments he offers on the poems the children wrote provide insight into what poetry is all about.

Lyman, Helen Huguenor. *Reading and the Adult New Reader.* Chicago: American Library Association, 1976.

In this now classic work in library literature, Lyman discusses books and reading in relation to the evolving needs of adult new readers and encourages librarians to reach out to populations who are not traditional library users.

Oliver, Mary. *A Poetry Handbook.* San Diego, CA: Harcourt Brace & Co., 1994.

Intended as a handbook for all aspiring poets, those new to poetry as well as those with notebooks full of verse, this book describes the craft of writing poetry. With her clear and precise language, prize-winning poet Oliver shows us poetry as a powerful and memorable means of expression, making this book an excellent introduction for any reader.

Rose, Mike. *Lives on the Boundary: The Struggles and Achievements of America's Underprepared.* New York: The Free Press, 1989.

Rose, himself an underachieving student who was "rescued" by a few conscientious and perceptive teachers, became a teacher and director of the writing program at UCLA. He writes with insight, compassion, and extraordinary grace about what it is like to be a failing student and what kinds of educational intervention can really make a difference.

Rosenthal, Nadine. *Teach Someone to Read: A Step-by-Step Guide for Literacy Tutors.* Belmont, CA: Fearon Education, 1987.

An excellent manual for tutors, this book presents a complete outline for an instructional program that is student-centered and built on reading from meaningful contexts. It is particularly adaptable to a library-centered literacy program.

Rossman, Mark H., Elizabeth C. Fisk, and Janet E. Roehl. *Teaching and Learning Basic Skills: A Guide for Adult Basic Education and Developmental Education Programs.* New York: Teachers College Press, 1984.

The authors discuss the physiological and psychological nature of the adult learner, as well as appropriate teaching methods. They also include sections on asking questions and simplifying materials.

Smith, Frank. *Reading Without Nonsense.* New York: Teachers College Press, 1978.
Smith presents a highly readable book about the nature of reading and how it should be taught. He argues strongly for teaching methods that emphasize the importance of meaning over word recognition skills.

Soifer, Rena, et al. *The Complete Theory-to-Practice Handbook of Adult Literacy: Curriculum Design and Teaching Approaches.* New York: Teachers College Press, 1990.
Along with an explanation of the whole language approach to teaching reading, the authors provide several illustrative lesson plans. Chapters on computers and adult literacy, staff selection, and program management are also helpful.

Resources for Library Literacy Programs

Johnson, Debra Wilcox, Jane Robbins, and Douglas L. Zweizig *Libraries: Partners in Adult Literacy.* Norwood, NJ: Ablex Publishing Corp., 1990.
While exploring the many facets of the library's role in adult literacy, the authors include a review of the literature 1979–1988, a survey of various types of libraries on their involvement in literacy, and case studies of model programs.

Johnson, Debra Wilcox, and Jennifer A. Soule. *Libraries and Literacy: A Planning Manual.* Chicago: American Library Association, 1987.
Intended for libraries deciding whether or in what way to participate in literacy activities in their communities, the manual gives an overview of the problem of illiteracy and discusses all aspects of a library's involvement, including building collections, working with literacy providers, publicizing literacy activities, and evaluating programs.

Lyman, Helen Huguenor. *Literacy and the Nation's Libraries.* Chicago: American Library Association, 1976.
Lyman was among the first and most eloquent advocates for library involvement in literacy programs. In this book intended primarily for librarians, she discusses the problem of illiteracy and the role that libraries can play in helping to eliminate it. She offers many specific suggestions for

developing literacy programs in libraries and establishing contacts with other agencies. Even after twenty years, Lyman's voice still carries a powerful message.

Monroe, Margaret E., and Kathleen M. Heim. *Partners for Lifelong Learning: Public Libraries and Adult Education.* Washington, D.C.: Office of Library Programs, United States Department of Education, 1991.
This volume contains two historical reviews of the involvement of libraries in adult education. Monroe's article covers the years 1900–1966, and Heim's carries on from there until 1991. Together they serve as a reminder that the collaboration of libraries with literacy and other adult education efforts is a long and fruitful one.

Weibel, Marguerite Crowley. *The Library as Literacy Classroom: A Program for Teaching.* Chicago: The American Library Association, 1992.
This book presents a library-based program for teaching adults to read. It discusses the teaching methods most commonly used, then links those methods to specific library resources. It offers several sample lessons and selected bibliographies, and it discusses ways in which libraries and literacy programs can work together to raise the literacy level of their community.

Resources for Family Literacy Programs

Butler, Dorothy. *Babies Need Books.* New York: Atheneum, 1985.
Butler describes the first five years of a child's life and recommends specific books to help both child and adult grow through each developmental stage. The author, a mother and grandmother many times over, sprinkles her book with humorous and insightful anecdotes from her rich personal experience. Although many additional titles have become available since 1985, most of the selections discussed are still in print or available at the library. Even without the book lists, however, Butler's impassioned encouragement of reading to children and her understanding of the parent-child relationship make this book an important addition to the family literacy library.

Cullinan, Bernice E., and Lee Galda. *Literature and the Child.* 3rd ed. Fort Worth, TX: Harcourt Brace College Publishers, 1994.
Cullinan provides an excellent sourcebook on children's literature for family literacy programs. The book discusses all genres of literature, from alphabet books to historical fiction, and gives many examples of each type. Specific

books are highlighted, both for their intrinsic quality and their value for children at particular developmental stages. Numerous profiles of authors and illustrators will give readers useful insights into their work. Extensive bibliographies follow each chapter.

Hearne, Betsy Gould. *Choosing Books for Children: A Common Sense Guide.* Rev. ed. New York: Delacorte Press, 1990.
Hearne writes with a blend of enthusiasm, common sense, and a thorough knowledge of children's literature. She discusses books of different types and books for different age groups. Each chapter ends with a helpful annotated bibliography.

Lipson, Eden Ross. *The New York Times Parent's Guide to the Best Books for Children.* Rev. and updated. New York: Times Books, 1991.
This extensive annotated bibliography of more than 1,000 titles of children's books, both new and old, was written by the children's book editor for *The New York Times.* Lipson includes books for all ages, from babies through young adults. Particularly helpful are the indexes that list books by appropriate age level and by special subject.

Marantz, Sylvia, and Kenneth Marantz. *Multicultural Picture Books: Art for Understanding Others.* Worthington, OH: Linworth Publishing Inc., 1994.
The two authors are a teacher-librarian and an art educator, both of whom have been particularly interested in picture books for many years. Sections include books about the countries of Asia, Africa, the Middle East, and Latin America, as well as books reflecting the experiences of European immigrants and Native Americans. The quality of the story and illustrations were major considerations for inclusion in this list, and the result is a useful resource for librarians and teachers looking for good children's books, whether they want them to represent a particular culture or not.

Quezada, Shelley, and Ruth S. Nickse. *Community Collaborations for Family Literacy Handbook.* New York: Neal-Schuman Publishers, 1993.
This handbook is based on a sixteen-month project which examined collaborative strategies for family literacy in six counties in Massachusetts. The result is a discussion of funding, strategic plans, model programs, and other lessons learned in the process. This handbook will be very useful to any organization attempting to establish a family literacy program.

Trelease, Jim. *The New Read-Aloud Handbook.* New York: Penguin Books, 1989.

The first half of this book is an eloquent plea to parents, teachers, and librarians to read aloud frequently to children of all ages. The second half presents a "treasury" of books suitable for reading aloud, organized by type of book and age level. Trelease's enthusiasm is infectious, and his knowledge of the world of children's literature is encyclopedic.

Additional Book Lists

Books for the Teen Age. New York: Office of Young Adult Services of the New York Public Library, 1995.

For over sixty-five years, this list has been created annually by youth services librarians of the New York Public Library. There are over 1,000 titles, both fiction and nonfiction, categorized by subjects such as cars, crime and justice, true adventure, crafts and hobbies, poetry, and many more. Each entry is briefly annotated. Many of the titles are suitable for adult new readers. This list is available for a small fee from the Office of the Branch Libraries, The New York Public Library, 455 Fifth Avenue, New York, NY 10016.

LiBretto, Ellen V., ed. *High/Low Handbook: Encouraging Literacy in the 1990's.* New York: R.R. Bowker, 1990.

This book is intended for teachers, librarians, and others working with reluctant teenage readers, but the discussions of selecting and evaluating materials will be helpful to those working with adult new readers as well. The well-annotated bibliography contains many potential crossover titles that will appeal to adult literacy students.

McBride, William G., ed. *High Interest-Easy Reading: A Booklist for Junior and Senior High School Students.* Urbana, IL: National Council of Teachers of English and the Committee to Revise High Interest-Easy Reading, 6th ed., 1990.

This booklist for reluctant readers contains over 400 annotated entries for fiction and nonfiction organized into 23 categories of subject interest. Many titles will be of interest to adult new readers. It is available in some library reference collections and from the National Council of Teachers of English, 1111 Kenyon Rd., Urbana, IL 61801.

Rochman, Hazel. *Against Borders: Promoting Books for a Multicultural World.* Chicago: American Library Association, 1993.

At the outset of this annotated bibliography, Rochman establishes two principles: multiculturalism is an inclusive term that crosses cultures and includes all, not just people of color. She recommends books as a means to help students better understand their own culture as well as the cultures of others and as a way of finding "home" in ideas and stories, not just in a familiar physical place. Intended to help teachers and librarians find books for young people, this bibliography will also be useful to adult literacy teachers. Its organization, based on cultural areas of the world, makes it particularly useful for ESOL teachers looking for books to introduce students to the various cultures represented in their classroom. Rochman is an editor for *Booklist,* and the annotations in this book have the same high quality as the reviews found in that journal.

Wurth, Shirley, ed. *Books for You: A Booklist for Senior High Students.* Urbana, IL: National Council of Teachers of English and the Committee on the Senior High School Booklist, 1992.

Compiled by a committee of teachers and librarians, this list is updated every four years. This edition contains more than 800 titles, fiction and nonfiction, covering a wide range of interests. All entries are annotated. It is available in many library reference collections and also from the National Council of Teachers of English, 1111 Kenyon Rd., Urbana, IL 61801.

Young Adult Library Services Association. *Best Books for Young Adults.* Chicago: American Library Association, 1995.

Published annually, this pamphlet lists about 100 titles, fiction and nonfiction, recommended by young adult librarians. Many titles will be suitable for adult new readers. Entries are briefly annotated and categorized by subject. It is available from the American Library Association, 50 E. Huron St., Chicago, IL 60611.

Title Index

Author Index

Subject Index

Age

American Culture

American History

American Landscape

Animals

Appalachia

Childhood and Family

Geography

Health and Disease

Historical Fiction

Love and Friendship

Music

Native Americans

Stories, General Collections

Urban Life

War

Work